PRAISE FOR
IF KENNEDY LIVED

"It can be an enlightening exercise to challenge the belief that what happened had to happen. Usually it didn't. In his diverting *If Kennedy Lived*, Greenfield, the veteran political commentator, asks how things might have played out had John F. Kennedy survived in Dallas."

—*The New York Times Book Review*

"On the fiftieth anniversary of JFK's assassination, this is the book to read. An intelligent, often haunting book about what America and the world would have looked like if John Kennedy had lived. . . . It's a clever, moving book."   —Fareed Zakaria

"Due to his extensive research and interviews with experts in Kennedy's life, Greenfield brings authenticity to the book, and provides a fascinating spin on what might have been."   —The Associated Press

"Greenfield grounds his fictional history in research and interviews with some of the era's experts and, as in his previous excursion into alternative history, offers an ending that the reader will not see coming. . . . Kennedy-era followers will enjoy this book."

—*Library Journal*

"Unquestionably well researched and written."   —seattlepi.com

"Greenfield does good service in demythologizing JFK to suggest that, had he indeed lived, his second term might have been marked by scandal and controversy, a Camelot undone by the president's own proclivities as much as by the events of the time. . . . Well researched and thought through—an interesting, plausible exercise in pop history."   —*Kirkus Reviews*

continued . . .

PRAISE FOR
THEN EVERYTHING CHANGED

"Shrewdly written, often riveting, gripping. . . . Thanks to Mr. Greenfield's own familiarity with American politics and a lot of energetic research, he turns these twists of fate into accelerating historical snowballs that rumble through our recent history, altering the social landscape in ways both small and large."
—Michiko Kakutani, *The New York Times*

"Not only thoughtful and sophisticated, but marked by the author's enthusiasm. Greenfield is having fun here, and you can feel it on every page. His scenarios are relentlessly grounded in plausibility. This is a book political junkies will adore."
—Bryan Burrough, *The Washington Post*

"Satisfying, entertaining, insightful. The key to Greenfield's success is that he knows his politics and the strengths and weaknesses of leaders. Greenfield's storytelling is compelling and his research superb."   —*The Miami Herald*

"Historians have long been tantalized by the what-ifs of history. In the hands of this tremendously gifted storyteller, *Then Everything Changed* will captivate the reader every step along the way."
—Doris Kearns Goodwin

"You expect intelligence and a devilish sense of humor and a profound knowledge of political history from Jeff Greenfield. But there is a deeper, haunting quality to this book as well. By adding a simple twist of fate, Greenfield brings fresh—and exhilarating—insights to the history of our times."   —Joe Klein, columnist, *Time*

"Jeff Greenfield has taken the 'what-if' game and turned it into something else entirely—a trio of thought-provoking, interesting, and downright clever scenarios that remind us just how much individuals do matter."   —Bob Schieffer, moderator, *Face the Nation*

ALSO BY JEFF GREENFIELD

NONFICTION

The Advance Man (with Jerry Bruno)

A Populist Manifesto (with Jack Newfield)

No Peace, No Place: Excavations Along the Generational Fault

The World's Greatest Team

Television: The First Fifty Years

National Lampoon's Book of Books

Playing to Win: An Insider's Guide to Politics

The Real Campaign

"Oh, Waiter! One Order of Crow!"

Then Everything Changed: Stunning Alternate Histories
of American Politics: JFK, RFK, Carter, Ford, Reagan

FICTION

The People's Choice

IF KENNEDY LIVED

THE FIRST AND SECOND TERMS OF
PRESIDENT JOHN F. KENNEDY:
AN ALTERNATE HISTORY

JEFF GREENFIELD

NEW AMERICAN LIBRARY

New American Library
Published by the Penguin Group
Penguin Group (USA) LLC, 375 Hudson Street,
New York, New York 10014

USA | Canada | UK | Ireland | Australia | New Zealand | India | South Africa | China
penguin.com
A Penguin Random House Company

Published by New American Library, a division of Penguin Group (USA) LLC.
Previously published in a G. P. Putnam's Sons edition.

First New American Library Trade Paperback Printing, November 2014

 REGISTERED TRADEMARK—MARCA REGISTRADA

New American Library Trade Paperback ISBN: 978-0-451-47132-1

THE LIBRARY OF CONGRESS HAS CATALOGED THE HARDCOVER EDITION OF THIS TITLE AS FOLLOWS:
Greenfield, Jeff.
If Kennedy lived: the first and second terms of
President John F. Kennedy: an alternate history/Jeff Greenfield.
p.   cm.
ISBN 978-0-399-16696-9
1. Kennedy, John F. (John Fitzgerald), 1917–1963.   2. Imaginary histories.   I. Title.
E841.G653   2013   2013030929
973.922092—dc23

Printed in the United States of America
1   3   5   7   9   10   8   6   4   2

Designed by Gretchen Achilles

FOR DENA

CONTENTS

THE LIVES AND DEATHS OF
JOHN F. KENNEDY

It was Thursday, July 14, 1960, in Room 9333 of the Biltmore Hotel in Los Angeles, and Kenny O'Donnell was furious at the man he had just helped nominate for president of the United States.

Again and again, John Kennedy had assured the unions, the civil rights leaders, the liberals and intellectuals whose support he needed, that Texas senator Lyndon Johnson would not be his choice for vice president. For those constituencies, the majority leader of the Senate was too tied to the corporate interests of his home state, too willing to weaken or abandon strong civil rights legislation, too much the symbol of wheeler-dealer insider politics.

Yet now, little more than twelve hours after Kennedy had won a first ballot nomination with a razor-thin margin of five delegates, he had offered the second slot on the ticket to Johnson—and Johnson had accepted.

"I was so furious I could hardly talk," O'Donnell remembered years later. "I thought of the promises we had made . . . the assurances we had given. I felt that we had been double-crossed."

So O'Donnell demanded to confront Kennedy face-to-face, and

the nominee complied, taking O'Donnell into the bathroom for a private conversation and assuring him that the job would actually diminish Johnson's power by placing him in a powerless, impotent job.

"I'm forty-three years old," Kennedy said, "and I'm the healthiest candidate for president in the United States. You've traveled with me enough to know that I'm not going to die in office. So the vice presidency doesn't mean anything."

The man who gave his disaffected aide this reassurance had already lost a brother and a sister in airplane crashes; had almost died when his ship was destroyed in the South Pacific during World War II; had been stricken with an illness so serious in 1947 that he had been given the last rites of his church; had undergone a life-threatening operation in 1954 to save him from invalidism—an operation so serious that he was away from his Senate seat for nine months; and had been living with a form of Addison's disease—hidden from the press and public—that required a regular dose of powerful medicine and made him live virtually every day in pain.

For a man so often described as "fatalistic"—who on the day of his murder mused to his wife, and to that same Kenny O'Donnell, about the ease with which "a man with a rifle" could kill him—Kennedy's blithe assurance about his invulnerability to fate seems astonishing. If nothing else, his immersion in history must have taught him that seven presidents had died in office, three violently; that FDR had barely escaped assassination in 1933; and that Harry Truman had been the target of assassins in 1950. Kennedy himself would escape death at the hands of a suicide bomber less than five months after speaking those comforting words.

Maybe, though, Kennedy's words are not so astonishing. They reflect an impulse deep within the human spirit: to push aside the power of random chance in favor of a more orderly, less chaotic universe. Even someone like John Kennedy, who had come close to death more than once, could casually dismiss the whole idea of considering that possibility when choosing the man to stand "a heartbeat away."

Many historians take the same approach in dealing with the what-ifs that drive excursions into "alternate history." For them, it is at best a parlor game, at worst a nuisance. "What *did* happen," they argue, "is what matters. Playing the alternate history game is like asking, 'What if Spartacus had had a jet?'"

I take a different view. Historian H. R. Trevor-Roper wrote:

"At any given moment in history, there are real alternatives . . . How can we '*explain* what happened and *why*' if we only look at what happened and never consider the alternatives . . . ?"

The alternatives, however, are not boundless. Asking "What if JFK had become a born-again evangelical?" or "What if a Soviet scientist had invented the Internet in 1965?" might make for an entertaining piece of fiction, but it violates the single most critical element of alternative history: *plausibility*. Harvard historian Niall Ferguson (who prefers the term "virtual history") says, "By narrowing down the historical alternatives we consider to those which are *plausible* . . . we solve the dilemma of choosing between a single deterministic past and an unmanageably infinite number of possible pasts."

If you're going to argue that history would have been very different if someone else had occupied the White House in a time of crisis, you have to show why: *what* in this individual's character, beliefs, impulses, and past actions would have made the difference. In *Then Everything Changed*, my previous excursion into alternate histories, the small twists of fate that would have seen John Kennedy killed before ever taking office, or that would have saved Robert Kennedy from assassination, or that would have seen Gerald

Ford keep the presidency in 1976, were all rooted in hard facts. And the hugely consequential changes that would have flowed from those small twists of fate were based on the beliefs, impulses, and character traits of these men and their contemporaries, gathered from biographies, oral histories, interviews, and memoirs.

I've brought this same approach to a question that is as prominent in the what-if realm as any: What if John Kennedy had not died in Dallas? The very small alteration of meteorological history that would have saved his life is well-known already—indeed, many in Dallas were painfully aware of it within minutes of the shots— and it is completely, deeply plausible.

And after that tiny twist of fate saves the President? I've sought to keep that plausibility as my polestar. As I did in *Then Everything Changed*, I've consulted biographies, oral histories, and memoirs (my debt to them is explained specifically in the afterword). I've also conducted interviews, in person, on the telephone, and via e-mail, with a variety of observers, including Dick and Doris Goodwin, Michael Beschloss, Norm Ornstein, Walter Shapiro, Meryl Gordon, Tom Hayden, Fred Kaplan, David Talbot, and Todd Gitlin (though they bear no responsibility for the speculative history I offer). Most of the fictional events presented have their origins in reality: the "facts on the ground," as they existed in November 1963. The opinions, the speeches, the conversations I recount from the days and months and years leading up to November 22 did in fact occur. More broadly, the political currents that shape the 1964 Kennedy reelection campaign, the decisions about Vietnam and the cold war, the forces that reshape America's culture, the threats to Kennedy's political survival and reputation, all were in place before Kennedy went to Texas. The question I try to answer is: How might John Kennedy's instincts, his understanding of history, his core impulses, have led him to deal with these forces? For instance, John

Kennedy tended toward a dispassionate, detached, analytical approach to issues; he was in this sense the polar opposite of Lyndon Johnson, who saw political threats and opportunities through an intensely personal prism. A detached, dispassionate president might not have had the commitment to fight hard for a civil rights bill or commit the nation to "war on poverty." But that same detached, dispassionate approach might have prevented a president from escalating a war out of a refusal to be "the first president to lose a war" (as LBJ once famously put it). This does not mean that my version of what happens is "right," but it does mean that it starts from what is *known*.

Two final notes: First, I essentially put aside the question of whether Lee Harvey Oswald acted as part of a conspiracy. For what it's worth, I've always thought that the evidence of Oswald's guilt is strong, but to plunge back into decades of speculation would simply overwhelm everything else. This book is about what happens after the assassination attempt *fails*.

Second, the story I tell here is neither hagiography nor pathography. Anyone seeking to imagine an eight-year Kennedy presidency has to come to grips with his strengths and weaknesses, his admirable and deplorable character traits. My intention here is to do just that, and to suggest how that mix of traits might have altered one of the most turbulent periods in our history.

IF KENNEDY LIVED

CHAPTER ONE

DALLAS, TEXAS, NOVEMBER 22, 1963, 7:30 A.M. CENTRAL STANDARD TIME

I t's raining, Mr. President."

"I'm up," he said to his valet, George Thomas, through the door of the master bedroom of Suite 850, and walked to the window. His hosts had borrowed priceless paintings from local museums—a Monet, a Picasso, a Van Gogh—but his eyes were drawn to the gloomy weather, and to a large crowd gathered on the sidewalk eight stories below: a fitting blend of bad and good news for this trip.

He'd come to Texas because it had seemed a state crucial to his reelection next year. Its twenty-four electoral votes, won with a margin of only 46,000 votes, had provided a badly needed cushion three years earlier—without them, his election would have rested on a highly questionable 8,000-vote margin in Illinois—and with twenty-five votes this time around, Texas might well have to be his firewall in the South, where his embrace of sweeping civil rights legislation had made his prospects below the Mason-Dixon Line thin at best. It was important enough that he'd persuaded Jackie to join him: her first political trip since 1960, and one that came just three and a half months after the death of their infant son.

At every stage of the visit so far—from the dedication of the United States Air Force School of Aerospace Medicine in San Antonio, to a Houston dinner for Congressman Albert Thomas, to the motorcade route to and from the airports—the crowds had been large and enthusiastic. *If we get a break in the weather,* he thought, *we can let the crowds get a good look at us here and in Dallas and Austin; maybe that'll shake some cash loose from the big-money boys.*

Only . . . there were clouds hanging over this Texas visit that had nothing to do with the weather.

For one thing, the Democratic Party was in the middle of a full-fledged civil war between conservative Democrats, led by Governor John Connally, and liberals led by Senator Ralph Yarborough. Just before leaving Washington to join the President on Air Force One, Yarborough had learned that he'd been denied a seat at the head table at the big $100-a-plate fund-raiser in Austin and had not been invited to the Governor's reception later that evening. He'd taken his anger out on Vice President Lyndon Johnson, a key Connally ally, repeatedly refusing increasingly desperate requests from the President's political team to ride in the motorcades with Johnson.

That had produced exactly the kind of headline John Kennedy did *not* want to see, splashed across the front pages of the Dallas papers: YARBOROUGH SNUBS LBJ, with others inside no better: PRESIDENT'S VISIT SEEN WIDENING STATE DEMOCRATIC SPLIT.

What is it with Lyndon? he wondered. He'd put him on the ticket in 1960 in the face of puzzlement, even anger, from his liberal and labor supporters, not to mention some of his closest political aides. Kenny O'Donnell had been in shock; Bobby, whose contempt for the Texan didn't just border on outright hatred but had crossed that border years ago, had tried three times to talk Johnson off the ticket. *Thank God he hadn't.* Johnson, riding the "Cornpone Special" across the South, had kept Texas in the Democratic column, and had likely made the difference in the Carolinas and maybe even Missouri. As for rumors that Kennedy might dump Johnson in '64, he'd brushed them aside: just this week, on a swing through Florida, he'd told his old friend Senator George Smathers, "Lyndon's going to be my vice president because *I need him!*" But if Lyndon didn't even have the power to hold Texas Democrats together, and if the civil rights issue was going to make the South a lost cause, then just how much did he need him? Last night he'd summoned Johnson to his suite and told him in no uncertain terms that this public spat between Connally and Yarborough had to be healed, and healed *now.*

Besides, there were these rumors out of Washington and New York that might turn out to be more than just rumors. Johnson's longtime protégé, Senate secretary Bobby Baker, had just resigned, and the rumors suggested that some of the stories about payoffs and kickbacks were getting very close to the Vice President. And some of the stories were about more than money: they were about prostitutes—"party girls" used to win the favor of important politicians. (He was more than familiar with that side of the story— uncomfortably so.) And one of his reporter friends in the Time-Life empire had passed along to Pierre Salinger another unsettling rumor: *Life* magazine was looking into Johnson's money—how had a man on the public payroll all his life become a multi-millionaire?

I wonder which one of my geniuses decided to end this trip with a barbecue and an overnight at the LBJ ranch . . . Maybe I can get Rusk or McNamara to gin up a crisis and get me the hell out of there.

He walked across the living room into Jackie's bedroom, where there was a better view of the crowd on the street below. Her presence was a gift, he knew; the crowd was here as much for her as for him, and he thought he'd rephrase the line he'd used on their European trip: "I am the man who accompanied Jacqueline Kennedy to Paris." She and the kids were potent political weapons, and those photo spreads in *Look* magazine—John-John frolicking in the Oval Office, Caroline and her cousins at Hyannis, piling into a golf cart as he drove them for ice cream—were pure gold. God knows, he was going to need the affection of the voters next year . . . because the track record of his administration was something less than overwhelming.

Yes, the economy was good—no inflation, unemployment under 5 percent—but there was a real concern from his economic team that things could be slowing down without a tax cut, and in Congress his own Democratic committee chairs were spooked by the idea that a tax cut was a liberal gimmick that would mean deficits. The civil rights bill he'd embraced was going nowhere; even that huge, peaceful March on Washington last summer hadn't budged the Southerners who ran the Congress, and the country still told the pollsters that Negroes were pushing too hard, too fast. Things in D.C. were so paralyzed that the press corps had begun to use terms like "gridlock," "breakdown," even "constitutional crisis."

And while there'd been real progress on the foreign front—the Nuclear Test Ban Treaty, signs of a thaw in the cold war after the Cuban missile crisis of a year ago—there were troubles from one side of the globe to the other. The CIA's attempts at covert action in Cuba had been as futile as that insane Bay of Pigs invasion; Bobby had been up in their face for two years, and all they'd come up with was to try and depose or kill Castro with the help of American gangsters. He'd begun to think it was time for something different, some kind of live-and-let-live understanding with Castro. That French journalist, Jean Daniel, was meeting with Fidel now; he'd asked Daniel to get back to him and let him know what Castro was thinking.

And South Vietnam? For almost three years, his advisors had been giving him such conflicting advice that he'd once asked two of them, "Are you sure you went to the same country?" Is the South Vietnamese army, with the help of 15,000 American advisors, making any headway against the Viet Cong guerrillas? Is the government of Ngo Dinh Diem "winning the hearts and minds of the people"? Diem and his brother had seemed more interested in suppressing the Buddhist majority than in dealing with the corruption and incompetence in their government; which is why, three weeks ago, a band of generals (with U.S. support) had overthrown the brothers in a coup—a coup that was *supposed* to leave Diem and Nhu unharmed. Instead, they'd been shot to death in the back of a truck.

And while his Joint Chiefs, and Rusk at State, and Bundy in the White House were telling him, "We can't let South Vietnam fall; it will endanger all of Southeast Asia," others—Ken Galbraith, his Indian ambassador; Senator Mike Mansfield, who knew the region; and General de Gaulle—were telling him, *It's a quagmire, if you go in with an army, you'll never get out.* His own George Ball had said flatly, that if the United States went in with ground troops, it would have 300,000 or more in a year or two. (That idea was nuts, of course—he'd told George that—but still . . .) As for his own instincts? Well, just yesterday in Washington, at the end of a meeting with a young State Department aide, Mike Forrestal, he'd beckoned him back into the Oval Office.

"Wait a minute," he'd said. "After the first of the year, I want you to organize an in-depth study of every possible option we've got in Vietnam, including how to get out. We have to review this whole thing from the bottom to the top."

But he was also a man of finely honed political instincts, and they told him he couldn't cut his losses now, even if he wanted to— not with an election coming up, not with the prospect that the Republicans would yell "Who lost Vietnam?" just the way they—and a lot of Democrats—had yelled "Who lost China?" at Truman back in '49 (hell, as a young congressman, he'd been one of them). That's why he'd told O'Donnell, Mansfield, and everyone else that nothing was going to happen until *after* he was reelected. For God's sake, all anyone had to do was look at the full-page ad in the *Dallas Morning News*, bordered in black, paid for by H. L. Hunt and a group of Dallas businessmen on the far right, more or less accusing him of treason.

"We're heading into nut country today," he'd said to Jackie, not mentioning to her that his UN ambassador, Adlai Stevenson, had been met with such a violent demonstration at a recent speech that Adlai had passed the word to the White House that it might be just as well for the President not to go to that city. But there was no way he was going to Texas without a stop in its second biggest city.

And as for that reelection? He knew what the polls were saying: that his job approval rating had dropped sharply, from 76 to 59 percent, most of it coming from the South's response to civil rights. He knew that racial splits were opening up—over jobs, housing, crime—in the big cities of the North, dividing white working-class voters from blacks and thus cleaving the old Roosevelt-Truman coalition further. (Was Alabama's segregationist governor George Wallace serious about running against him in Democratic primaries outside the South?)

And he also knew that he could not count on the Republicans to nominate Arizona senator Barry Goldwater, the conservative hero whose pronouncements about nuclear weapons were bound to paint him as a figure outside the mainstream. "If Barry's the nominee," he'd said a week ago to his political team, "I won't have to leave Washington." A candidate like New York's Nelson Rockefeller or Michigan's George Romney, though . . . that could be a problem.

But if he was concerned that his hold on the White House was not as firm as he might wish it to be, there was comfort, a kind of reassurance, in remembering how often pure, random chance had governed his life; so many times in the past, going back years— even decades—a small turn of fate would have ensured that he never made it to the White House at all.

IT WAS SUPPOSED TO BE JOE

Joe was the firstborn son of one of the country's wealthiest men, who had once pondered the presidency for himself before his ally turned nemesis Franklin Roosevelt ran for a third term. No less than a nobleman of other times and realms, Joe Kennedy Sr. embraced primogeniture, and in his namesake son, Joseph P. Kennedy Jr., it seemed as if the gods had agreed. Tall, muscular, strikingly handsome, he projected assurance, confidence, command. At Choate, he'd been a leader in the classroom and on the field and earned the Harvard Cup, given to the student who embraced excellence in scholastics and athletics. At Harvard, he'd been a star in football, rugby, crew. And he made no secret of his intentions, telling one of his tutors—a young economist named John Kenneth Galbraith— "When I get to the White House, I'm taking you with me."

His father's counsel to him over the years had always been given with an eye on the main prize. He'd persuaded Joe to switch his major from philosophy to government. When Joe was at Harvard Law School, he wrote: "Get yourself signed up and possibly make some speeches in the fall in the campaign throughout Massachusetts. It would be a very interesting experience and you could work up two or three subjects you wanted to discuss throughout the state." When Joe Sr.'s father-in-law, John "Honey Fitz" Fitzgerald entered a primary battle for the U.S. Senate in 1942, father wrote son that Fitz's primary opponent was facing "a lot of criticism by the Catholic women that [he'd] married a Protestant . . . I am thoroughly convinced that an Irish Catholic with a name like yours, and your record, married to an Irish Catholic girl, would be a pushover in this State for a political office."

But there were complications. Joe Jr. was very much his father's son, far more so than his younger brother; he embraced Joe Sr.'s anti-interventionist views, joining organizations closely allied with the America First movement, cautioning that the U.S. military was simply not ready for war. Privately, at least as a young man, he had reflected some of his father's antipathy toward Jews. Writing Joe Sr. from Germany in the summer of 1934, he'd argued:

"The German people were scattered, despondent, and were divorced from hope. Hitler came in. He saw the need of a common enemy. Someone of whom to make the goat . . . It was too bad that it had to be done with the Jews, [but] this dislike of the Jews was well founded."

So while any politically ambitious young man would have sought a military record once World War II broke out, it was even more crucial for Joe Jr. to separate himself from his father's long record of appeasement, and to erase any questions about his own stands. He was drafted out of Harvard Law, signed up as a naval aviator, and by 1944 had flown more than twenty-five missions, surviving a number of dogfights with the Luftwaffe in the process. That was more than enough to entitle him to come home, but something was keeping him in combat—quite possibly the emergence of his younger brother Jack as an authentic war hero, celebrated in front-page newspaper stories after his PT boat was sunk in the Solomon Islands a year earlier. (Jack had mordantly noted once that "it would be good for Joe's political career if he died for the grand old flag, but I don't believe he feels that is absolutely necessary.")

Whatever the motive, Joe Jr. signed up for a mission that war historians later described as "near suicidal"—even pulled rank to get the task. He was to pilot a stripped-down B-24 Liberator bomber loaded with high-level explosives toward the site of a Nazi rocket site in northern France, and parachute out of the plane as the robotically controlled Liberator and its 22,000 pounds of Torpex crashed into the site.

He never made it. Because of a miscommunication between the U.S. Navy and British radar installations, a radar beam triggered the explosives while Joe was at the stick. His remains were never found.

And if Joe had lived . . . ?

It would have been Joe who came home to an open House seat, made vacant when the sitting congressman, Boston legend James Michael Curley, vacated it to seek a return to the mayor's office. (Somehow, Curley's massive debts from past campaigns had suddenly, miraculously been paid off by a mystery benefactor.) It would have been Joe who took on Senator Henry Cabot Lodge Jr. in 1952, with limitless sums from his father's treasury.

As for himself? John Kennedy's own tastes had run to a more contemplative, more analytical life. His health battles had made books his constant companions, and his personality was far less outgoing than Joe's. He'd been drawn to journalism, and thought at one point that a job as a foreign bureau chief of a major newspaper or magazine would be to his liking. He'd even turned his senior thesis about British fecklessness in the run-up to World War II into a book, *Why England Slept*, that became a best seller. (He'd had a small army of helpers, including *New York Times* columnist Arthur

Krock—one of the many benefits of being the son of a very wealthy, well-connected man.)

"I never thought at school or at college that I would ever run for office myself," he said later. "One politician was enough in the family, and my brother Joe was obviously going to be that politician. I hadn't considered myself a political type, and he filled all the requirements for political success." Their father agreed: he described his second son as "shy, withdrawn, and quiet. His mother and I couldn't picture him as a politician. We were sure he'd be a teacher or a writer."

But when Joe Jr. died, Jack was next in line, and for the patriarch, that was enough.

"It was like being drafted," Jack said. "My father wanted his eldest son in politics. 'Wanted' isn't the right word. He *demanded* it. You know my father."

So it was Jack who struggled through awkward meetings with voters and badly given speeches all through 1946, until he finally found his footing, and—with the limitless flood of his father's money—won that House seat and began his fourteen-year journey to the office his father long ago had vowed a Kennedy would one day occupy . . . a journey that almost ended when one of his lifelong health afflictions struck.

HE WAS LUCKY TO BE ALIVE . . .

He had almost died in the war a year before Joe did, surviving a days-long ordeal in the Solomon Islands after the PT boat he was commanding was split in two by a Japanese destroyer. That much was well known to the country; his father and a brace of journalists had seen to that. The story of his heroism, his close brush with death, had been spread across the front pages of newspapers, chronicled by John Hersey in the pages of the *New Yorker* and later *Reader's Digest*. The tie clip in the shape of his PT boat was the calling card of his aides and allies.

That was the life-threatening story that was a key to his political rise. What was just as important was the succession of threats to his life that had begun almost from birth—and that he, his family, and his doctors worked so hard to conceal.

He'd been sick from infancy, not just with the normal ills of childhood. He'd come down with scarlet fever at age three, spending two months in a sanitarium in Maine. His prep school days were marked by constant visits to infirmaries and hospitals; his afflictions ranged from colitis to "flu-like symptoms" to a blood count so low his doctors feared he had leukemia. And all the medical care money could buy could not protect him from treatment that may well have posed the greatest threat to his health and life. He'd been prescribed "corticosteroids" for his colitis, in the form of pellets lodged just under his skin. But the drug in all likelihood severely weakened his backbone, and triggered a form of Addison's disease—an adrenal insufficiency that left him prone to infections of every sort.

At every stage of his life, ill health stalked him. He spent weeks in infirmaries and hospitals all through his school years; became so sick coming back from Europe in 1947 that he was given the last rites of the Church on board the *Île de France*. But it was in 1954 that he faced the gravest threat to his future—political and otherwise. His doctors told him bluntly that without a spinal fusion operation, it was very likely that he'd be unable to walk in a year or two. But because of his susceptibility to infection, the operation could very well prove fatal.

Don't do it, his father had advised. *Look at Roosevelt: won four terms from a wheelchair.* But Jack was adamant: *I'd rather die than live that way,* he'd said. And from a bluntly political view, it was hard to imagine how a prospective president whose root message was youth, energy, vigor, the future, could succeed campaigning from a wheelchair, or on crutches. So, on October 21, he underwent a three-hour operation, during which the surgical team embedded metal screws into his spine. As feared, he developed infections; once again he was given the last rites of the Church. It took nine months of further surgery and recovery before he was able to return to the Senate.

In the nine years since, with the help of a compliant series of doctors and a determination to dissemble, he'd been able to hide the truth of his ill health from the press and the public. His campaign team denied he had "classic" Addison's disease (it was a variation). When he tapped the services of Dr. Max Jacobson, widely known as "Dr. Feelgood" for the amphetamines he supplied, the doctor was kept off his list of appointments. ("I don't care if it's horse piss," he said to brother Bob, who expressed concern about the medication. "It works.") And now, thanks to the insistence of Admiral George Burkley, the White House physician, a regimen of exercise and relaxation had provided a decent measure of relief, although he still spent literally every day in considerable pain.

But what if that 1954 operation hadn't worked? Suppose he hadn't survived, or had been forced into retirement? It wasn't just his career that would have ended. Yes, his father would have looked to Bobby or Teddy to step in, but that would have been an impossibility: in the fall of 1954, Bobby would have been twenty-eight years old, and thus constitutionally ineligible for a Senate seat. (Teddy would have been twenty-two—not even old enough for a seat in the House.) And without a brother in the White House to smooth the way to political success, as he later did for Teddy in

1962, neither Bobby's thin accomplishments nor his abrasive personality would have been enough—even with Dad's money.

The operation had been a coin flip. Had it landed the other way, there would not only have been no President Kennedy; there would have been no Kennedy dynasty at all. And he would not have found himself, in October of 1960, in a fight for the White House he was by no means certain to win.

IT CAME DOWN TO TWO TELEPHONE CALLS

The path to the White House had brought him to the edge of a cliff, over and over again. More than once, a single misstep or even a different decision by one of his opponents would have sent him over that edge.

He'd had to prove to the skeptical kingmakers in his party that his youth and religion were not disabling liabilities. So he'd gone into West Virginia, where the Catholic population was 4 percent, and where suspicions about his faith ran strong. And with an eloquent appeal to tolerance, and the help of his father's money (which, in the words of campaign worker Leo Racine "came in satchels—it just kept flooding in"), he won in a landslide. He'd braced himself for competition from the most powerful of Democrats, Senate majority leader Lyndon Johnson, and the most beloved of Democrats, two-time nominee Adlai Stevenson, the representative of the liberal heart and soul base of the party. Had Adlai said yes, or had Johnson stepped into the race a few months or even a few weeks earlier, Kennedy would almost surely have been denied a first-ballot victory. And once the kingmakers retreated behind the doors of their hotel suites, the young Senator's chances for the nomination would have all but disappeared.

Now, in the campaign's final weeks, there was one central factor that could decide the campaign—a factor that had divided the United States, literally, from before there *was* a United States. It was race. And when it came to race, John Kennedy was walking a tightrope. The Democratic Party's uneasy coalition of liberals in the North and Midwest and hard-shell segregationists and outright racists in the South had been coming apart for more than a decade. A segregationist presidential ticket headed by South Carolina governor J. Strom Thurmond had won four Southern states in 1948. A Democratic nominee without the lion's share of the South's 122 electoral votes faced an almost insurmountable path to the presidency.

But . . . too much attention to Southern sensibilities could pose a different political danger. The Republican Party was a serious contender for the Negro vote. Republicans were some of the strongest civil rights champions in the Congress, while Democratic powers like Russell of Georgia, Byrd of Virginia, and Eastland of Mississippi were the latest in a century-long line of Democrats determined to keep blacks in a state of near bondage and peonage. The Republican nominee, Richard Nixon, had so impressed Martin Luther King Jr. with his commitment to equality that most of King's associates were betting that he'd endorse Nixon for president. In fact, Martin Luther King Sr., the young reverend's father and one of the most influential black ministers in America, had signed a newspaper ad endorsing Nixon—out of fear of a Catholic in the White House.

"Imagine Martin Luther King having a bigot for a father!" Kennedy said to campaign aide Harris Wofford. Then, grinning, he added, "Well, we all have fathers, don't we?"

Then, on October 19, King was arrested at an Atlanta sit-in for trespassing, spending the night in jail for the first time in his life.

When he appeared a few days later before a militant segregationist judge, he found himself charged with a trumped-up parole violation and sentenced to six months in jail at the Georgia State Penitentiary at Reidsville, hundreds of miles from Atlanta; his wife feared he would never come out of there alive. She called Wofford, who in turn pressured Sargent Shriver, Kennedy's brother-in-law, who, after carefully making sure that none of the candidate's top aides were within hearing range, persuaded Kennedy to call Mrs. King to express his concern.

The reaction within the campaign was explosive. Bobby was so furious that he phoned Shriver and tore into him with such vehemence that it opened a years-long rift. Summoning Wofford and Louis Martin, the top Negro in the campaign, he said: "Do you know that three Southern governors told us that if Jack supported Jimmy Hoffa, Nikita Khrushchev, or Martin Luther King, they would throw their state to Nixon? Do you know that this election may be razor close and you have probably lost it for us?"

What Bobby *didn't* tell them was that, on the advice of the secretary of the Georgia Democratic Party, *he* had already called the judge who had thrown King in prison and urged him to release the minister on bond. Along with pressure from the Governor, the judge did exactly that, and that's when King's father stepped front and center.

He didn't just officially endorse Kennedy; he did much more.

"I had expected to vote against Senator Kennedy because of his religion," Daddy King said. "But now he can be my President, Catholic or whatever he is. It took courage to call my daughter-in-law at a time like this. He has the moral courage to stand up for what he knows is right. I've got all my votes and I've got a suitcase and I'm going to take them up there and dump them in his lap."

Almost immediately, Louis Martin began calling black journalists around the country. (He scrupulously avoided the white press.) Papers like the *Pittsburgh Courier* and the *Washington Afro American* prominently featured the story. For its part, the campaign distributed some 2 million pamphlets under the name of the "Freedom Crusade Committee" with the headline "NO COMMENT" NIXON VERSUS A CANDIDATE WITH A HEART, SENATOR KENNEDY. (For Nixon, the frustration must have been palpable; he'd urged the Justice Department to intervene, only to be told that it was a matter for the state of Georgia to resolve.)

It was impossible to *prove* the impact of those phone calls, or Daddy King's statement, or the massive distribution of that pamphlet in black neighborhoods across the country; the analytical tools of 1960 weren't that sophisticated. But here's what *was* known. In a black enclave in Philadelphia, where Stevenson had won about 75 percent of the vote, Kennedy won almost 85 percent. In a black neighborhood in Pittsburgh, where Stevenson had won two to one, Kennedy won four to one. In New York's most heavily black neighborhoods, Stevenson had won two-thirds of the vote; Kennedy won three-fourths of the vote. In New Jersey, some 125,000 blacks had voted for JFK: he won the state by 30,000 votes, a margin of less than 1 percent. As for Illinois, where Kennedy won by 8,000 highly dubious votes, one aide noted, "Without the Negroes, it wouldn't have been close enough to steal—not that I'm saying we stole it." Even in the South, the black vote was critical; for all the talk of LBJ as the key to Texas, the black vote in Houston, which had given Stevenson 12,000 votes, gave Kennedy more than 22,300 votes. And the Negro vote in Louisiana and the Carolinas was crucial to Kennedy's narrow victories there.

The link between those phone calls and his historically close victory was not obvious. But there were times when he allowed himself to think: if he had not called Coretta Scott King, if his brother had not called the judge, if Daddy King had not expressed his gratitude so powerfully, if the black vote had not come out as enthusiastically as it did . . . then Richard Nixon would likely have won the White House.

And what would a President Nixon have done if he had been confronted with Soviet offensive missiles in Cuba? It had taken every ounce of presidential insistence to keep Kennedy's advisors—military *and* civilian—from launching an air strike with God knows what consequences. With a Nixon in the White House . . . ? Incredible that Kennedy's presidency, and the fate of the world, might have hinged on a couple of telephone calls. Then again, it might also have hinged on how his wife had been feeling on a Sunday morning almost three years ago . . .

SHE CAME TO THE DOOR TO SEE HIM OFF . . .

It was Sunday morning, December 11, 1960, and he was at the family's oceanfront Palm Beach home on Ocean Avenue. He was working on his tan and—more important—his inaugural address, after surviving one of the closest elections in American history. Now he was getting ready to head to St. Edward Church, a gesture politically necessary even for a Catholic as secular as he was. He headed for the front door, where the Secret Service would be waiting to drive him the short distance.

Parked just down Ocean Avenue was a 1950 Buick in which Richard Pavlick, a seventy-three-year-old retired postal worker, sat behind the wheel, holding a switch wired to seven sticks of dynamite.

He had been stalking Kennedy across the country, driven by hatred of the Catholic Church and the conviction that Joe Kennedy had stolen the presidency for his son. He'd been sending threatening postcards back to his hometown of Belmont, New Hampshire, promising that they'd soon be hearing from him "in a big way." Now, to save the country from papist tyranny, he was preparing to ram his car into the back of Kennedy's automobile and detonate his explosives.

And the Secret Service was, inexplicably, completely indifferent to his presence. Pavlick had a clear, unimpeded path to Kennedy's car—and, in the words of a shaken Secret Service chief, "enough dynamite to level a mountain."

And then, as Kennedy was leaving, Jacqueline Kennedy came to the door with their three-year-old daughter, Caroline, to see him off.

It was the most casual, insignificant of gestures. On another morning she might have stayed in bed; it was, after all, little less than a month since the difficult birth of John Kennedy Jr. She might have been reading the Sunday papers or been chatting on the phone with a friend or relative.

But she came to the door. And Richard Pavlick . . . did nothing. He was a man of firm if twisted conviction—he spent endless hours protesting the mishandling of the American flags that flew around his hometown—and the idea of killing a man, even a Kennedy, in front of his wife and small child was simply unthinkable. He would wait for another time, perhaps next Sunday. He was arrested four days later when a postmaster from Belmont alerted Florida authorities to the threats he'd been mailing back home. The story barely merited more than a brief mention in the press.

And if Jackie had not come to the door? We were, the Secret Service chief said to his shaken staff, "seconds away" from the first-ever murder of a president-elect—and a full-fledged constitutional crisis. John Kennedy in fact was *not yet* the president-elect, not officially. That designation wouldn't apply until after 270 electors had cast their ballots for him at the fifty state capitols a week from Tuesday. If Kennedy had died, what were his electors supposed to do? What were they allowed to do? What if the election were thrown into the House of Representatives? What if Southern congressmen voted for Senator Harry Byrd or Senator Richard Russell and said they'd tie the system up in knots unless Johnson—or Hubert Humphrey or whomever the Democratic insiders chose—agreed to back off civil rights?

And suppose the country had wound up with Lyndon Johnson in the White House? He'd seen Johnson during the missile crisis—seen him reflexively follow the lead of the military men and the more hawkish of his advisors. If there was one thing Kennedy's years in the White House had reaffirmed, it was his instinct to put himself in the other fellow's shoes; back during those thirteen days, he was always looking to give Khrushchev a path out of the crisis, always looking as well to avoid his biggest fear: miscalculation. For Johnson, everything was personal; the fights were about his need to dominate, his need to avoid humiliation, his need to crush the spirit of the other guy. If Johnson had been president then . . .

Damn good thing Jackie came to the door . . .

He went back to the master bedroom and began to dress, beginning with the back brace and the elastic bandage that he wound around his waist and thighs. It was awkward, but it was better than the intense, chronic pain that would otherwise strike him throughout the long day of speeches, rallies, and motorcades. After he'd put on the crisp white shirt with the short straight collar, the red tie, the dark blue Paul Winston two-button suit, he looked down across the street, where he'd be speaking in a few moments.

Just this morning, right after he'd told Jackie, "We're heading to nut country," he'd added, "but if someone wants to shoot me with a rifle through an open window, there's nothing anyone can do about it, so we might as well not worry about it." He'd said almost exactly the same thing to Kenny O'Donnell as he pointed out the window to the stage where the labor rally would take place.

"Look at that platform. With all those buildings around it, the Secret Service couldn't stop someone who really wanted to get you."

He went downstairs and walked across the street through a light drizzle to a labor rally where 5,000 supporters had gathered in the early morning damp. When some in the crowd began yelling for Jackie, he offered a mock apology.

"Mrs. Kennedy is organizing herself. It takes her a little longer, but of course she looks better than we do when she does it."

He was grateful for her willingness to make this trip, especially just a few months after the death of their infant son, Patrick Bouvier. He was grateful to her for other reasons as well: had his compulsive, sometimes reckless behavior driven her from the marriage, his political career would have stalled if not ended. Maybe it was because her own mother had ended her marriage because of the philandering of her father; maybe Jackie had looked at her father, and Jack's father, and decided that it was just the way men are. What was clear was that, without her forbearance, he would never have become president.

Then, after a breakfast speech to the Fort Worth Chamber of Commerce, they had driven to the Fort Worth Airport for the ten-minute flight to Dallas. He climbed up the stairs to Air Force One, angling slightly to ease the pain of his back. There'd be no time to rest on the short flight to Dallas, but there would be time for a quick, blunt chat with Governor Connally. As soon as the plane took off, he summoned the Governor into his cabin, and after a three-minute conversation the Governor agreed to put Senator Yarborough at the head table for the Austin fund-raiser and invite him to the post-dinner reception at the governor's mansion. Sure, it would just paper over their blood feud, but at least the headlines on Saturday wouldn't trumpet that feud.

OF COURSE HE WAS GOING TO DALLAS

There was uneasiness about visiting the city from some of his staff and political allies. It was ground zero for the far right in Texas; the John Birch Society, whose founder Robert Welch had gained fame (or infamy) by branding President Eisenhower "a dedicated, conscious agent of the Communist conspiracy," had a highly visible presence, and a celebrity supporter in the form of retired major general Edwin Walker. (A few months ago, some unknown assailant had taken a shot at Walker through the window of his home with a high-powered rifle; the shooter, whoever he was, had escaped, and the trail had long grown cold.) On a visit to Dallas on October 23, UN ambassador Adlai Stevenson had been jostled and spat on by a crowd of demonstrators.

But Dallas was the second-biggest city in the state, home to some of the most powerful corporate and business interests anywhere in the region. If he had any hopes of winning Texas in '64, he needed the support, not just from the liberals and the labor folks in the state, but from Governor John Connally's conservative wing as well.

So, yes, he was going to Dallas, but that didn't mean the visit would be free of the bitter intraparty split. Hell, even the location for the President's luncheon speech was a source of endless contention.

For Connally and his allies, the only place for the luncheon was the Dallas Trade Mart, a five-year-old, $12.6 million, 980,000-square-foot architectural gem located on North Stemmons Freeway just north of the city's downtown center, in the Dallas Market Center. It was a magnet for Dallas' establishment—at least for those not convinced that John Kennedy was a dangerous leftist eager to sell America out to the Russians.

Kennedy's own team preferred another site: the Women's Building, located on the site of the state fairgrounds, southwest of the downtown center. Because it could hold 4,000 people—twice the capacity of the Trade Mart—it could easily accommodate the Kennedy supporters from the liberal-labor-minority wing of the Texas Democratic Party. That was precisely what Governor Connally and his allies in the State Democratic Party did not want. On November 18, Kennedy's top political aide, Kenny O'Donnell, called advance man Jerry Bruno and told him, "We're going to let Dallas go. We're going to let Connally have the Trade Mart site."

So the Trade Mart was selected as the luncheon site; invitations went out on behalf of the Dallas Citizens Council, the very embodiment of the conservative white establishment.

And there was one more consequence of that site selection. Had the Women's Building been chosen, the route from Love Field to the site would have taken the motorcade east through downtown Dallas—on a more southerly route hundreds of feet farther away from the Texas School Book Depository on the corner of Houston and Elm Streets. And because the President always sat in the right rear of the presidential limousine, anyone looking at the motorcade—say, from the sixth floor of the Texas School Book Depository—would have found Mrs. Kennedy between him and the President.

Just after 11:00 a.m. central standard time, a twenty-nine-year-old reporter for the *Dallas Times Herald* walked to a fence at Dallas' Love Field and picked up a telephone linked by an open line to the paper's downtown office. Normally, Jim Lehrer covered the "federal beat"—the FBI, IRS, courts, that sort of thing—but with the President coming to Dallas, and with the tight deadlines of an afternoon paper, all hands were deployed for the visit. Lehrer was to follow the motorcade through downtown to the Trade Mart, cover Kennedy's speech, and follow the motorcade back to Love Field, where Air Force One would depart for Austin and the big fund-raising dinner.

On the other end of the phone was Stan Weinberg, the rewrite man who would turn Lehrer's observations and notes into the finished story.

"Look," Weinberg said, "I'm going to be writing this story under a lot of pressure later. Do they have the bubble top on the President's car?" The rain that had been falling all morning in the Dallas–Fort Worth area was on the minds of more than just the President.

"Well, I don't know," Lehrer replied. "I can't see his car. Let me go look and see."

He walked down the ramp where the President's limo, a highly modified deep-blue 1961 Lincoln Continental SS-100-X, was parked, and where Forrest Sorrels, the Secret Service agent in charge of the Dallas bureau, was standing. The bubble top was still on the car.

Lehrer and Sorrels were familiar to each other, so the reporter approached the agent, saying: "Rewrite wants to know if the bubble top's going to be on or not."

"Don't know," said Sorrels, and called out to a subordinate. "Why don't you check downtown, see if it's still raining."

It was a matter of the purest chance. On another day, a small, insignificant shift in pressure of wind would have moved the bad weather out, and sunshine would have broken out over Dallas. "Take off the bubble top," Sorrels would have told his men, and the President and Mrs. Kennedy and Governor and Mrs. Connally would have been driving through downtown Dallas at high noon in an open car, waving to the cheering crowds that lined the streets, crowds pressing in, slowing the motorcade down, the open convertible giving everyone in the crowd—anyone looking out a building window—a clear, unobstructed view.

But on this day the weather did *not* change. On *this* day the answer that came from downtown was: "Still raining here, and no sign of clearing. Better leave it on."

"All right," said the chief. "It stays on."

And Jim Lehrer walked back up the ramp, went over to the fence, picked up the open line, and told Stan Weinberg what he'd learned.

"The bubble top's staying on."

No one—not Weinberg, not Lehrer, not Sorrels, not one of them—gave it a second thought . . . for another hour and eight minutes.

CHAPTER TWO

DEALEY PLAZA, DALLAS, TEXAS, 12:30 P.M. CENTRAL STANDARD TIME

They were in downtown Dallas now, and the thin crowds that had clustered along the motorcade route in the industrial suburban streets were gone; in their place were big crowds cheering as the midnight-blue Lincoln drove by. The steady, light rain hadn't kept them away, and while the umbrellas blocked the view of those behind the first rows of spectators, the enthusiasm of the crowds was unmistakable. This was why the motorcade was driving through downtown Dallas, after all: it would have been much quicker to take Lemmon Avenue to the North Dallas Tollway to Stemmons Freeway; but, as the Secret Service had come to understand with the Kennedy White House, "politics trumps protection." In 1964, Governor Connally would be running for reelection on the same ticket as Kennedy; it was crucial that he saw the President as an asset, not a liability, and the bigger the crowds, the louder the cheering, the more likely that outcome was, and the more likely that the wealthy Texas Democrats would start opening their wallets for the President's reelection campaign.

The President and Governor Connally were waving to the crowds; Jacqueline was clutching a dozen red roses she had been given at Love Field. The bouquet was visible even through the mist and the bubble-top canopy.

The motorcade proceeded down Houston Street through the canyon formed by the office buildings that lined the route. From the windows, people were waving and cheering (though when they passed the headquarters of H. L. Hunt, the billionaire who had helped pay for the full-page ad in the morning paper, Hunt and his subordinates watched in silence, then turned their backs on the procession). At street level, the crowds pushed against the police barricades, straining for a glimpse of the First Couple, compressing the route and forcing the motorcade to slow and slow again. As it reached the corner of Lamar and Main Streets, the procession was traveling at barely five miles an hour. In a moment they would pass under a triple overpass, onto Stemmons Freeway, and right to the Trade Center . . . and some relief from the increasingly uncomfortable heat of the Lincoln's interior. When the bubble top was on, there was simply no way to avoid the disagreeable interior climate. That climate may have been the cause of Mrs. Kennedy's discomfort, but for John Kennedy the discomfort was of a political nature. He knew what it meant when he could interact with the crowds face-to-face; he'd seen it in West Virginia in May of 1960; seen it in Paris, where a million turned out in 1961; seen it early this fall on the swing through eleven Western states. "Kennedy weather," Dave Powers and Kenny O'Donnell called it; when the sun was bright and the skies were blue, the cheers seemed louder, the crowds more frenzied.

Just not our day, he thought, and then the Governor's wife, Nellie, pointed out the window, and said, "Well, Mr. President, rain and all, you can't say Dallas doesn't love you . . ."

And then there was a loud crack, and hundreds of pieces of plexiglass exploded into the air; and the President grabbed the left side of his chest, slumped toward his wife, and shouted, "My God, I'm hit!"

Roy Kellerman, the Secret Service agent detailed to the President on the Dallas leg of the Texas trip, was sitting in the right front seat. As soon as the bubble top shattered, he knew what had happened.

"I can't honestly say what I might have thought or done if there'd been only the sound to go by," Kellerman said many weeks later. "You don't want to be in a position of overreacting to a firecracker, or the backfire of a car, or the snapping of a tree branch. It might have taken a few seconds, or even a second shot, God help me, to make it clear what was going on. But as soon as the plexiglass exploded all around us, there was no doubt that someone was shooting at the President."

His immediate instinct was to throw himself over the right front seat of the Lincoln and cover Kennedy with his body. But he couldn't. The center partition of the SS-100, and the jump seats on which Governor and Nellie Connally were sitting, effectively blocked him from the President.

What he did do was to yell to the driver, Agent William Greer, "Let's get out of here! We've been hit! To the hospital, to the hospital!" while radioing the same urgent directive to the lead car. The Lincoln sharply accelerated, following close behind the lead car, an unmarked white Ford driven by Dallas police chief Jesse Curry, and carrying Dallas County sheriff Bill Decker and Dallas Secret Service chief Forrest Sorrels. By the time a second shot was fired, the Lincoln, powered by a hand-built 350-horsepower, 450-cubic-inch engine, was moving at close to forty miles an hour, hundreds of feet away from where the first shot had struck the bubble top; that second shot struck the right rear of the Lincoln just above the rear wheel housing.

It took the Lincoln, now moving at eighty miles an hour, less than three minutes to travel the 3.7 miles from Dealey Plaza to Parkland Memorial Hospital, just off the Stemmons Freeway. On its heel, flanking it on both sides, were the four motorcyclists from the Dallas police force. Close behind was the *"Queen Mary,"* the armored vehicles carrying Secret Service agents, along with Kenny O'Donnell and Dave Powers, and the convertible that held Vice President Johnson and Senator Yarborough. Part of the planning of any presidential trip was to locate the nearest, best-equipped hospitals at every stage of the trip; Parkland was just two miles from the Trade Mart, where Kennedy was to give his speech. They knew exactly where they were going.

They had no idea of what they'd find when they got there: a wounded president of the United States—or a dead one.

At 1:45 p.m. central standard time, Malcolm Kilduff Jr., White House deputy press secretary, walked into Nurses' Classroom 101–102 on the ground floor of Parkland Memorial Hospital. Dozens of reporters, cameramen, and officials were jammed into the room, bright with the glare of the camera lights, heavy with the dense clouds of cigarette smoke. Just outside the room, reporters clustered around a bank of pay phones, the only link between the hospital and the world outside. There was an elaborate press facility with open phone lines back to the city desks of major newspapers, TV networks, and wire services, along with microwave relays that could carry live television signals to local television stations and then, via telephone long lines, back to New York network headquarters—but that was all at the Dallas Trade Mart a mile away. As for the millions turning on their television sets as they heard the first hints of what had happened, they would witness the enormous power, and the stark limits, of mid-century information technology.

The CBS soap opera *As the World Turns* had just begun its broadcast when the rotating globe was replaced by a slide reading: BULLETIN BULLETIN BULLETIN. The crisp voice of anchor Walter Cronkite intoned: "From Dallas, Texas, shots were fired at President Kennedy's motorcade as it rode through downtown streets. First reports say the President was apparently hit . . . more information now coming in . . . the bubble top that covered the President's car was shattered into pieces, the President recoiled in apparent pain, and the limousine sped off as a second shot apparently struck the rear of the car. More details as soon as they become available."

And then viewers saw an elegantly produced commercial for "Nescafé . . . a *new* kind of coffee," and several minutes of *As the World Turns*, until the network cut to a shirtsleeved Cronkite wearing thick black horn-rimmed eyeglasses in the middle of the CBS newsroom, reaching beyond camera range for the sheets of wire-service copy.

On NBC, a trio of their most familiar faces—anchor Chet Huntley and correspondents Frank McGee and Bill Ryan—clustered around a single desk, clutching phones, trying to put the words of Robert MacNeil on the air from Dallas, grappling with an amplifier that did not work, finally listening to MacNeil and repeating his words phrase by phrase.

From the Dallas Trade Mart came images of the guests who had come to lunch, some sitting, stunned, some wandering through the cavernous hall looking for information. KRLD's Eddie Barker, who was at the Trade Mart to anchor the local station's live coverage of Kennedy's speech, noted, "It is ironic in a way that one of the traveling White House advance men just half an hour ago expressed his disappointment that the weather had not cleared off here as they had hoped. Earlier forecasts had called for the possibility of rain throughout the presidential visit. But it was only shortly prior to his jet touching down at Love Field that it became clear that the weather would not break through, which would have made it possible for the President to ride in an open convertible rather than the plexiglass top that was used."

There was only one question anyone really cared about, and it was a question no one in the press was in any position to answer. There was no live coverage of the motorcade, no way to transmit video from the scene of the shooting directly back to the networks, no videotape of the shooting. So the newsmen at their desks in New York and Washington read from wire-service copy, or recounted the fragmentary information from their reporters on the scene: "The President lurched forward . . ." ". . . Mrs. Kennedy reached for him . . ." ". . . Governor and Mrs. Connally leapt from their jump seats to the floor of the car . . ." ". . . witnesses at the hospital reported that the President was carried in on a stretcher . . ." ". . . two priests entered the hospital . . ."

At the same time, the first still photos of the President and Mrs. Kennedy, and of the limousine surrounded by pieces of the bubble top, arrived via wire, and desk assistants in the newsroom mounted them on cardboard and ran them over to the reporters, who held them up; but the newsroom cameras lacked the ability to zoom in, so viewers could barely make out the smiling, waving

First Couple, or the nature of the wounds the President might have suffered.

Then deputy press secretary Kilduff stepped onto a small platform in front of a blackboard in the nurses' classroom. He drew a long breath, then flashed a quick, small smile.

"At approximately 12:30 p.m. central standard time, President Kennedy sustained a bullet wound in his upper left back midway between his spinal cord and his shoulder. He is at this moment in surgery; his condition is critical but stable. Neither Mrs. Kennedy, Governor Connally, nor Mrs. Connally sustained any gunshot wounds; Mrs. Kennedy and Governor Connally did suffer minor cuts from the plexiglass bubble top, but none were deemed serious.

"The President did receive the last rites of the Catholic Church"—there were clearly audible gasps and moans—"from the Very Reverend Oscar L. Huber, but I am assured that this was strictly a precautionary measure." Kilduff paused, took another deep breath, and said, "While I will have no further information until the surgery is completed, I *can* say that as to the prospects of the President's recovery, there is—and I am quoting the President's personal physician, Admiral George Burkley—'every reason to be optimistic.'"

That was, indeed, what Admiral Burkley had authorized Malcolm Kilduff to say. And it was true . . . as far as it went.

But there were other facts that Admiral Burkley had no intention of sharing with Kilduff, or with the press, or with anyone else—ever.

Something very strange was going on at Parkland Memorial Hospital.

Dr. "Pepper" Jenkins was having lunch with members of his anesthesiology department when he heard a page: "Dr. Shires, stat." The head of surgery is almost never paged, he recalled, and never with the injunction "stat."

Dr. Bill Midgett, an OB-GYN resident, was trying to take the history of an emergency room patient when he heard someone screaming for a gurney. As he ran outside pulling one end of a gurney, he saw the presidential limousine pulled up to the entrance to Parkland's emergency room, surrounded by men with automatic weapons. Four Secret Service agents pulled Governor Connally out of the car and lifted the President out of the backseat, out of the arms of Jacqueline Kennedy, and onto a stretcher. The President had been semiconscious during the quick journey to Parkland, but as he was wheeled inside he lost consciousness, and his face took on a gray pallor. That told the half dozen doctors inside Trauma Room 1 that he had gone into shock, likely from internal bleeding . . . which meant that emergency surgery was required to find the source of the bleeding and stop it if they were going to save Patient 24740.

They quickly cut and stripped off his clothes, removed the back brace and elastic bandages that covered his torso and thighs, checked him for vital signs: shallow breathing, a very weak pulse, a fever of 99.6. Dr. Charles Carrico put his hands under the President's upper back and quickly located the bullet wound between the President's left shoulder and chest. The surgical team had just begun inserting two intravenous lines for blood transfusions and fluids when someone walked quickly into the room.

"I'm Admiral George Burkley, the President's personal physician. You need to get him some steroids."

"Steroids? Why?" asked Dr. Charles Baxter.

"Because he's an Addisonian," Admiral Burkley said.

No physician could misunderstand. If President Kennedy had

Addison's disease, it meant a deficiency in his adrenal glands that left him acutely vulnerable to infections, to stress of all sorts; without steroids, an operation could kill him. If they had been followers of political campaigns—"junkies," as they came to be called in later years—they might have remembered that, shortly before the Democratic convention in 1960, two of Lyndon Johnson's campaign aides had accused Kennedy of hiding this condition from the public, a charge the Kennedy campaign had furiously denied.

"Give him one big bolus," Carrico ordered, and set 300 milligrams of Solu-Cortef, a cortisone-based steroid, into Kennedy's arm intravenously. Within minutes the President was under heavy anesthetics and the team opened his chest, finding a cracked rib and, more seriously, a nick in his subclavian artery, causing the heavy internal bleeding. After a two-hour operation, the artery was repaired and a substantial piece of the bullet was removed. A KUB X-ray of his abdomen found another fragment lodged in Kennedy's lower chest and that was removed, lessening the possibility of a postoperative infection.

"I think that's going to do it," one of the physicians said to Admiral Burkley. "But my God, the way his lumbar region looks, I'm surprised he can even walk."

"Well, he can—and, thanks to you and your team, he will," Burkley said. "And as I'm sure you realize, all of the records of the procedures here will come under the purview of the Secret Service. The details of the President's health have national security implications that—"

"Understood," the doctor said, "understood."

A few minutes after Mac Kilduff's briefing, after he had phoned in the details to Weinberg at the city desk, Jim Lehrer stepped outside the entrance to Parkland's emergency room for a few breaths of fresh air. There, standing by the presidential limousine, was Dallas

Secret Service chief Forrest Sorrels. They glanced at each other, and Sorrels, looking like a man just pulled back from the abyss, shook his head and pointed to the plexiglass shards of the bubble top.

"Thank God it rained, Jim; thank God it rained. If the sun had come out, he'd be a dead man."

Robert Kennedy was eating a tuna fish sandwich on the patio of his home in suburban Virginia, chatting with some of his Justice Department colleagues, when he was told that J. Edgar Hoover was on the phone. The Attorney General and the FBI director despised each other; for Hoover to call Robert Kennedy at home was an instant sign of bad news. Maybe another rumor had surfaced about Jack; maybe he was asking for more surveillance of Martin Luther King Jr.

"I have news for you," Hoover said in a voice stripped of any trace of emotion. "The President's been shot."

"Yes," he replied to Kennedy's first, stunned question. "It appears to be serious. I'll call when I know more."

Robert Kennedy hung up the phone, then spoke as though he had been struck hard.

"Jack's been shot . . . It's serious." Then, to Ed Guthman, one of his senior Justice Department aides: "There's been so much hate . . . I thought they'd get one of us . . . I thought it would be me."

His first thoughts about his brother were protective—in two senses. First, he called national security advisor McGeorge Bundy and had the locks changed on the President's files. *If Lyndon Johnson is the president, there's no way he's going to get his hands on those files.*

Second, even before he knew his brother's fate, he began asking the same question to a dozen different people: "Who did this?"

He summoned CIA director John McCone to his Hickory Hill home and asked if his agency had done it. (No, said McCone, and invoked their shared Catholic faith to underscore his assertion.) He asked his contact in the Cuban exile community if the exiles' anger over JFK's "no invasion" pledge in the wake of the Cuban missile crisis had triggered the attack; he asked his top investigator, Walter Sheridan, whether Teamsters president Jimmy Hoffa, on trial for jury tampering, had done it. What about organized crime? There were plenty of tapes of Mafia bosses swearing bloody vengeance on Kennedy for his crusade. And what about Fidel, who had told an AP reporter just two months ago that "U.S. leaders should think if they are aiding terrorist plans to eliminate Cuban leaders, they themselves will not be safe"? Bobby knew damn well that "U.S. leaders" were doing just that—because he was one of them.

It was forty-five minutes later when his wife, Ethel, beckoned him to the phone. It was Kenny O'Donnell from Dallas. O'Donnell had been with Jack since his first campaign for Congress in '46, had helped put him in the Senate and then the White House, and Kenny was weeping and laughing and telling Bobby, "He's in surgery—but it looks like he's going to make it. It looks like he's going to be okay. And Jackie's fine; I mean, not fine, but—"

"Ed!" he said to Guthman as he hung up the phone. "Let's go."

Seven minutes later, Robert Kennedy was speeding down George Washington Memorial Parkway; fifteen more minutes and he was heading down Alabama Avenue, then waved through gates by the Air Force guards. Shortly after 3:30 p.m. eastern standard time, an eight-seat military transport jet was taxiing down the runway at Andrews Air Force Base.

Someone had tried to kill his brother. He was going to find out who he—or they—were . . . and why.

Shortly before 2:00 p.m. central standard time, the screen at the Texas Theatre on West Jefferson Boulevard in Dallas went black; the matinee showing of *War Is Hell* was shut off, the lights went on, and the handful of patrons looked up to see a dozen police officers, armed with shotguns, deployed throughout the theater. Officer M. N. McDonald began to walk down the left aisle, toward the front of the theater, searching patrons as he went.

Unlike the vast majority of Dallas police at that moment, they weren't searching for the gunman who had shot President Kennedy. They were looking for the man who had shot Officer J. D. Tippit on Tenth Street—a shooting witnessed by several eyewitnesses (one of whom begged the police to leave him out of their investigation, as he had been visiting his lover for an afternoon fling). The gunman had fled down Jefferson Boulevard and stopped briefly in the foyer of Hardy's Shoe Store, where manager Johnny Calvin Brewer, deciding that the man "looked suspicious," followed him as he ducked into the Texas Theatre.

"Did that man who just ran in here buy a ticket?" Brewer asked clerk Julia Postal. When she realized the man had slipped inside, Postal—who had heard a radio flash about the Kennedy shooting—told him, "I don't know if this is the man they want in there, but he is running from them for some reason." Minutes later Brewer was onstage with police officers and was pointing a man out to Officer McDonald.

When he was ordered to stand, the man put up his hands, then yelled, "Well, it is all over now!" punched the policeman in the face, and pulled a pistol out of the waistband of his slacks.

And Officer McDonald, faced with the threat of imminent

death, pointed his service revolver at his assailant and fired two shots. The man clutched his stomach and collapsed.

When the ambulance arrived barely a minute later, the police carried the wounded man out of the theater, and Detective Paul Bentley pulled a wallet out of the man's left hip pocket.

"Who is he?" asked Officer C. T. Walker.

"Well, this ID says he's A. L. Hidell. But this one says he's Lee Harvey Oswald. We may have to wait awhile to find out who he really is."

"Or who he *was*," Walker said.

For 100 million Americans, the shooting and the survival of John Kennedy became, in the words of the *Times* of London correspondent Louis Heren, "a collective national experience surely unprecedented anywhere in the world and anytime in history . . . [C]lustered around millions of television screens, most Americans were involved in the fate of Kennedy to a degree unimaginable before the age of electronic communications." From the first scattered reports interrupting the early afternoon soap operas, to the countless clusters of passersby peering into the windows of appliance stores to follow the news, to the cautious optimism and then confident assertions of his survival, the now-dominant medium of television that might have become a repository of national mourning became instead a source of national relief and exhilaration.

That first afternoon and evening, viewers saw surgeons and physicians, holding enlarged images from anatomy textbooks, explaining where the President had been hit, how his subclavian artery had been repaired, where his rib had been cracked, along with highly incomplete accounts of John Kennedy's medical history. They saw footage from the day: the speech to a labor rally and the chamber of commerce in Fort Worth; the reception at Dallas's Love Field, Jackie in her two-piece pink suit and pillbox hat, clutching a large bouquet of roses, still photos of the First Couple waving to the crowd; then a grainy image of the bubble top exploding and the President clutching his upper left chest. The networks carried the press briefings from Parkland—microwave relays had been hastily installed to permit live coverage—and viewers saw and heard Admiral Burkley assert that "the President has been in excellent health, which should help ensure his recovery," and that there was "no reason" to fear any long-term injury.

They saw footage of Attorney General Robert Kennedy arriving at Parkland Hospital at 8:00 p.m., surrounded by a phalanx of Dallas police and Secret Service; heard reports from Washington that the plane carrying six cabinet officers and Pierre Salinger, the White House press secretary, on its way to Tokyo for a major economic conference, was safe. They heard historians talk of past attempts, successful and failed, to kill presidents, and heard one wonder aloud about whether the absence of more than half the cabinet had been timed to create maximum chaos.

"Remember," he said, "the conspiracy to kill Lincoln—and it *was* a conspiracy—also involved an attempt to kill the Vice President and Secretary of State."

And increasingly that first evening, the networks turned their attention to Lee Harvey Oswald, the twenty-four-year-old who had been pronounced dead on arrival at Methodist Dallas Medical Center after being shot in that Texas Theatre scuffle with Officer McDonald. He had worked at the Texas School Book Depository, from which a raft of witnesses said the shots had been fired; he'd been the head—and apparently the *only* member—of the Fair Play for Cuba Committee, an organization supporting the Cuban leader and urging an end to embargoes and confrontations with the country. He'd served in the Marine Corps; defected to the Soviet Union, where he'd lived for three years; married a Russian woman; returned to the U.S. a year and a half ago. And if the eyewitnesses were right, he'd shot and killed Dallas police officer J. D. Tippit on a street in the Oak Cliff neighborhood after the officer, hearing a description of the alleged Kennedy assailant, had beckoned him over to his police car. The more that was learned about Oswald, the less he seemed to fit the narrative that had emerged in the first moments after the shooting: Dallas was a center of the white-hot radical right. That very morning a full-page ad in the *Dallas Morning News* had all but accused the President of treason. In the first moments after the shooting, the "climate of hate" in Dallas became something of a theme.

But Oswald? Neighbors and acquaintances—he didn't seem to have many friends—were telling the press he was a self-taught Marxist. A search of his rooming house turned up copies of the *Militant*, a publication of the Socialist Workers Party. His wife, Marina, was telling the police that he had been trying to visit Cuba, perhaps return to the Soviet Union. It just didn't seem to fit . . . unless Oswald wasn't who he seemed to be.

The speculation about Oswald, and the mounting evidence of his guilt—he'd ordered the 6.5-millimeter Mannlicher-Carcano model 91/38 by mail under an assumed name; he'd posed in a photograph holding the rifle; his palm print had been found on the rifle—was intense. But it would soon be overwhelmed by the images that defined that "collective national experience." The nature of television was that it conveyed national leaders in a personal, intimate way, almost as if these once distant Olympian figures were members of a family. And what America experienced in the following days was a family member's narrow escape from death.

On Sunday, November 24, the front page of virtually every American newspaper carried a photograph of a smiling John Kennedy, in pajamas and bathrobe, standing next to his wife, Jacqueline. The photo, taken by White House photographer Cecil Stoughton, was powerful, compelling, and incomplete; it had been cropped to eliminate a nurse holding a bag connected to the President's chest. But it set the tone for what followed: Sunday was just four days before Thanksgiving, and the timing guaranteed that in almost all of the 300,000 churches in the country, there were sermons and celebrations giving thanks that Kennedy had not died. In a hastily arranged nationally televised appearance at the University of Illinois basketball arena—site of the yearly InterVarsity Christian Fellowship's Urbana student missions conference—the Reverend Billy Graham told a crowd of 16,000 that "surely no one can doubt that it was the hand of Providence that saved the life of our President with that sheltering rain; indeed, God did 'shed his grace' on our blessed land."

Over the next two weeks, the White House press office, with Pierre Salinger now a daily presence in the makeshift press briefing room, supplied a steady stream of news all built around one theme: President Kennedy was the functioning head of state. There were pictures of him on the phone with British prime minister Alec Douglas-Home, French president Charles de Gaulle, and Germany's new chancellor, Ludwig Erhard. He accepted with thanks the public good wishes of the Soviet premier, Nikita Khrushchev (and a private, urgent message assuring him that the Soviet Union "had nothing to do at all with this dastardly crime" and promising the full cooperation of Moscow in "any investigation into the history of L. H. Oswald"). He talked by phone with his key aides: O'Donnell, who had remained in Dallas; Ted Sorensen, speechwriter and advisor; and Larry O'Brien. He conferred at least half a dozen times a day with Robert Kennedy, who had returned to Washington after three very eventful days in Dallas; their conversations were not the subject of any White House press releases. He met once, for seven minutes, with Vice President Johnson, who was told, "You might want to go to the ranch. We'll let you know if the President needs you here."

Every day, he signed a piece of (routine) legislation, or issued a new (routine) executive order. On December 3, the Tuesday after the Thanksgiving holidays, Kennedy "met" with his cabinet, using a speakerphone, beginning by saying, "That's the last time I let half my cabinet leave town at the same time."

Without question, though, the moment that remained in every-one's memory happened shortly after 4:00 p.m. on Wednesday, December 11, on the White House lawn. The President left Parkland Hospital at 9:30 a.m.; photographers were allowed a brief moment to snap pictures of the President, standing and smiling, his wife by his side. When they left, Kennedy slowly, painfully maneuvered himself into the waiting limousine for the ride to Love Field. No one was permitted near Air Force One—"for security reasons," the White House explained—so no one saw the President being carried up the stairs by four Secret Service agents.

Four hours later, at 4:00 p.m. eastern standard time, Air Force One landed at Andrews Air Force Base, and fifteen minutes later, the Marine One helicopter touched down on the White House lawn. There, six-year-old Caroline and three-year-old John Jr. were wait-ing. And as the President stepped down from the helicopter, John stood at rigid attention and offered his father a crisp military salute before running with his sister across the lawn and into his arms.

"I think of myself as a pretty composed reporter," Walter

Cronkite said later. "But I'm very grateful the camera wasn't on me just then. My heavens, if you didn't have tears in your eyes at that moment, what kind of human being are you?"

That night, from the Oval Office, John Kennedy gave his first public remarks since the shooting. It was, as Ted Sorensen said later, "vital that the President reject the notion that the shooting was somehow evidence of a national sickness, that there was any kind of collective guilt for what had happened."

So he began by expressing his thanks "to the doctors, nurses, and staff at Parkland Hospital, and to the people of Dallas and all of Texas for their warmth and good wishes. The actions of a single deranged individual cannot be permitted to define that city or that state. So it is my firm pledge to return to Texas at the earliest possible time, to convey my thanks in person.

"Nor can we permit this single act to define us as a nation. There will always be dissident voices heard in the land, expressing opposition without alternatives, finding fault but never favor, perceiving gloom on every side and seeking influence without responsibility. Those voices are inevitable.

"But those strident voices cannot be allowed to drown out that great silent majority that understands that we are a strong *and* peaceful people who indeed seek 'liberty and justice for all.' May God grant us success in that effort."

By the end of 1963, the shock of what had happened—and what had almost happened—on November 22 had begun to ease. But for some, what America had escaped was very much on their minds. One of them, former secretary of state Dean Acheson, found himself musing about what it might have meant had John Kennedy not survived that morning in Dallas.

"It would not have been bewilderment at the loss of a great and tried leader, as with FDR, because JFK was not that," Acheson wrote to a British friend. "What his death would have evoked was . . . fear from the utter collapse of all sense of security which lay at the bottom of the emotion . . . If a leader is old and should die of a heart attack, as Ike might have done, we would be upset. But if this young and vibrant man had become a corpse within an hour, the vast factor of chance and insecurity in all our separate lives as well as in our collective life would have become oppressive and paralyzingly terrifying. In this sense, President Kennedy's survival spared us, not a constitutional crisis, but a profound wound to the spirit. Thank God we will not have to learn at what cost."

CHAPTER THREE

THE SECOND CASUALTY

The Vice President of the United States was not having a good day when November 22 began.

But then, he had not been having many good days lately.

As he rode through the streets of Dallas, he was seventy-five feet behind the President and Governor Connally, the distance prescribed by the Secret Service. Really, though, he was much, much farther away from the President.

The morning papers were filled with stories of The Snub—Senator Yarborough's adamant and repeated refusal to ride in the same car as Johnson. It was a deliberate, calculated, and successful exercise in humiliation, and humiliation was what Lyndon Johnson had feared all his life, back to his childhood days when his neighbors would look pitifully on his once-prosperous and successful father, who had been reduced to menial labor. He still bore the sting of last night's tongue-lashing from John Kennedy in the President's Fort Worth hotel suite. The Secret Service agents guarding the suite said Johnson had bolted from the room, face flushed with fury or embarrassment or both. It was the latest, full-frontal example of what he had endured for almost three years: the scorn and the mockery of the well-born, well-educated Kennedy clan ("Rufus

Cornpone," they called him behind his back); the exclusion from any hint of power or responsibility; the refusal to listen to his advice on how to work the Congress that he knew so well and had mastered for so long.

It wasn't Jack Kennedy who was doing this, he was sure; it was that snot-nosed runt Bobby, the man who had tried to throw him off the ticket after Jack picked him, the man who'd humiliated him time after time at meetings of the Equal Employment Opportunity Commission, the man who'd reduced him to the stature, as he put it to friends, of "a cut dog." Well, maybe he'd had enough. More than once he thought about chucking it, going back to Texas, maybe running his old alma mater, Southwest Texas State Teachers College. He'd even told an old friend that this Friday evening he was going to tell Jack that he wasn't going to run again in '64. (Then again, threatening to quit was something he'd said at one time or another in just about every campaign he'd ever run.)

Now Senator Yarborough was sitting beside him—the President had more or less ordered him to do so on pain of political isolation—but he refused to say so much as a word with Lyndon, or with Lady Bird. For her part, Lady Bird was obsessing over the impending visit of the Kennedys later that evening to the LBJ Ranch after the Austin fund-raiser. Would they have the right food, the right liquor, the right wine, the right bath soap? Would the entertainment be welcomed, or scorned as the stuff of rubes, hicks?

Nor was Johnson in any mood to exchange pleasantries. His thoughts were back in Washington, where a threat to his political future was growing more serious by the day. His longtime Senate protégé, Bobby Baker, a young man he'd installed as secretary of the Senate, his vote counter, his dispenser of campaign cash and favors of every sort, had become caught up in a firestorm. A small legal dispute over a vending machine contract—Baker owned a piece of the company—had exploded into charges of influence peddling, pay-to-government contracts. The press began asking how a man with a net worth of $11,000 in 1954 could have a net worth of nearly $1.8 million nine years later while serving full-time on the government payroll. And then sex had been added to the combustible mix: Baker owned the Carroll Arms Hotel, close by Capitol Hill, where, the stories went, important government officials and prostitutes found common ground.

From the moment the Baker story surfaced, Johnson had panicked; he'd cut short an official visit to Europe and used his clout in Texas to make sure none of the state's papers published a story by a Washington journalistic gadfly named Sarah McClendon (the story appeared in an obscure wire service, but that was enough to put the tale in circulation). Johnson then tried to distance himself from Baker; he claimed he barely knew the man, that his fellow Democrats had chosen Baker as secretary of the Senate, but the idea was laughable on its face (Baker's nickname on the Hill was "Little Lyndon"), and when *Life* magazine published a cover story on the scandal— THE BOBBY BAKER BOMBSHELL: CAPITAL BUZZES OVER STORIES OF MISCONDUCT IN HIGH PLACES—the piece made prominent mention of the close ties between Baker and Johnson.

So on this late morning of November 22, riding through the light rain in downtown Dallas, the Vice President of the United States was not having a good day.

What he did not know was that he was having a much, much worse day than he could have imagined.

In Room 312 of the Old Senate Office Building, a Maryland insurance executive named Don Reynolds was being questioned by the

Democratic and Republican staff lawyers of the Senate Rules Committee. Reynolds claimed that in return for selling Johnson a $100,000 insurance policy on his life—a policy difficult to get for a man who'd had a near-fatal heart attack a few years earlier—Reynolds had been compelled to buy advertising time on the Johnson-owned Austin TV station and had been forced by Baker to buy Johnson a high-end stereo set. What had begun as an investigation into a staff aide was now directly implicating the former Senate majority leader and current vice president.

And as the lunch hour grew near, Reynolds produced two checks; one to KTBC for the advertising time, one to the Magnavox Company for a stereo, to be delivered to the Johnson home.

And then a secretary burst into the room, sobbing hysterically, barely able to get the words out . . .

Two hundred miles to the north, on the ninth floor of the Time & Life Building on Manhattan's Fifty-First Street, a dozen reporters and editors were meeting in the office of managing editor George Hunt. *Life* magazine's look into the finances of Bobby Baker had yielded a much richer vein of inquiry: if it was a mystery how Baker had accumulated a net worth of nearly $2 million, it was an even deeper mystery how Lyndon Johnson, who had been on the public payroll all his adult life, had managed to accumulate a network many times greater—an estimated $14 million worth. How had he managed to win a license for the only radio station in Austin, Texas, back in 1943 (his wife, Lady Bird, was the nominal owner, but everybody knew who really ran it), and how was it that the Johnsons now owned the only commercial TV station in the town? How had the company managed to build such significant holdings in other radio and TV stations, in banks, in real estate?

And then the phones started ringing, all of them, every line at once.

In the moment and hours when John Kennedy's survival was in doubt, the same thoughts had filled the minds of everyone in that Washington hearing room, and everyone in the executive offices of *Life* magazine.

What if he's about to become president? Don't we have to give the guy a chance? What will it mean to the country if they hear that their new leader is a crook in the middle of a national crisis? Without question, the Washington investigators and the New York editors would have quietly stepped back and let the allegations settle for a while . . . a good, long while.

But when it became clear that John Kennedy would live, a very different thought took hold: *Lyndon Johnson is a heartbeat away from the White House. He came close, very close to becoming president. We've got to get the facts out on the table now.*

Life magazine, like every other major news publication, spent the next two weeks covering the attempted assassination of Kennedy— coverage that gained worldwide attention when the magazine published frames from a home movie shot by Abraham Zapruder, a fifty-eight-year-old women's clothing manufacturer, that showed the plexiglass bubble top exploding, the President clutching at his upper chest, Jacqueline's pink suit spattered with flecks of blood. But in its January 8 issue, which went on sale just after the holidays, *Life* hit the stands with a cover story: LYNDON JOHNSON'S MILLIONS—HOW DID A LIFELONG PUBLIC SERVANT GET SO RICH?

The story created a press firestorm (no one was using the word "media" then). When word of the impending publication broke, the wire services, New York newspapers, and TV networks sent messengers up to the R.R. Donnelley & Sons printing plant in Old Saybrook, Connecticut, to grab advance copies of the issue.

("What do you want me to do?" a *Life* editor yelled at a friend at the *New York Times* who pleaded for an early look. "Should I try to stuff the magazine into the phone so you can read it when it comes out the other end? It's *print*, Arthur!")

The news from Washington was even worse for the Vice President. From the moment the Bobby Baker story emerged, it had drawn the attention of Delaware senator John Williams, who regarded government waste and corruption as among the deadliest of sins, and who had made himself into something of a one-man FBI. He'd exposed rampant corruption in the Wilmington branch of the IRS; forced one of Harry Truman's top aides out of the White House for arranging for Mrs. Truman to receive a Deepfreeze from a government contractor; and driven Eisenhower's chief of staff, Sherman Adams, out of public life for accepting gifts from a wealthy financier. Now, armed with the canceled checks from Don Reynolds, and fueled by the *Life* magazine revelations, Williams took to the Senate floor on a daily basis, asking the same question every day: "What is the Vice President worth, and how did he earn it?"

After weeks of obsession with John Kennedy's health and the motives of the alleged shooter, the country was ready for a new story. The details of Lyndon Johnson's fortune might be complex—FCC license allocation hearings, real estate transactions with straw purchasers and dummy corporations—but the core of the *Life* magazine story was easy to understand: a public servant had used his power to accumulate a vast private fortune. The Washington end of the story was even easier to grasp: that same public servant had used one of his closest aides to pry campaign cash and luxurious gifts for himself as the price of doing business with the government. It was so easy to grasp, in fact, that it leached into the popular culture.

On January 10, NBC launched a new half-hour topical political comedy program, *That Was the Week That Was*, an American adaptation of a successful BBC broadcast. It was a sharp departure for American TV, whose most daring foray into politics came when Ed Sullivan had booked JFK impressionist Vaughn Meader and his feather-light jibes at the Kennedys.

But in its debut broadcast, *TWTWTW* featured a sketch portraying Lyndon Johnson as Senator Midas King ("Every bill he touches turns to gold—for him!") and ended with a pointed version of "The Yellow Rose of Texas":

> *He's the richest politician*
> *That Texas ever saw,*
> *And he gets even richer,*
> *Every time he writes a law.*
> *How did he get so wealthy*
> *Working for the U.S.A.?*
> *It's really very easy*
> *If your name is LBJ!*

Johnny Carson followed suit. The *Tonight Show* host rarely dealt in political humor, so it was telling that on January 11 he began his monologue by announcing, "We've just learned what Vice President Johnson will be having for dessert tonight at dinner—*impeachment* pie."

Faced with a mortal threat to his political survival, Lyndon Johnson became ill—a response utterly unsurprising to his lifelong aides and supporters. He'd been struck with an appendicitis attack two days before Election Day as a twenty-nine-year-old candidate for the U.S. House of Representatives; bad political news had hospitalized him with depression during his first campaign for the U.S. Senate in 1941; he'd come down with a powerful case of kidney stones in his second Senate campaign in 1948 and almost pulled out of the race. Now, facing public embarrassment and a congressional investigation, convinced that his humiliation was being orchestrated by his mortal enemy who held the post of U.S. attorney general, he awoke in the middle of the night on January 15 sweating profusely and complaining of severe abdominal pains and an accelerated heart rate. The doctors at Walter Reed Army Medical Center recommended "extended bed rest"—but it was the recommendation of two lawyers that proved decisive.

On the evening of January 16, two of the most significant inside players in Washington slipped quietly into the hospital and into the Vice President's VIP suite. Abe Fortas, a onetime New Deal liberal crusader, had built one of the most politically powerful law firms in Washington. He'd been a friend and counsel to Lyndon Johnson for years, and saved his political life by persuading Supreme Court justice Hugo Black to leave Johnson's name on the ballot for senator in '48, despite powerful evidence of blatant voter fraud. Clark Clifford, the elegantly dressed, soft-spoken onetime Truman aide, was a master at exercising behind-the-scenes influence, doing more with a single phone call than most lawyers did with a hundred-page brief.

They spoke in sympathy and in sorrow; agreed that Bobby Kennedy had embarked on a ruthless, unprincipled vendetta; acknowledged that old Joe Kennedy had consorted with gangsters and bought his boy the White House; sat mute as Johnson remembered telling Clare Boothe Luce why he'd taken the vice presidency ("One out of every four presidents has died in office; I'm a gambling man, darlin', and this is the only chance I've got"). But they were firm in their counsel.

Which is why, when President Kennedy stepped to the rostrum in the House of Representatives on January 21 to deliver his delayed State of the Union speech, House speaker John McCormack and Senate president pro tempore Carl Hayden were seated behind him. Lyndon Johnson, the former vice president, was home in Texas . . . where, two months before, he'd come within inches of becoming the thirty-sixth president of the United States.

CHAPTER FOUR

THE FIGHT FOR
FOR A SECOND TERM

M is-tah Speak-ah . . . the President of the United States!"
He walked into the House chamber behind doorkeeper William "Fishbait" Miller, flanked by the ceremonial welcoming committee of congressional leaders—Mansfield, Dirksen, Albert, Halleck, and with them the junior senator from the state of Massachusetts, Edward Moore Kennedy—and at the moment Fishbait spoke the last words of his incantation, the chamber exploded into cheers that seemed to shake the galleries. Never in the history of Congress had they welcomed into their hall a president who had narrowly escaped assassination; all of them knew what this moment would mean to the country, which was why, for the first time, they had moved the State of the Union speech from midday to prime time. When the President walked in, still a little careful with his tread, their relief—their *exultation*—was overwhelming. They were all on their feet, of course, but that was protocol; when the President walked in, you stood. But the force of the clapping, the stomping of feet—this was something unseen and unheard before. There was Arizona's Barry Goldwater, the man most likely to run against

him next fall (and who shared with Kennedy a mutual affection): the tears were streaming down his cheeks, and he was shouting, "Jack! Jack! Jack!" There was Georgia's Richard Russell, the ardent segregationist whose mastery of Senate rules had tied the administration in knots on vote after vote, and the usually stoic Russell was trembling with emotion.

In the front row where the cabinet sat, the Attorney General of the United States stood, his hands clapping softly, his face almost expressionless. But then Jack walked by, on his way to the rostrum, and Bobby took his hand and gave a small nod of his head. Up in the First Lady's box, Jacqueline Kennedy was standing, applauding, clad in a new black double-breasted mink coat over a gray Alaskine silk-and-wool day suit designed by Oleg Cassini; next to her was Caroline. There were others in the box, but none of the reporters recognized the faces; they were not the usual family friends and political allies who had claim to the prized seats.

"Members of the Congress," Speaker McCormack intoned, "I have the high honor, and the distinct, *joyful* privilege, of introducing the President of the United States." And the chamber rocked with cheers and applause again; reporters noted the break with tradition in McCormack's introduction—"joyful" was not part of the litany—and it came from a fellow Massachusetts politician whose nephew had lost a nasty Senate primary a year earlier to the President's youngest brother, Ted. None of that mattered, at least for now, and it was a long time before the cheers finally died down.

"Mr. Speaker," Kennedy began, "it was our great wartime friend and ally Winston Churchill who once observed, 'There is nothing as exhilarating in life as to be shot at without result.' While I cannot claim to have enjoyed that precise experience, I can embrace his sentiment. As I did once before, twenty years ago, from the other side of the world, I have returned home . . . to the welcome of colleagues, friends . . . yes, and adversaries . . . and most of all to my family." The audience stood and cheered, as they would two dozen times before his speech was done.

"Let me say at the outset that I would not be standing here today were it not for the physicians, surgeons, nurses, and staff of Parkland Memorial Hospital. I have invited some of them here this evening, so that I might acknowledge them publicly." And five men and women seated in the box section reserved for the First Lady and her guests stood and waved. (It was the first time a president had singled out members of the audience for recognition. In years to come, Kennedy and his successors would continue what became a tradition; the guests, often used to make a political point about an issue or a program, would become known as "Parklanders.")

As the President spoke, one observer—one highly interested observer—found his thoughts drifting . . . to what he had learned in the first days after he heard the news . . .

From his seat in the House chamber, Robert Kennedy joined in the applause and the standing ovations, but his mind was back in Dallas, on what he'd learned as his brother recovered at Parkland Hospital. Someone—maybe more than one person—had almost killed his brother, and from the first moments he had learned of the attack while at his Hickory Hill home, he had compiled a mental list of plausible suspects. It was unimaginable to him that a single insignificant twerp of a man like Lee Harvey Oswald could have struck the most powerful figure in the world. But the more he and his team of investigators looked, the harder it was to fit any of the likely suspects into the facts.

There was little doubt that Oswald had fired the shot that had wounded Jack. The bullet had been traced to the Mannlicher-

Carcano rifle that had been found on the sixth floor of the Texas School Book Depository, where Oswald worked; the rifle had been bought by mail order under an assumed name Oswald frequently used. His wife, Marina, produced a photograph he had insisted she take, of Oswald posing with the rifle in his backyard. That same rifle, police discovered, had been used in an attempt on the life of retired general and right-winger Edwin Walker. Witnesses saw a man fitting Oswald's description in the sixth-floor window of the Depository moments before and just after the shooting. And there was the undeniable fact that Oswald had shot and killed police officer J. D. Tippit and had tried to kill the police officer who had arrested him inside the Texas Theatre. But was Oswald the whole story? Could others, with an obvious motive to kill the President, be involved? Fidel Castro surely had a motive: the Kennedy administration, with Bobby the chief enthusiast, had tried for almost three years to remove Castro from power, with tactics that ranged from a (bungled) invasion to subverting Cuba's economy to outright attempts at assassination. The very day Kennedy was shot, a CIA agent in Paris was awaiting delivery of a poison pen to be used by a Cuban military officer named Rolando Cubela, yet another would-be assassin. Hadn't Fidel himself warned the United States that *their* leaders might find themselves facing the same kind of threats? Wasn't Oswald the lone member of the New Orleans branch of the Fair Play for Cuba Committee, who had sought to travel to Cuba two months ago, a vocal supporter of Castro?

Yes, but . . . Jean Daniel, the French journalist Kennedy had met with shortly before his Texas trip, had been with the Cuban leader in Havana when an aide burst in with the news that Kennedy had been shot. Castro's distress was palpable; and when the aide returned with the news that he was apparently going to live, Castro exclaimed: "Then he's reelected!"—and there was no doubt, Daniel said, that his reaction was genuine. Fidel went on to express the hope for some kind of reconciliation with Washington.

What about *anti*-Castro Cubans? They'd never forgiven Kennedy for aborting the Bay of Pigs invasion, nor for giving Castro a no-invasion pledge as the price of resolving the missile crisis. Could Oswald have been a double agent, professing support for Castro while acting on behalf of his enemies? Well, Oswald's only link to the exile community was a clumsy effort to infiltrate their ranks. Everything else about him—his defection to the Soviet Union, his subscriptions to Marxist newspapers and magazines, the strident positions he had taken in arguments with his few friends— suggested a (not very well) self-educated leftist with an inflated view of his political wisdom. And his attempted assassination of General Walker surely spoke volumes about his political leanings and his propensity for violence.

Organized crime? Yes, the Kennedys' relentless pursuit of the Mafia and its allies, like the Teamsters' Jimmy Hoffa, had brought no shortage of threats against John and Robert, plenty of declarations that "we're going to take them out." But when it came time to connect the dots between organized crime and Oswald . . . there were no dots. The same was true of the far right; *H. L. Hunt and company might take out full-page ads denouncing the President, might pass out leaflets along his motorcade route. And all of these people might well have cheered the news that Jack had been shot,* Bobby thought, *might have raised glasses had he died, but a conspiracy to murder the President? That's a reach.*

Besides, there was the undeniable factor of . . . sheer happenstance. Oswald had applied for two other jobs before finding work at the Texas School Book Depository; either of those jobs would have placed him far from the motorcade. And that job in the Depository? It was his landlady, Ruth Paine, who had a contact in the building, who'd gotten the job for Lee . . . a job he'd taken weeks before anyone knew the route of the motorcade.

It was the President, speaking from his Parkland Hospital bed, who had made the point to Bobby.

"If you're looking for a conspiracy, try 1865," he had said. "Booth and his friends were out to get Lincoln, Andrew Johnson, Seward; they were out to decapitate the whole federal government. But the man who shot McKinley? Czolgosz? A self-taught anarchist. Zangara, who almost killed Roosevelt? Same thing. That nut who tried to blow me up in Palm Beach—Pavlick? Just a lunatic who hated the Church and Dad. I know you'll keep looking, Bobby. And maybe you'll find something. But I doubt it."

In fact, Bobby had found something: not about who had tried to kill his brother, but what had been done—and not done—to try to stop it. What he found in Dallas was a level of carelessness, negligence, and ineptitude on the part of the CIA and the FBI that bordered on the criminal.

The CIA had been tracking Oswald ever since his return from the Soviet Union in 1959. They were aware of his pro-Castro activities and, more important, his visits to the Cuban and Soviet embassies in Mexico City just a few months before the shooting of the President. Yet, somehow they had lost track of Oswald when he returned to Dallas. As for the FBI, their Dallas agent, James Hosty Jr., had had a direct exchange of sorts with the suspected shooter. After Oswald learned that Hosty had been interviewing his landlady, he'd stormed into the Dallas bureau and left a note for the agent, threatening to blow up the FBI and Dallas police headquarters. None of that information reached the Secret Service, which might have been interested in knowing that this individual worked in a building right along the President's motorcade route.

What *really* got Bobby's attention was that, when he confronted

Hosty three days after the shooting, the agent admitted that he'd destroyed the threatening note Oswald had written on the direct order of J. Edgar Hoover. Bobby nodded, said nothing, but left with a grim sense of satisfaction. For three years he and Hoover had dealt with each other with mutual, intense, barely concealed contempt. To Hoover, Bobby was an arrogant, spoiled brat protecting his degenerate brother. To Bobby, Hoover was a blatant racist and "a psychopath" to boot. And both were at the mercy of the other. Hoover knew too many details of John Kennedy's private life. The Kennedys knew one big secret about Hoover's private life. Neither could strike at the other without imposing fatal damage to himself. If, however, word got out that Hoover's own bureau had been flagrantly derelict, and that Hoover had tried to cover up the failures, then the press and the Congress might drop their fawning adulation of the FBI director; might even insist that he follow the mandatory retirement age he'd reach in 1965. At the least, Bobby would have a powerful club to hold over Hoover—and, for that matter, the apparatchiks in the CIA who thought nothing of launching dangerous operations without the permission, or even knowledge, of the President.

That might make a second term worthwhile in and of itself, he thought, and stood with the rest of the cabinet for another standing ovation.

The drama of John Kennedy's reappearance on the political stage overwhelmed the substance of his talk. It was dominated by two themes: an appeal to the Congress to pass his stalled legislative agenda (a tax cut, a civil rights bill, medical care for the elderly, federal aid to education), and a promise to pursue "peace through strength" by combining continued increases in defense spending with new agreements with the Soviet Union. In the eyes of his audi-

ence and the press, though, there was no question about the real
import of his speech: it was the opening round of his fight for a
second term.

And it was a fight he was not at all sure he could win.

He had come to the presidency by the narrowest of margins: one-
tenth of 1 percent of the popular vote, a difference of 112,827 out of
69 million votes cast. It was a fact that was never far from his thinking; he carried that number with him on a slip of paper, and when
a *Time* magazine piece described his staff as "corsucatingly brilliant," he noted: "A few thousand votes the other way, and we'd all
be coruscatingly stupid."

A week before he left Washington for Florida and Texas, on November 13, Kennedy convened the first meeting devoted to his
1964 campaign. Along with Bobby, Sorensen, O'Donnell, O'Brien,
and brother-in-law and campaign manager Steve Smith, Kennedy
brought in Richard Scammon, director of the U.S. Census Bureau
and—more important—a man with an encyclopedic knowledge of
voting demographics. What they confronted was a glass half full,
half empty.

On his side, he had the twin pillars of any incumbent reelection
strategy: peace and prosperity. The chill of the 1962 Cuban missile
crisis had been replaced by the Limited Nuclear Test Ban Treaty,
which the Senate had approved by a wide (80–19) margin. Unemployment had been under 6 percent all year, and inflation was all
but nonexistent—1.3 percent in the latest numbers.

That was the good news.

The trouble came when the view from 30,000 feet was replaced
by the view on the ground. *America* didn't elect a president; fifty
states did. And the picture was gloomier on the ground. The South

and the border states held more than 120 electoral votes, and his popularity in the region was under 40 percent; even New York governor Rockefeller, with a commitment to civil rights clearer than his, was running ahead of him in the region. Washington columnist Roscoe Drummond had written of "a Republican iceberg of unknown force" threatening Democrats in the region they had dominated for almost a century. (A few months earlier, Kennedy had described his Southern dilemma more pungently when he said to Pennsylvania governor David Lawrence, "I can kiss the South good-bye next year.") No wonder he was heading to Florida and Texas in late November: the thirty-nine electoral votes of those two states were critical. The West was also troubled turf: of the eighteen states west of the Mississippi River he'd won only New Mexico (barely) and Nevada in 1960; and in Arizona senator Barry Goldwater the West would have a native son with a message about the overbearing, intrusive federal government that had powerful regional resonance. So the forty electoral votes of California—a state he'd lost by less than 1 percent in 1960—would be critical. (At the end of the '60 campaign, he'd said to Kenny O'Donnell, "Well, it's all over. I wish I'd spent forty-eight hours more in California.")

There was unsettling news as well from places he'd *won* in 1960 and had to win again this time. A year ago, the 1962 midterms had seen moderate Republicans win governorships in three big states: New York, Pennsylvania, and Michigan. Each of those governors, Rockefeller, William Scranton, and ex–auto industry executive George Romney, had appeal across party lines that would serve them well in a presidential campaign. The Kennedy team was unworried about Rockefeller this time around. He'd dithered in 1960 about running when he'd had an excellent chance at the White House—"Nobody had any doubt he could beat me in 1960. I knew that," Kennedy had told the *Post*'s Ben Bradlee—but Rockefeller had recently divorced his wife of thirty-two years to marry a woman eighteen years his junior. It was Michigan governor Romney, a devout Mormon, who was their chief concern.

"People buy that God-and-country stuff," Bobby said.

"You have to be a little suspicious of somebody as good as Romney," the President added. "No vices whatsoever . . ."

That was not, some on the team may have noted to themselves, an issue with John Kennedy.

By contrast, Kennedy said with a laugh, "Give me Barry. I won't even have to leave the Oval Office."

Kennedy had come to this political gathering with the idea of making poverty a central campaign issue. He'd been inspired by *The Other America*, a detailed look by Michael Harrington at the millions living in poverty. They could, he thought, "deracialize" the poverty issue by linking poor whites in rural America with poor blacks in the inner cities. That, he'd told O'Donnell, was how he wanted to campaign.

But Census Bureau director Scammon thought otherwise.

"I wouldn't do that, Mr. President," he said.

"Why not?"

"You can't get a single vote more by doing anything for poor people. I was thinking of photographs with policemen in the cities. Then you should go to the new shopping centers on the highways. The voters you need, your people, men with lunch pails, are moving out to the suburbs."

Kennedy was intrigued. How much income, he wanted to know, did it take for Democrats to turn into suburban Republicans? Scammon said he'd find out.

"It's going to be a new kind of politics," Kennedy said.

"It's a new country," Scammon replied.

Then the President went to Texas.

In the first aftermath of the shooting in Dallas, John Kennedy's political prospects brightened dramatically. *Life* and *Look*, the mass circulation magazines with millions of readers, carried lengthy photo spreads of the recovering President, playing with his children, meeting with congressional leaders, convening an informal gathering of prominent religious leaders to examine the roots of intolerance in American life. The photos, taken under the rigorous eye of the White House Press Office, did not capture the slow, sometimes unsteady gait of the President, nor the frequent breaks he took for rest and medication. "You know all those Westerns where the hero is up on his horse two minutes after getting shot?" one aide remarked to a reporter. "Well, this is no Western. The President took a real hit, and his health wasn't exactly in A-1 shape in the first place—and that's so off the record that if I see a word of this conversation, you'll have to join a tour to see the inside of the White House again."

Life also featured a compelling joint interview with President and Mrs. Kennedy conducted by Theodore H. White, whose *Making of the President 1960* had cast the presidential campaign in a romantic, heroic light. The interview was notable for Jacqueline Kennedy's dramatic recollection of the moments after the shooting: "I remember reaching out, pulling him over to me, cradling him in my lap; for some reason, what flashed in my mind was that statue, *The Pietà*, with Mary holding the body of Jesus."

For the President, the goal was to damp down any talk of a plot involving the Soviet Union or Cuba, or to cast blame on a defect in the American spirit.

"Everything we know so far," Kennedy told White, "points to a single deranged individual with a twisted hunger to make his mark on history—the same impulse that drove other assailants in years past. Yes, there are voices of intolerance and extremism in the land; I'd intended to address that issue in the luncheon speech in Dallas. But it is wrong to indict a hundred ninety million Americans for what happened."

From the Congress came calls to deal with the trafficking in mail-order weapons: Should it really be that easy for a customer to buy a rifle by answering an ad in the National Rifle Association's magazine? The NRA didn't think so: it endorsed a bill by Connecticut senator Tom Dodd to eliminate such sales. In congressional hearings, NRA executive vice president Franklin Orth supported a ban on mail-order sales, saying, "We do not think that any sane American who calls himself an American can object to placing into this bill the instrument which almost killed the President of the United States." (After angry protests from its members, the NRA encouraged them to oppose the bill with letters and phone calls; the bill died in committee.)

In the wake of such coverage, the countless prayers of thanksgiving offered up in churches and synagogues for Kennedy's survival, the photo spreads in women's magazines of the Kennedy family, the CBS special on *The Men Who Saved the President's Life*, the emotionally gripping State of the Union speech, it was unsurprising that Kennedy's favorability rating soared above 90 percent in the first weeks of 1964. But by the spring it was clear that John Kennedy's *political* survival was no sure thing. His dilemma, the Achilles' heel of his reelection prospects, was the primal issue that had the potential to upend all the conventional wisdom about the invincibility of an incumbent president in a time of peace and prosperity.

It was race.

The impact of the issue was starkly clear in the South. However tepid the White House response had been to the sit-ins and Freedom Rides; however much John and Robert Kennedy treated the demonstrations as international embarrassments and domestic political nuisances, rather than as the product of legitimate outrage; however much the administration tried to placate the Southern segregationists who ran Congress by appointing racist judges to the federal bench, much of the white South had come to see John and Robert Kennedy as leading a Second War of Northern Aggression against their most cherished institutions: first and foremost, white supremacy. "Raul," they had started calling the younger Kennedy, in a mocking reference to Fidel Castro's brother. And when federal marshals and troops fought bloody clashes with mobs of whites in Oxford, Mississippi, in the fall of 1962, as James Meredith became the first black student at Ole Miss, the anger at the Kennedys had hardened into outright hatred—and the political consequences became clear in the 1962 midterms. The Republican share of the Southern votes jumped from 660,000 in 1958 to more than 2 million; a Republican won a Texas Senate seat, and another nearly picked off a powerful Democratic incumbent in Alabama. A year later, after the White House introduced a far-reaching bill to block discrimination in hotels and restaurants, the President's popularity in Dixie cratered. A Gallup poll in September of 1963 showed that in the eleven states of the Confederacy (plus Oklahoma and Kentucky), Barry Goldwater would swamp Kennedy by a 59–41 margin.

But it wasn't just the South.

Race was beginning to look like a "wedge" issue, cleaving two of the Democratic Party's core elements: working-class whites and Negroes. In the big cities of the Northeast and Midwest, crime rates were beginning to rise—50 percent between 1960 and 1964—despite economic good times; and in these cities, crime and race were tightly interwoven. So was the issue of welfare. So was the issue of school integration: in most Northern cities, blacks and whites were segregated not by law but by neighborhoods. In New York, Negro leaders like Reverend Milton Galamison were organizing school boycotts and demonstrations to demand integration; white parents in Queens had formed a parent-teacher association to push back against those demands. In Boston, pressures to end the deeply embedded school segregation led to a massive response by whites—"backlash," they were beginning to call it—and Boston School Committee chief Louise Day Hicks won a landslide reelection by promising to preserve neighborhood schools. In the suburbs, where the increasingly prosperous working class was moving in ever larger numbers, the demand for "fair housing" laws from Negroes and liberals stirred primal fears of declining property values and rising crime. The voters in liberal cities like Seattle and Berkeley had repealed local fair-housing ordinances, and in California a measure would be on the 1964 ballot to nullify a fair-housing law.

The primal political threat to Kennedy's party had been bluntly expressed more than a year earlier in a letter from liberal Michigan congresswoman Martha Griffiths, who warned about the impact of a federal fair-housing law:

"No Democratic congressman, from suburbia, to whom I have talked, believes he is in any danger of losing colored votes; but he does feel such an order [to integrate] could cost white votes. [If] I lose this election . . . can I have the next Supreme Court vacancy, where I can legislate in safety far from the prejudices of the precincts?"

By the time Kennedy went to Texas, Griffiths's warning seemed prescient. Even after the massive, peaceful March on Washington, half of *all* Americans thought he was pushing civil rights too hard. Alabama governor George Wallace, who had "stood in the schoolhouse door" in 1962 to symbolically resist the integration of the state university, embarked on a speaking tour across the North. He delighted in taunting Northerners for hypocrisy, asking them: "You see Jack and Bobby and Teddy putting their little children on buses to send them into colored neighborhoods? You see a lot of black faces in the newsrooms of the *New York Times*, the *Washington Post*, the *Boston Globe*? If you're so eager for integration, why don't you try it in your schools, your neighborhoods, instead of telling us in the South how to live our lives?"

The Harvard students might boo and taunt Wallace, but the cops sent to protect him, the cabdrivers bringing the audiences to his speeches, they were cheering him on; by early 1964, Wallace had declared his intention to run in Democratic presidential primaries outside the South. In city after city, nervous mayors and Democratic county leaders were sending warnings back to the White House: *Our homeowners, our craft union workers, our parents, are listening to Wallace.* And if this crude Southern demagogue could win their cheers, there was a real danger that an Arizona senator, without any tint of personal racism or thuggery, might be able to win their votes. No wonder *Look* magazine, which devoted so many pages to endearing photos of the President and his family on Cape Cod, titled a story: "JFK Could Lose." No wonder that *Time* could report that "Barry Goldwater could give Kennedy a breathtakingly close race."

And if white working-class defections from the Democrats made a huge black turnout imperative, the spring of 1964 brought little encouragement on that front. Yes, he'd introduced sweeping legislation in 1963; yes, he'd been the first president to pronounce civil rights "primarily a moral issue"; but he and his White House had proved no match for the Southern committee chairs in the House and Senate with their mastery of the rules and control of the machinery. Just before the Easter recess, with Kennedy's bill hopelessly stalled in both houses of Congress, Senator Richard Russell sat with a few colleagues and shared a thought that would never leave the inner sanctum of his office.

"We should be very grateful that Oswald fellow was a poor shot," Russell said. "We couldn't have beaten a President Lyndon Johnson on civil rights. A Southerner with Lyndon's skills making the cause a martyr's legacy? No, we couldn't have beaten Lyndon. But beat John Kennedy? Yes, we will."

Without question, the Kennedy White House had committed some serious missteps. Back in '63, Vice President Johnson had warned Ted Sorensen, "Don't send up civil rights until you've got your other bills cleared; otherwise they'll tie up your whole legislative agenda." But they hadn't listened—they never listened to Lyndon on anything—and now the congressional machinery had come to a dead stop: not just on civil rights but on aid to education, the tax cut, pretty much everything Kennedy was planning to run on. That paralysis, in turn, had triggered a fever of pessimism among academics and journalists about the health of the American governing process. Historian James MacGregor Burns wrote a whole book whose title summed up the concern: *The Deadlock of Democracy*. The most influential columnist in the country, Walter Lippmann, suggested the paralysis was nothing less than "a grave danger to the Republic." *Life* magazine said it "put our whole system of parliamentary democracy in question." In that climate, it would not be hard for a challenger to turn Kennedy's 1960 argument—"Let's get America moving again"—against him.

No wonder Robert Kennedy, in the midst of a strategy session in mid-May, looked up and said flatly, "Civil rights is something around our neck." And no wonder there was real concern in the White House that a credible Republican candidate—a big-state governor with broad voter appeal—could pose a serious threat to Kennedy.

In February of 1964, it was that threat that brought the Kennedy political team into the Oval Office—an office whose new red rug and pale curtains bore the mark of Jacqueline Kennedy's hand. The President sat in his high-back black leather chair, cradling a book on his lap.

"Let me ask you all something," he began. "Have many of you actually *read* Teddy White's book—apart from looking at the index to see how many times you were mentioned?"

There were embarrassed chuckles.

"When Teddy wasn't turning us all into the Knights of the Round Table," he said, "he did some pretty interesting reporting with the census numbers, especially about the Negroes. Our fine Southern statesmen have made life so inhospitable that Negroes have fled en masse: half of all the young Mississippi Negroes fled the state in the last twenty years. They've been uprooted, packed into slums, shut out of jobs. That's meant an epidemic of crime, welfare, broken families; he says that almost a *fifth* of all black children are illegitimate. And you know what federal welfare laws say? You can only *get* help if there's no man in the house.

"He also raised a political question we might think about." Opening the book, he began to read.

"'The abrasions and frictions of urban life in the Northern big cities have begun to rub off in politics. No Northern political boss has yet begun to make political capital of these frictions as race-blind Southern politicians have done for decades; yet more than one Northern big-city boss has privately considered the matter.'"

He clapped the book closed.

"And we can be goddamn sure that Governor Wallace is considering the matter. He's going to tuck it to me pretty good in some of these primaries."

"It's a web White's talking about," Bobby Kennedy said. "I see it every time I walk the streets about a mile from here: no work in the ghetto, no jobs, an economy built on welfare checks, no men in the house to raise the sons . . . You know who the kids have to look up to? The gang leader and the drug dealer." He shook his head. "And when you listen to our liberal friends . . . Hubert and Douglas and Hart and Javits . . . it's not just the politics of integration and open housing that are so awful . . . I just don't know why they think their ideas are going to help the people they say they're trying to help. If you are going to take ten thousand black people and move them into Orange County or Westchester or Cicero . . . you take them out where 40 percent of them don't have any jobs at all, that's what you are talking about. But if you are talking about hitting the problem in a major way—taking those people out, putting them in the suburbs where they can't afford the housing, where their children can't keep up with the schools, and where they don't have the skills for the jobs—it's just going to be catastrophic."

"I think we have to face the facts," the President added. "A lot of these people are going to live in the ghettos for another several decades. And they can't live under the conditions that exist there. So, Bobby, why don't we see if somewhere in the two and a half million people in our civilian workforce there's someone who has an idea or two."

And there was.

When Daniel Patrick Moynihan wrote of broken families and a hardscrabble life, it was not the product of academic research. His father had left when he was six months old, leaving a wife and three children to fend for themselves. They moved from tenement to tenement in New York's Hell's Kitchen, with Pat working as a shoeshine boy in Times Square, then finding work as a longshoreman after high school. He'd found his way to New York's City College, where tuition was free, then to a life in the academy, then to politics and the Kennedy campaign. By 1964, he was an assistant secretary of labor with a special interest in urban and minority group issues, and co-author of *Beyond the Melting Pot*, a widely praised book about racial and ethnic tensions. When the President asked him for a memo, Moynihan's first words were blunt.

"The racist virus in the American bloodstream still afflicts us," the memo began. "What afflicts the Negro family today is the product of that virus." And the key to strengthening that family, he argued, was to put black men to work: on public works projects, in schools as teachers, in job-training and apprenticeship programs. Put men to work, he argued, and they will be more likely to marry the mothers of their children and stay to raise those children. If they stayed, their children were less likely to turn to street gangs for a sense of purpose, more likely to stay in school. If neighborhoods grew safer, stores and businesses would be more likely to locate in those neighborhoods, replacing a vicious circle with a virtuous one.

"All well and good," the President said three days later. Moynihan was in the Oval Office, where Robert Kennedy, Labor secretary Arthur Goldberg, Health, Education, and Welfare secretary Anthony Celebrezze, and the political team heard the President's response. "Done right," he said, "this could be politically potent. But done wrong, it could be politically damaging."

"So," the President said. "First, this *cannot* be a 'Negro' program. I want to cut a ribbon in Appalachia or Macomb County for every office we open in Harlem or Watts. Second, we need to frame this idea as an anti-welfare program as much as a jobs program."

"Might get some pushback from the black caucus on that," Larry O'Brien said. "In fact, you might get some pushback on the whole picture this will paint about Negro families and neighborhoods: crime, welfare, illegitimacy . . . 'Blaming the victim,' they'll say."

"It's not blaming the victim," Moynihan interjected. "It's diagnosing the disease."

"That's right . . . but so is Larry," Kennedy said. "You've done great work, Pat, but it will be wasted if this becomes a bunch of white men in suits acting like missionaries to darkest America. We need to think this through a lot more carefully. And when we *do* have something to propose . . . keep it small at the start; keep the language modest. 'A Marshall Plan for the cities' sounds great until people start asking how much it's going to cost and whether the folks in the suburbs are going to pay for it."

It was mid-May when a White House Conference on Jobs and the Family was convened, under the chairmanship of Dr. Kenneth Clark, professor of the City College of New York, whose psychological tests of black children's self-worth helped convince the Supreme Court to outlaw segregation. Clark's credentials as a prominent Negro academic and a fervent integrationist made the conference's findings broadly palatable. ("If this had been *The Moynihan Report* instead of *The Clark Report*, we'd have had the first White House sit-in," Moynihan himself remarked.) Kennedy managed to finesse the end-welfare-as-we-know-it case by casting welfare as a case of white condescension.

"These men might have wanted a job," he said in his remarks to the conference. "We have given them a check and told them there is no meaningful work for them to do. Of all the injustices that have befallen the Negro in America, this remorseless indifference may rank among the worst."

There was no illusion at the White House that this approach would eradicate the political threat of racial discord. It would be months before the first concrete, modest steps toward a clear-eyed jobs program would begin. Still, for all the justified political concern, there was a strong counterpoint of optimism; and one of those most optimistic about the President's prospects was John Kennedy. His optimism rested on two key foundations: first, the issue he believed would be at the center of his campaign; second, the identity of his opponent.

If race was the "iceberg" that could sink Kennedy's second-term hopes, there was one issue that could conceivably melt it. It had emerged, almost by accident, in the weeks before his near-fatal journey to the South. In September, he'd embarked on a "conservation" tour of eleven states, mostly in the West, where he'd been all but shut out in 1960 and where he'd likely not have time to visit in 1964. There were dams to be dedicated, national parks to be celebrated; but then, on September 25, at the Yellowstone County Fairgrounds in Billings, Montana, came one of those increasingly rare unscripted political moments. Kennedy, in praising Montana senator (and majority leader) Mike Mansfield, had singled him out, along with Republican leader Ev Dirksen, for their work in winning Senate approval of the Nuclear Test Ban Treaty, and cheers erupted for a long, long moment. The next day, in Great Falls, he touched on the same theme, and the cheers once again were loud and long. And that night, in Salt Lake City, Utah, in a state where he'd lost decisively in 1960, he'd devoted much of his speech to peace, to the need to understand the limits of American power, to the dangers posed to children's health of radiation in the atmosphere. And from a block away, Kennedy's chief advance man, Jerry Bruno, could hear cheers as loud as he had ever heard for his boss. By the time he'd returned to Washington, Kennedy was convinced he'd found the key to his reelection; an issue that had become even more primal, personal, visceral, than race.

A year earlier, for thirteen days in October 1962, Americans had watched their television sets and listened to their radios, wondering if the crisis over Soviet missiles in Cuba would lead to a nuclear war. High government officials were being briefed on when and how to leave the capital for relocation to a post-nuclear government headquarters, built deep into a mountain in White Sulfur Springs, West Virginia. On the campus of the University of Wisconsin, a teaching assistant told his philosophy seminar, "Your assignment for next Thursday—if there *is* a next Thursday . . ." No longer was this a matter of diplomatic exchanges and ponderous foreign policy debates and *New York Times* columns that nobody read. Now the specter of nuclear war had come home, posing a threat to the United States that not even World War II could equal. (American boys might be dying on faraway beaches and waters in 1943, but no one in America feared that their neighborhood or city might be reduced to rubble and ash.)

In the autumn of 1963, during the Test Ban Treaty debate, Americans had learned of radiation—"strontium 90," it was called—that could wind up in the teeth and bones of their children. An ad backing the treaty featured an internationally famous baby doctor with the headline: DR. SPOCK IS WORRIED. In the same sense that race had migrated from a distant concern about peaceful demonstrators seeking basic rights to pressing issues of personal safety and the value of a home, peace had migrated into the homes and neighborhoods of the American family. The audiences on his Western tour had brought that home to Kennedy. More and more, he began to make that the central focus of his campaign. If it was true, as *U.S. News & World Report* wrote in the spring, that "it's been a generation or more since the world was as quiet as now," Kennedy intended to turn that quiet into his major campaign theme.

On a gray, wet April 22, he opened the New York World's Fair in Flushing Meadows Park with a lighthearted "salute" to the Unisphere, the twelve-story-high globe built with 900,000 pounds of stainless steel.

"It was supplied, I understand, by U.S. Steel—at a very reasonable price," he laughed, recalling the bitter fight he'd had in 1962, when he'd forced U.S. Steel and other companies to roll back their price increases.

Then he turned serious.

"Twenty-five years ago," he said, "President Franklin Roosevelt opened an earlier World's Fair on this same site, and offered a prayer that 'the years to come will break down many barriers to intercourse between nations.'

"Neither he nor anyone else foresaw that, barely four months later, the world would be devastated by war, or that millions of the helpless would be slaughtered. No one foresaw power that was capable of destroying man, or a cold war that would bring conflict to every continent.

"Now, after a conflict that brought us perilously close to a war that could have wiped out all of the achievements past, present, and future that we celebrate today—a war that could literally have threatened human existence—we may be at the start of a new era that replaces conflict with cooperation. But to achieve that new era, we must deal with the world as it is—not as we might wish it to be.

"We must first of all recognize that we cannot remake the world simply by our own command. When we cannot even bring all of our own people into full citizenship without acts of violence, we can understand how much harder it is to control events beyond our borders.

"Every nation has its own traditions, its own values, its own aspirations. Our assistance from time to time can help other nations preserve their independence and advance their growth, but we cannot remake them in our own image. We cannot enact their laws, nor can we operate their governments or dictate our policies." *I sure hope they heard that in Saigon,* he thought.

Two weeks later, he took that message to the other side of the world, to Japan—the first American president to do so since World War II (a 1960 visit by Eisenhower had been canceled in the wake of massive student protests). He traveled to the Diet along Tokyo streets lined with hundreds of thousands of spectators, and in his speech he began by thanking the Japanese "for your invaluable contribution to my political career by turning a lowly junior officer into an involuntary hero." He struggled to render a Japanese proverb— *Juu-nin to-iro*: "Different strokes for different folks"—to argue that "not every nation will follow the path to democracy that our two nations walk, but this does not mean we cannot find common ground on which to stand . . . No nation knows more than yours about the horrors of nuclear war; today, with fearsome weapons a thousand times more lethal, it is our moral obligation to find that common ground."

It was another trip, a month later, that demonstrated just how much John Kennedy intended to make peace the central theme of his reelection . . . a trip that would radically reshape the destinies of guest and host.

It was born by accident, during a visit to the Soviet Union by Bill Walton, a journalist turned painter who was a friend and confidant to both John and Jacqueline Kennedy—close enough to the President to act as escort for a number of women who would visit the

White House; close enough to the First Lady to serve as her companion at parties and occasional off-the-radar trips to Cape Cod. Walton was supposed to travel to Moscow on November 22 as part of an exchange between Soviet and American artists but postponed that trip when he learned the President had been shot. When he traveled to Russia a week later, his mission had grown dramatically: he had a message to deliver to the leaders of the Soviet Union from the leaders of the United States; and those Soviet leaders had a message for him to deliver back home as well.

It was at a luncheon at a Moscow restaurant where Walton sat down with Georgi Bolshakov, a high official with the GRU, the intelligence wing of the Soviet military. For almost three years, Bolshakov had been stationed at the Russian embassy in Washington, where he and Robert Kennedy had formed an extraordinary back-channel relationship—so extraordinary that Bolshakov would sometimes show up at the Department of Justice and walk into the Attorney General's office without an appointment. During the Cuban missile crisis, Robert Kennedy had passed assurances to the Kremlin through the Bolshakov connection that the United States was prepared to remove Jupiter missiles from Turkey in exchange for the removal of Soviet missiles in Cuba . . . assurances that could not be made public for political reasons.

Now Walton and Bolshakov were exchanging confidences both reassuring and alarming.

"The President and the Attorney General want to reassure Chairman Khrushchev that we know your government had nothing whatever to do with the events in Dallas," Walton began. "They believe that since the resolution of the Cuban conflict, there have been significant steps in improving relations, and they have high hopes for further progress."

"You should know," said Bolshakov, "that when Khrushchev

heard of the shooting, he was distraught, in tears—and when he
learned that the President would live, he wept for joy. Our fear
however is that there were powerful forces in reactionary circles
that may have tried to kill the President . . . We know that your
generals, your financiers who profit from the weapons trade, your
'Birchers,' may have wanted the Texan with his oil friends in the
White House. But"—and here Bolshakov lowered his voice—"your
President is not the only leader who is threatened in his own house.
The Chairman has his enemies as well; they think him too eager to
deal with the United States, too eager to embrace ideas that do not
fit their orthodoxies. Some of them never forgave him for exposing
the crimes of Stalin—they tried to remove him six years ago—and
after the missile crisis, some of them condemned the settlement as a
defeat."

"Let the Chairman know that some of *our* top military men said
the same thing about President Kennedy," Walton said.

"What is important," Bolshakov said, "is that your President
knows that the Chairman's political survival is very much at issue in
the next year. Anything that improves the material situation of the
Soviet people will improve his chances to remain in power. We may
not have the same political process as you do," he said with a smile,
"but it's not as it was with Stalin. The Presidium members would
think twice about removing a leader who has the support of the
people."

Six months later, on June 1, John Kennedy, along with his wife,
members of his cabinet and national security staff, and a group of
congressional leaders, stepped off Air Force One into the chilly afternoon at Vnukovo airport in Moscow, where Chairman Khrushchev, Foreign Minister Andrei Gromyko, and a carefully assembled
crowd of onlookers greeted them. It was a trip surrounded by controversy from the moment it had been announced. Barry Goldwater

called it "another step on the President's misguided march to Munich." Richard Nixon wrote in a column for *Time* magazine, "While of course I wish the President well, I have real concerns that political and public relations considerations may lead him into ill-considered agreements that would have serious repercussions for the security interests of the United States." Columnist William F. Buckley Jr. was less diplomatic:

"Back in the days when Vice President Henry Wallace was looking at the Soviet Union through his rose-pink-colored glasses, Congresswoman Clare Boothe Luce labeled his delusions 'globaloney.' We now offer a modest addendum to her vocabulary: President Kennedy will soon embark on an exercise in 'summ-itiocy.'"

There were cautionary notes from the press as well: *Time* magazine pointed to "the abject disaster of the first Kennedy-Khrushchev confab in Vienna, where the rotund, bellicose Kremlin boss browbeat the untested, ill-prepared Kennedy—which led to a wall in Berlin, and Soviet missiles on our doorstep." Columnist Joseph Alsop, a friend of the President's and a militant hawk, urged the President to reconsider his "foolhardy mission to Moscow, where his hunger for an election-year success poses a real danger of long-term strategic disaster."

The White House surrounded the trip with built-in safeguards. Kennedy brought with him congressional leaders from both parties: Senate minority leader Dirksen, Aiken of Vermont, Kuchel of California, and Saltonstall of Massachusetts were among the Republicans; so was North Dakota's Milton Young, whose presence was explained by the agreement to sell 6 million tons of grain to the Soviet Union over the next three years—a boon to the wheat-growing farmers of the Midwest. And on his way to Russia, the President stopped off in Warsaw, where he was greeted by a crowd of 300,000 in Krasinski Square, who serenaded him with "Sto Lat!

May You Live a Hundred Years." (He sang to them what he called "a traditional American song, 'When Polish Eyes Are Smiling.'") His speech, carefully vetted to avoid unsettling Moscow, spoke of "the irrepressible spirit of the Polish people, which no would-be conqueror will ever dominate." It was a speech aimed more to Milwaukee, Chicago, and Cleveland than to Warsaw. He also met with a gathering of Poland's Catholic leaders, including the forty-four-year old archbishop of Kraków, Karol Wojtyla, whose striking looks and youthful energy had made him a hero to the city's young.

"They tell me you're called 'the John Kennedy of the Church,'" the President said. "If you plan to seek higher office, give me a call."

"Well, Mr. President," Wojtyla said, "our religion would not be a problem as it was for you, but my geography might be."

Then came four days of official formality and private conversations: dinner in the Great Hall of the Kremlin, a visit to Leningrad's Piskariovskoye Memorial Cemetery to honor the fallen during the World War II Nazi siege, and an evening at the Bolshoi Ballet that tested the President's back and his patience.

"My God, the things I do to avert a Third World War," he groaned.

The heart of the trip was a string of agreements between the two nations—on cultural exchanges, increased trade, and a preliminary effort toward limiting the spread of nuclear weapons and the stockpiling of nuclear arms. In an unprecedented address on Soviet television, Kennedy recalled the words of his inaugural address.

"Your country and mine," he said, "have different traditions, different beliefs, different ideas of what a just and free nation looks like. But just as we joined together to fight a common enemy twenty years ago, so we can join together to fight the common enemies of man: tyranny, poverty, disease—and war itself."

The most important words were spoken in private—words exchanged by the two leaders in three separate meetings, with only their interpreters present; words spoken by two men who had brought the world to the brink of annihilation, and who had been profoundly shaken by that experience. They spoke of China's growing militancy, its contempt for Khrushchev's overtures to the United States, its casual acceptance of a nuclear war that might kill 300 million people as long as it ended in a Communist triumph.

"Our schism began," Khrushchev said, "when I refused to share our nuclear weapons technology with them. But our intelligence services tell me they will have the bomb soon—maybe before the year ends."

"Perhaps," Kennedy said, "instead of a joint space venture, we might launch a joint venture to ensure that doesn't happen . . . I mean that in jest, of course."

"Too bad," said Khrushchev.

Kennedy's address to the Soviet people—broadcast on all three American TV networks—was a message aimed squarely not just at the Soviet leaders but at the broad American electorate, designed to confront the opponent he was most likely, and most eager, to face in November. Kennedy's political calculus was simple: if the Republicans nominated a candidate with a reputation for caution and good judgment, they could neutralize or at least minimize the peace question and give voters the freedom to vote on other issues, like the paralysis in Washington, or the growing racial divide. But if the 1964 campaign could be cast as a choice between a careful, prudent president, and a challenger who seemed casually indifferent to the dangers of nuclear weapons, the contest would be over before it started.

And in his fervent hope, Kennedy had no stronger allies than those who were working most feverishly for just that opponent.

They weren't going to let it happen again.

For a quarter century and more, they'd seen their Republican Party—the party of the Main Street shopkeeper, the farmer and rancher, the third-generation owner of a small factory, the school board member, the town doctor—railroaded by the big Eastern banks, the corporate giants, the newspaper and magazine titans, the Wall Street law firm partners with Roman numerals after their names, the blue-blooded families of Beacon Hill, Park Avenue, Philadelphia's Main Line, the men who sat on the governing boards of Harvard and Yale. They'd seen their hero, Ohio senator Robert Taft, denied the presidential nomination three times, losing to a millionaire utility executive, Wendell Willkie; to a Wall Street lawyer, Tom Dewey; and, in 1952, to a war hero who hadn't even decided he was a Republican until that year. Taft had come to that convention with more than enough delegates to win, but the East Coast didn't want a solid Midwestern conservative; so the *New York Herald Tribune*, *Time* and *Life*, New York governor Dewey, and the big banks cooked up a naked power grab, a "fair play" resolution that took away his Texas and Georgia delegates and gave them— and the nomination—to Ike.

"Every Republican nominee since 1936," Taft had said afterward, "has been picked by the Chase Manhattan Bank."

Sure, Ike had won the White House, but so what? In eight years, he hadn't undone a single piece of the New Deal—even *added* a cabinet department; sent troops to Little Rock to force blacks and whites to go to school together; shoveled as much foreign aid abroad as Truman had ever done . . . even invited Soviet dictator Khrushchev to visit the United States.

Well, not this time. Four years ago, Barry Goldwater had declined to fight Richard Nixon for the 1960 nomination—it was too late anyway—but he'd told conservatives to "grow up" and take the Republican Party back. And that's what they were doing precinct by precinct, county by county, state by state. They'd actually openly borrowed a tactic from the hard left, packing meetings, staying late, wearing out their opponents with parliamentary warfare, until they'd grabbed control of so much of the party's apparatus that the fight was over before it had officially begun. They'd had a moment of doubt, even panic, on November 22 when they first heard the news that the President had been shot; if John Kennedy had died in Dallas, their efforts might have been wasted.

"America's not going to change presidents twice in one year," they nervously told each other as they waited for news about Kennedy's condition. But he'd lived . . . which meant they were looking at a clean sweep in the South, a strong showing in the mountain West, and some real possibilities in the Midwest, where middle-class folks were getting an unappetizing taste of what an overbearing, intrusive government could do to their schools, their homes, their values. And who better than Barry Goldwater to run against a slick, rich, glamorous aristocrat whose father had bought him the White House? Maybe Americans did admire the Kennedys—their youth, their good looks, their wealth—but the other side of admiration is envy, even resentment, and if that resentment were to feed anxiety, that could even trump a low jobless rate and a growing economy. As Clif White, the strategist who organized the Goldwater insurgency, put it, "Pocketbook issues can take a backseat if you're afraid someone's going to steal your pocketbook on the way to the grocery store."

Besides, even if electing Goldwater was an uphill battle, better to lose with a leader who *fought* the battle than to win with someone who *surrendered* before the first shot was fired—someone who captured the conservative cause boldly.

"I have little interest in streamlining government or in making it more efficient," he'd written, "for I mean to reduce its size. I do not undertake to promote welfare, for I propose to extend freedom. My aim is not to pass laws, but to repeal them." On civil rights, his personal views diverged sharply from his political positions. In Phoenix, he'd desegregated his family's department store and led the efforts to integrate local schools and restaurants and the state's National Guard. But he'd been telling Southern audiences for years that the federal government should not enforce school segregation by force, because the Supreme Court's decision "was not grounded in law." And he'd opposed Kennedy's public accommodations civil rights law as an intrusion on a private citizen's right to do as he wished with his own property.

His foreign policy approach was equally uncompromising. *Why Not Victory?* he'd asked in a book title. Why not challenge the Soviet Union's conquest of Eastern Europe? Why not unleash Chiang Kai-shek and give him the support to retake China from the Communist rulers? Why not put the full force of American might behind the toppling of the Cuban dictator who'd established a Communist beachhead ninety miles from Miami? He'd been openly contemptuous about Kennedy's no-invasion pledge that helped end the Cuban missile crisis. "We locked Castro's communism into Latin America and threw away the key to its removal," he said. And if Goldwater was untroubled by the idea of nuclear weapons as useful tools for the U.S. military, that was no different from the views of the Joint Chiefs and other key military men. "Disarmament" was a Soviet ploy to end America's nuclear superiority, a critical counterweight to the massive Red Army spread out across Eastern Europe. "Let others talk about test bans; I want the ability," Goldwater said, "to lob one into the men's room of the Kremlin."

To his fervent supporters, these and other views—ending diplomatic recognition of the Soviet Union, repudiating the Test Ban Treaty, making Social Security voluntary (which would effectively end the system)—were squarely in the mainstream of muscular, patriotic conservatism. To the broader electorate, which had lived through three decades of a moderate-liberal consensus and twenty years of a cold war framed by a balance of power, they sounded odd, eccentric, dangerous. Throughout the nominating season, moderate and liberal Republicans warned again and again that the nomination of Barry Goldwater would split the party and ensure the reelection of President Kennedy. And the conservatives replied, again and again: *You don't understand America; there's a conservative majority that's stayed home in November because they've never had a candidate of their own.* Hell, one of FDR's original brain trusters, Raymond Moley, was making the same argument. Besides, the quarter century of frustration at the power of the Eastern liberal Republicans was not about to be deterred. So when Goldwater won the winner-take-all California primary on June 2—helped immeasurably by the birth of a son to Nelson and Happy Rockefeller just three days before—the fight was essentially over.

On July 15, President Kennedy and his inner circle watched Barry Goldwater win the Republican nomination from the family compound at Hyannis Port.

They'd watched the convention all but boo Nelson Rockefeller off the podium when he argued for a convention plank denouncing extremism. They'd nodded with professional admiration when Goldwater made a politically savvy choice of a running mate. Michigan's Gerald Ford—fifty-one years old, Eagle Scout, war veteran, football star, fifteen-year veteran of the House of Representatives— had an engaging smile, and a broad regular-guy/Main Street appeal. (Ford also supplied the comic moment of the convention when he picked up the oversize gavel to proclaim that "when this campaign is over, John Kennedy will never know what had hit him!"—an unfortunate, unintended reference to the events in Dallas—and then lost control of the gavel, which flew out of his hand, over the stage, and wound up opening up a nasty gash on the forehead of former senator William Knowland, chair of the California delegation.)

The next night they heard Goldwater, in his acceptance speech, assail the President's foreign policy: "He has talked and talked and talked and talked the words of freedom. Now, failures cement the wall of shame in Berlin. Failures blot the sands of shame at the Bay of Pigs. Failures mark the slow death of freedom in Laos. Failures infest the jungles of Vietnam." They heard him denounce the spiritual and moral climate of the nation.

"Tonight there is violence in our streets, corruption in our highest offices, aimlessness among our youth, anxiety among our elders, and there is a virtual despair among the many who look beyond material success for the inner meaning of their lives."

("Exactly!" shouted a young Goldwater supporter, Hillary Rodham, as she watched from her parents' home in Park Ridge, Illinois. "I'll remember that line if I ever get to give a speech.")

And they heard him issue an unprecedented challenge to Kennedy, a challenge stemming from some informal conversations the two men had had.

"Mr. President," Goldwater said, "you and I have a historic opportunity to turn this political campaign into a civic crusade; to take politics out of the hands of the Madison Avenue hucksters, the cynics who would substitute sixty-second slogans for real debate. I propose that you and I travel the nation together and engage in a series of debates on the great issues confronting us. I do not fear the outcome of an open clash of ideas. Do you?"

("We're going to have to finesse that debate issue," O'Donnell said.)

And, with unanimous delight, they heard Goldwater answer critics of his allegedly "extremist" view by proclaiming, "Extremism in the defense of liberty is no vice and . . . moderation in the pursuit of justice is no virtue."

As Goldwater's speech ended—with images of liberal Republicans like New York senator Ken Keating leaving the convention floor—the President raised a bottle of beer.

"Gentleman," he said, "I propose a toast to the Republican National Convention. Tonight, they've given us exactly what we've asked for."

In fact, in nominating Goldwater, the Republicans gave John Kennedy something more, something neither he nor any of his aides even imagined. With the Goldwater nomination, the Republicans had unknowingly protected him from the gravest threat to his presidency . . . a threat that was brewing not in the ranks of the opposition, but inside his own house.

For more than three years the Kennedy administration had been at war with itself, a war whose roots were in the contradictions the new president had brought to the office. He was skeptical of the assumptions that underlay American foreign policy: the monolithic view of communism; the support for every foreign ruler, no matter how brutal, as long as he protected U.S. interests; the dismissal of nationalism as a powerful source of revolt. But he also saw international affairs as a global contest between Moscow and Washington, looked for new ways to engage the cold war struggle through counterinsurgency, launched a campaign of subversion against Castro's Cuba, and touted a nonexistent "missile gap" with the Soviets as a motive for inflating the defense budget.

Moreover, many of the highest-ranking members of his administration fully shared the foreign policy orthodoxies of the postwar American establishment. Dean Rusk at State, Mac Bundy at National Security, Walt Rostow, the top men at the CIA, the generals and admirals at the top of the Pentagon firmly believed that only the threat of overwhelming force ever deterred the Communists from their march to world domination; and if threats of force did not work, then force itself was required—up to and including America's vastly superior nuclear forces.

And by 1964 some of these men—small in number but not in influence—had come to the unsettling realization that President Kennedy did not share these bedrock convictions; worse, that he had embarked on a course that would, in their minds, pose a clear and present danger to the national security of the United States.

Yes, he'd given a steely inaugural address, promising to "pay any price, bear any burden" to protect freedom around the world. Yes, he'd pumped serious money into the Defense Department and enthused over a new breed of counterinsurgency warriors. But at the very start of his presidency, faced with the advice of the military and outgoing president Eisenhower to inject American forces into Laos, Kennedy refused, and shaped a highly shaky "neutralization" plan with Soviet leader Khrushchev. Three months later, when the Bay of Pigs invasion of Cuba was faltering, he refused to use any American forces to save the plan. It had been a huge black eye for the United States, a huge propaganda victory for Castro. And then the President fired CIA director Allen Dulles, and Richard Bissell, deputy director for plans. These were the men who'd overthrown

U.S. adversaries like Iran's Mossadegh and Guatemala's Arbenz. Now this callow, inexperienced president was ending the careers of men of proven judgment and effectiveness. And it got worse: in October 1962, Kennedy and his brother rejected the counsel of the Joint Chiefs, and wise men like Acheson and Nitze, who advised them to take those missiles out. "Moscow will understand it's our sphere of influence, they'll do what we did in Budapest in '56— nothing." And now a Communist dictator, fomenting subversion throughout Latin America, was shielded by a no-invasion pledge from the American president.

"The greatest defeat in our history," Air Force chief Curtis LeMay called it, and many of these men agreed. The resolution of the crisis had been, as Dean Acheson had it, a matter of "luck"; in the long run, they were sure, the United States would pay for such feckless leadership—if indeed you could call it "leadership" at all.

Some of these men did not.

"Kennedy is weak, not a leader," Allen Dulles was saying from his forced retirement.

"We have to face the fact that the United States has no leader," Acheson told former colleagues at a dinner.

Others were far more acerbic, at least in private. Richard Helms, a career CIA official who took Bissell's place as deputy director for plans, thought Kennedy weak, cowardly. Air Force chief LeMay despised the Kennedys, calling the President and his brother "vermin, cockroaches."

These views only hardened after the Cuban missile crisis, when Kennedy seemed embarked on a course of conduct that would effectively call a truce in the cold war. He'd given that speech at American University, asking Americans to "reexamine" their attitudes toward the Communist world, to acknowledge the limits of American power. He'd signed the Nuclear Test Ban Treaty with Moscow and, if Dean Rusk was right, he was looking to "normalize" relations with the Communist Chinese in a second term.

By 1964 a few of these men had come to believe that the policies and intentions of John Kennedy posed nothing less than a clear and present danger to the United States. Some of them—we will never really know—may have spent the time on November 22, 1963, between the shooting of the President and word of his survival with this assessment: *A President Lyndon Johnson, far more deferential to the orthodoxies of his time, far less engaged in foreign and military matters, would be far more likely to follow the wisdom that had guided the nation for twenty years or more.*

That hadn't happened. Kennedy had survived; Lyndon Johnson was gone, his spot on the ticket yet to be filled. But in the weeks and months before the Republican convention, they came to an understanding that it might be in their collective power to do politically what that bullet in Dallas had not done. Given the right dissemination of information—or disinformation—to the right people in politics and the press, a portrait could be painted of an administration paralyzed by incompetence. Confidential assessments by military and intelligence operatives—shaped for maximum political effect—could highlight weakness worldwide: an ally in South Vietnam increasingly threatened by collapse; allies in Europe doubting America's commitment to defend the continent against a Soviet assault; allies in Latin America who feared the United States had given Castro a free hand on the continent. If Kennedy in 1960 could turn polls about U.S. prestige abroad into a campaign weapon, then these assessments of American weakness, coming (under deep cover) from high counsels of power, could prove devastating.

Indeed, they'd had a very recent, unsettling example of just how far President Kennedy had drifted from his 1960 commitment to "pay any price, bear any burden, support any friend, oppose any foe" to resist the advance of communism. On August 2, the destroyer *Maddox* had engaged three North Vietnamese torpedo boats off the coast of North Vietnam. A brief sea battle erupted; the *Maddox* sustained light damage, the torpedo boats were heavily damaged. Two days later, when reports reached Washington of a second attack on the *Maddox* and the destroyer *Turner Joy*, President Kennedy and his top civilian and military advisors gathered to decide how to respond—most likely with a reprisal attack on North Vietnamese military installations.

And then Kennedy said no. For one thing, he argued, wasn't there some dispute about whether the *Maddox* was in international or North Vietnamese territorial waters? Hadn't the South Vietnamese navy been engaged in a series of coastal raids (perhaps, he thought silently, with the whispered okay of American agents)? As for the second "attack," there was no evidence at all that such an attack had even taken place. It could just as easily have been the faulty conclusion of a nineteen-year-old sonar operator on board the *Turner Joy*.

Remember what had happened during the missile crisis, he asked, when a Soviet sub thought we were dropping depth charges and almost launched a nuclear-tipped torpedo against the *Essex*? Miscalculation, Kennedy said, was the single biggest cause of military blunders—never more so than in a nuclear age.

"Well, Mr. President," Bundy, the national security advisor, interjected. "If the North Vietnamese *are* engaging us, it wouldn't be very difficult to get Congress to pass a resolution of support."

"Support for what?" Kennedy asked.

"Well," Secretary of State Rusk said, "for pretty much anything you thought necessary to—"

"You mean a blank check," Kennedy said. "Dean, that's the *last* thing I want. As soon as they write me a 'blank check,' I'm going to start getting flak, not just from Barry, but from our own party—Jackson, Dodd, Smathers—about when I plan to cash it. It's going to be tough enough to figure out what the hell to do there once this election's over. We start turning up the heat now, and it's likely to have a very bad outcome."

For the most zealous among these men, it was more evidence that, in John Kennedy, the United States had a president who simply did not understand what was necessary to protect the long-term national security of the nation he was leading.

This conviction, in turn, raised the possibility of an even more radical step. Apart from the potential use of military and defense intelligence, there was in the hands of a very few of them intelligence of another sort, intelligence that raised the most unsettling of questions about the President himself—questions of personal behavior and morality—though for most of those desiring the end of the Kennedy presidency that kind of information was something of a "nuclear option," as likely to injure those handling it as the intended target. Better to concentrate on serious issues of weakened national security and the unraveling of the cold war consensus.

These men might have pursued that path if the Republicans had chosen a different nominee, like George Romney or Bill Scranton or Nelson Rockefeller. The New York governor in particular was an attractive possibility: a strong-on-defense politician with an appetite for big increases in military spending (he'd pressured Nixon into endorsing just such spending as the price of his non-candidacy in 1960) who was comfortable enough with the concept of massive retaliation to propose a massive nationwide fallout-shelter building program. But Goldwater? He was too reckless with his language, like his talk of wanting the ability to "lob one into the men's room of the Kremlin," for heaven's sake; and while Curtis LeMay might find him a plausible president, the men who'd held the levers at State and Defense and CIA over the years—the "wise men" among current and former diplomats, journalists, House and Senate members, the men who formed an unofficial council of elders—did not. And besides, Goldwater was likely so weak a candidate that their efforts would fail to alter the outcome in November.

So they stayed their hand, and waited. If Kennedy continued on this dangerous path of appeasement, if he moved closer toward a naive accommodation with Moscow, then they could revisit how to render him politically impotent. Indeed, one key test would be coming very soon: whether and how to save an increasingly vulnerable South Vietnam, whose fall, they believed, would jeopardize all of Southeast Asia and whose survival required a large force of American troops, hundreds of thousands of them. If Kennedy faltered in South Vietnam after giving a clear commitment to saving the country, that would be conclusive evidence that Kennedy had to be stopped. And once he'd been reelected and was immune from accountability to the voters, the only effective weapon at their disposal would be that "nuclear" option.

They sat on an open porch under a clear blue, late August sky, in shirtsleeves and shorts, lunching on clam chowder, lobster rolls, corn on the cob, and beer, bemoaning the performance of the Boston Red Sox—eighteen and a half games out of first place—and choosing the man who would almost certainly become the next vice president of the United States.

From the moment Lyndon Johnson stepped down some seven months ago, speculating about the identity of John Kennedy's running mate had been one of Washington's favorite indoor sports. Some of it reached the outer limits of whimsy. In late spring, Kenny

O'Donnell showed the President an Art Buchwald column in which the humorist asked: "Why doesn't Bobby Kennedy move to New York, change his residency, and run with Jack? Think of all the money they could save on bumper stickers."

("Bobby as a New York politician? With his accent," the President laughed, "they'd run him out of town in a week.")

Now, just three days before the opening of the Democratic convention in Atlantic City, there was nothing whimsical about the conversation. With the Goldwater nomination, the Republicans had made the terms of their case clear: the Kennedy administration was committed to socialistic Big Government at home and paralyzed by weakness and indecision in the face of a worldwide Communist threat abroad. Kennedy and his team had little concern about the domestic argument: voters had shown their approval of an expansive government for thirty years. When Ike became the first Republican president in twenty years, he'd done nothing to undo the programs of the New Deal. But the charge of weakness in the face of a Communist foe? Yes, that had the potential to cause real political damage, especially given Kennedy's call for a dramatic reexamination of cold war thinking.

That's why the President was determined to keep a contentious issue like Vietnam off the political radar screen as much as possible; why he'd brushed aside the possible confrontation in the Gulf of Tonkin; why he'd told Senator Mansfield that he could do nothing about winding down America's role until after November. ("If I tried to pull out completely now from Vietnam, we would have another Joe McCarthy Red Scare on our hands, but I can do it after I'm reelected. So we had better make damn sure that I am reelected.")

It was also why Kennedy and his advisors agreed that the defense credentials of his running mate had to be unassailable—which pretty much ruled out Minnesota's Hubert Humphrey.

"He's been a good friend," O'Brien said. "Really pushed hard for our agenda in the Senate."

The President added, "And no one's better at standing up for us with the 'honkers,'" the term he used for the more assertive liberals.

But Hubert was an all-out advocate for peace. He'd been pushing for the Nuclear Test Ban Treaty for years; had called for a "hard look" at defense spending. Beyond the specifics, his very identification with the most liberal wing of the Democratic Party—civil rights advocates, intellectuals with a fondness for government planning—was not going to help Kennedy as he reached for independents and liberal Republicans for whom Goldwater was suspect goods.

By contrast, several Democratic senators were undeniably hawkish on defense matters; two of them had been serious contenders for the vice presidency four years ago. Washington State's Henry "Scoop" Jackson was a pro-labor, pro–civil rights liberal who was also a champion of ever larger military spending ("the senator from Boeing," he was called, after the aerospace and defense giant whose headquarters were in Seattle). His anti-Soviet credentials were impeccable, so much so that he'd forced Kennedy into significant concessions before signing on to the Test Ban Treaty. And that was a problem.

"I can't be campaigning on a promise of peace while my running mate is going all over the country promising to liberate Eastern Europe and unleash Chiang Kai-shek," Kennedy said.

Moreover, Jackson shared a liability with Humphrey: geography.

Because the legacy of the Civil War had made it impossible for a Southerner to win a presidential nomination, the Democratic Party was all but required to pick someone from a Southern or border state for the second spot on the ticket. Only FDR had broken that tradition when he chose Iowa's Henry Wallace in 1940; and when he dumped him four years later, it was Missouri's Truman who took his place.

It had always been Kennedy's intention, despite the rumors, to keep Lyndon Johnson as his running mate, to help him once again in Texas and the South. And when scandals forced Johnson off the ticket, he and his aides had looked first to the South for a running mate: to a progressive like North Carolina governor Terry Sanford or Tennessee senator Al Gore Sr. Neither, however, had the kind of national security credentials Kennedy was looking for, and in any event it was highly possible that the South was more or less a lost cause.

"Well," Kenny O'Donnell said, "I think we're back to Stu."

"Isn't this where we came in?" Sorensen cracked.

Four years ago in Los Angeles, Symington was widely assumed to be Kennedy's choice for running mate—so much so that he'd begun drafting his acceptance speech. There were still some around the President, including his brother, who insisted that the offer to Lyndon Johnson had been a formality, a courtesy, and that once Lyndon said no, they'd turn to Symington. Now the twin demands of policy and geography made him an even stronger choice. Domestically, he was in good standing with labor unions, big-city machines, and the civil rights movement. On defense, he'd been the first secretary of the Air Force during the Truman administration, and he fully embraced the argument that a loss of any nation to communism would send the dominoes crashing.

And he was from Missouri—a border state with twelve electoral votes that Kennedy had won by just 12,000 votes—a quarter of 1 percent—in 1960. If it wasn't the home run that LBJ had been for them in 1960, it was a prudent, safe choice, "just like the Hippocratic oath the doctors take," Sorensen said. "'First, do no harm.'"

It would be almost two years before Sorensen, and every other close Kennedy hand, realized how wrong that judgment was.

"Mr. President, I think we'll be getting to bed a lot earlier than we did last time," said Kenny O'Donnell. It was just after 8:00 p.m. on November 3, and they were settling in at the Hyannis Port family compound, shuttling back and forth between Jack's home and Bobby's, converted into an Election Night headquarters with dedicated phone lines and tickers from AP and UPI. They all remembered the endless night in 1960: the early lead from the East eroding, the bad news from Florida, Wisconsin, and Ohio, the razor-thin margins in Texas and Illinois, the agonizingly close loss in California. *Not this time,* the polls were saying.

He'd begun the day in Boston, driving with his wife from his official residence at 122 Bowdoin Street to the West End Branch of the Boston Public Library on Cambridge Street, carefully navigating the steps to the basement, where the voting booths were. They voted, smiled for the cameras, then flew by helicopter to the Cape, where the President soaked his chronically painful back in a hot tub, napped, played with his children outside in the brisk fall air. Pictures would be supplied to the wire services in time to hit the afternoon papers; if they inspired a voter to head to the polls and vote for the handsome young father with the adorable children, so much the better.

If he and his team exuded confidence this night, there was good reason. Presidents are almost never turned out of office in a time of peace and prosperity, and he had both working for him. The jobless rate was still under 6 percent, inflation was nonexistent, and in the words of *U.S. News & World Report,* "It's been a generation or more since the world was as quiet as now." The Republicans had never united behind Goldwater; traditional voices of the party, like the *New York Herald Tribune* and the *Saturday Evening Post*, either refused to endorse him or even backed Kennedy.

The Democratic Party's mid-August convention in Atlantic City was a model of civility—at least, compared with many past Democratic conventions. (Sure, it might have been better to hold it in Miami, given that Florida's fourteen electoral votes were up for grabs; but they could not risk disruptive, even violent demonstrations from Miami's Negro population or from the city's rapidly growing Cuban exile community.) There was only one potential for disruption in Atlantic City: the demand of an ad hoc integrated "Mississippi Freedom Democratic Party" to be seated in place of the all-white segregationist official delegate slate, headed by the unrepentant white supremacist senator James Eastland. The Kennedy White House had persuaded a broad coalition of civil rights groups to declare a moratorium on demonstrations to avoid stirring up white resentment, but an outbreak of disorder between white police and black residents in New York, Newark, and Philadelphia put the issue back on the front pages. For the White House, seating the integrated "Freedom Democrats" meant trouble: since they had organized outside party rules, the organization Democrats—the Mayor Daleys, the John Baileys, the Jesse Unruhs—were bound to be unhappy. What saved the peace was Kennedy's very weakness in the South. With little need to placate the region, it was easy to pass a strong civil rights plank and a pledge that, in 1968, no delegation would be seated unless it could demonstrate an open, unsegregated process. With that, the Mississippi delegation walked out, and five Freedom Democrats were seated as at-large delegates.

In a convention with no doubt about the identity of the nominees and no dispute over platform planks and credentials, the energy level was low, and vice presidential nominee Stu Symington's vapid acceptance speech did nothing to excite the crowd, provoking NBC's Sander Vanocur to comment, "They say in Missouri he tried to give a fireside chat and the fire went out"—a crack that earned him a formal censure vote from the Missouri Democratic Party.

That all changed when John Kennedy walked to the rostrum.

When the cheers and applause finally stopped after fifteen tumultuous minutes, he offered good-natured but pointed humor directed at his Republican rival.

"I note with some amusement," he said, "that my opponent has expressed a desire to debate. So let me suggest to my distinguished opponent that if he wishes to get a little experience under his belt before the 'main event,' he might start by debating the Republican governor of New York, the Republican governor of Pennsylvania, and the Republican governor of Michigan, all of whom have called his ideas and proposals wholly outside the mainstream of American thinking."

Then he turned to the major themes of his address. He'd told his speechwriting team he wanted to steer a middle course between blunt appeals to personal interest and sweeping, gauzy visions.

Back in the spring, White House aide Dick Goodwin had been taken with a phrase from older Progressive journalists like Herb Croly and Walter Lippmann: "The Great Society." It might be a way, he thought, to elevate the campaign with a vision of an America that went beyond a series of reforms and legislative ideas.

"No," Sorensen said. "Too grandiose; it's overreaching. It'd be fine for Hubert or Lyndon, but you need to remember," he added, "the President doesn't think the way you do or I do. In a sense, he's a conservative—in the real meaning of the word."

So in place of "the New Frontier," Kennedy called for "a New Patriotism." It was designed as an answer to the patriotic themes of the Goldwater campaign—"a real-life, grown-up version of that old playground game, 'Capture the Flag,'" as *Washington Star* reporter David Broder put it.

"The New Patriotism of which I speak," Kennedy said to the convention, "is clear-eyed, tough-minded, unafraid. It remembers that 'America the Beautiful' asks God not just to 'shed His grace on thee' but to 'mend thine every flaw.' It reveres our freedom so much that it seeks to ensure those freedoms to every one of our citizens, of every race and creed. It recognizes the patriots in uniform who stand on the watchtowers of freedom—and the patriots who are giving two years of their lives as Peace Corps volunteers, healing the sick, feeding the hungry, teaching the young, nurturing the old, on every continent of the globe. And next year we will be asking other patriots to join in that work in the inner cities and rural hollows of our own nation—when we launch AmeriCorps early in 1965."

He ended by reframing the most famous line from his 1961 inaugural.

"Four years ago," he said, "I asked Americans to 'ask what you can do for your country.' In that same spirit, I ask you tonight to consider not 'Are *you* better off than you were four years ago?' but 'Are *we* better off than we were four years ago? Is our land more just? Is the world at peace? Are we bringing hope to the hopeless?' That is the measure by which I ask you to judge these past four years. If you once again give us your hand, your heart, your voice, and your vote, I will spend every day so that four years from now, all of us can answer: 'Yes, we *are* better off than we were, because we have helped to build a world more peaceful, more just, more free.'"

For the next eight weeks, Kennedy pursued that theme relentlessly as his campaign never stopped reminding voters of the peril a

Goldwater presidency would mean. In what became the most controversial message of the entire election, a one-minute ad appeared
on daytime television on CBS and NBC on September 7, 1964, in
the middle of *Days of Our Lives* and *As the World Turns*: A four-year-
old boy wanders into a kitchen as his mother turns away; he walks
toward a stove where a pot sits, just coming to a boil; he reaches his
hand out to it. As his mother lunges to save him, the film cuts to a
massive nuclear explosion as an announcer's voice intones, "Every
mother knows . . . a moment's miscalculation can mean disaster for
her family. In a nuclear world, it can mean disaster for mankind. A
steady course is our best hope to avoid that disaster. On November
third, vote for President Kennedy. Stay the course."

The film—instantly known as the "Nuclear Kitchen" ad—only
ran for one afternoon as a paid commercial. But it was seen by tens
of millions on the evening newscasts as the Goldwater campaign
charged that Kennedy was "engaged in a slanderous attack on Senator Goldwater." A Kennedy campaign spokesman noted, "It's curious that his campaign would identify their own candidate with the
danger of miscalculation. The ad never mentioned Senator Goldwater at all."

On Monday, October 5, at 9:00 p.m., President Kennedy and Senator Goldwater walked into Studio 3A of Chicago TV station
WBBM and shook hands. Both were wearing dark-blue suits—
Goldwater advisor Stephen Shadegg had showed the Senator photos
of Richard Nixon at the first 1960 debate wearing a light-gray suit
that all but disappeared into the background—and the challenger
also wore a layer of makeup, much to his annoyance. ("I'm not
going to turn myself into a goddamn circus clown!" he'd snapped,
and Shadegg had to remind him again of Richard Nixon's fate four

years earlier. "All right, dammit," Goldwater said, "but if I win, we'll do the debates on radio in '68.")

There was unhappiness among millions of American teenagers about the broadcast: it preempted a *Perry Como's Kraft Music Hall* broadcast that was to feature Frankie Avalon and Fabian. Even more unhappy were many of President Kennedy's close aides: they hadn't wanted this debate to happen at all.

"You're thirteen points ahead," pollster Lou Harris had said a month earlier as he sat with President Kennedy and a half dozen men around the pool of the family home on Ocean Avenue in Palm Beach. "A decisive share of the public simply does not see Goldwater as a credible president of the United States. The minute you let him on the same stage as you, you're granting him that credibility."

"He's going to push you into defending a civil rights bill you couldn't pass and most of the country's against," said Florida senator George Smathers, one of the President's oldest friends. "He's going to push you into calling for open-housing laws, foreign aid to Communists like Tito, coddling rioters—that's spelled *N-E-G-R-O*, in case it's slipped your mind . . ."

"It worries me," Robert Kennedy said. "I go back to what Lou said. You step down from the presidency and you become just another politician grubbing for votes."

There was just one dissenter. Unfortunately for the group, it was the President.

"I think you're playing by old rules," he said. "*We're* the ones who decided to air my press conferences live. Remember what Scotty Reston wrote? He called it 'the goofiest idea since the Hula-Hoop.' Yes, people saw reporters asking some pretty impolite questions, saw me answering them on the fly. How do we think that worked out for us? They tell me there are college kids watching them like it's a quiz show. Pierre, how many times have we waited until Mrs. Kennedy was traveling so we could sneak a photographer in to get pictures of me and the kids playing? Anybody here think that 'demystified' the office? As a matter of fact, Teddy Roosevelt got a hell of a lot of mileage when he let the press photograph him camping out in Rock Creek Park.

"And one other point: Suppose we don't agree to debate; what's our explanation? That we're afraid I'll spill some damaging state secret? That doesn't exactly play to our argument that *I'm* the one with the steady hand on the tiller, does it?"

"Well," Larry O'Brien said, "it's up to the Congress to suspend the equal time rule so that you and he can debate without fifteen minor-party candidates. We could always blame them—"

"Come on, Larry," Kennedy said. "Is there anyone over the age of four who's going to believe I couldn't get Mansfield and McCormack to pass that bill in thirty seconds? Let's not forget that we were the ones pushing for a debate last time. The only argument anyone will believe is: 'It's not in our political interest.' And anyway"—he gave a small smile—"it's probably a good thing for the country. I once asked Macmillan how he felt about having to drag himself into the House of Commons twice a week to get pounded by the opposition. 'Keeps you on your toes,' he said. If we do it, I don't see how any future president will be able to say no."

"And Barry's idea of flying together to ten different cities, Lincoln-Douglas debates—"

"Ted, I have not taken complete leave of my senses," Kennedy said to Sorensen. "First of all, Lincoln and Douglas had audiences—competing mobs, really—shouting, heckling. I can't imagine anything more demeaning. Second, they talked for as long as ninety minutes at a stretch. I'm not interested in putting America to sleep.

We'll also want a panel of reporters. Let them break the shaft off in him; most of them think Goldwater's half nuts, and I'm sure they'll do their best to prove it—assuming they have any hope of a sit-down with me anytime in the next four years. And one or two debates will be plenty; we're not going to throw our campaign schedule out of whack. We'll fit it in, but you fellows can keep the negotiations going for as long as you need, like last time." (In 1960 the Nixon campaign had pushed for a fifth, late debate; the Kennedy campaign never refused but kept extending the negotiations until time ran out.)

Between the delays in Congress and the extended negotiations about format, there was time for only one debate; something Goldwater pounced on in his opening remarks, addressing Kennedy directly:

"I'm happy to be here with you, Mr. President. We've managed to maintain our friendship despite our differences. But I have to add a sense of disappointment that we'll only be meeting this one time. Four years ago, you and Vice President Nixon met *four* times, and the country got a real sense of where you both stood. We'd often talked about a series of real, substantive debates, and I say to-night what I've said throughout the campaign: I will meet you any-time, at your convenience, in the last month of this election.

"But I have to say," Goldwater said with a smile, "after looking at the record of the last four years, I can understand why you might not want to have to defend that record face-to-face. If I'd presided over a government that has grown ever bigger, ever more costly . . . if I'd advocated a massive federal intrusion into the rights of home-owners and parents . . . if I'd been at the wheel when violent crime rose dramatically, and when violence and disorder swept through many of our biggest cities . . . if I'd watched international communism take the offensive from Latin America to Africa to Southeast Asia . . . if I'd gone to Moscow to toast the Soviet dictator who's promised to 'bury' us and engaged in a slow-motion Munich appeasement strategy—I might not be all that eager to defend myself, either. I'd probably be spending my campaign trying to convince the American voter that my opponent couldn't wait to get his finger on the button and set off World War III. Although I think I'd have a heck of a time trying to explain how such a 'warmonger' could have the enthusiastic support of President Eisenhower."

The President began on a lighthearted note.

"Senator, I'm delighted to join you tonight. I realize this will be an exciting new experience for you, since just four months ago you declined an invitation to debate Governor Rockefeller, and just two months ago you refused every invitation to debate Governor Scranton, when he was your principal opponent for the nomination. I can tell you from personal experience it would have been a worthwhile endeavor for you . . . having debated Senator Humphrey in West Virginia, and the Senate majority leader at our last convention, and the sitting vice president of the United States four times last fall. And I've asked my campaign to meet with yours, to see if we can at this late date work out some mutually agreeable time for another debate."

("Maybe sometime in December," Salinger cracked from the Green Room backstage.)

"Senator Goldwater has talked of 'Munich,'" he continued. "I know those lessons well. They are the lessons of appeasement, of the failure to prepare. Those failures cost the lives of tens of millions in World War II. And mine was almost one of them.

"My administration has taken that lesson to heart. Since 1960, we now have 50 percent more Polaris submarines; 75 percent more

Minutemen; increased by 50 percent the portion of our strategic bombers on fifteen-minute alert forces; 60 percent more tactical nuclear forces deployed in Western Europe.

"But we also know that neither Europe nor any other continent relies on nuclear forces alone, whether they are strategic or tactical. We have radically improved the readiness of our conventional forces: increased by 45 percent the number of combat-ready Army divisions; increased by 100 percent the procurement of modern Army weapons and equipment; increased by 30 percent the number of tactical air squadrons; and increased the strength of the Marines.

"But history also teaches another lesson: the lesson of Sarajevo. Seventy years ago the world watched as a dispute between two nations exploded into the First World War—out of a series of miscalculations and false assumptions. Today we dare not let such miscalculations, such false assumptions, lead to a third world war in which hundreds of millions would die, and in which 'the living would envy the dead.'

"As for Senator Goldwater's ideas about how to deal with our adversaries, and with the world . . . If we were to resign from the United Nations, break off with all countries of whom we disapprove, end foreign aid and assistance to those countries in an attempt to keep them free, call for the resumption of atmospheric nuclear testing, and turn our back on the rest of mankind, we would not only be abandoning America's influence in the world, we would be inviting a Communist expansion which every Communist power would so greatly welcome. And all of the effort of so many Americans for eighteen years would be gone with the wind."

There was one moment from the debate that was the source of both puzzlement and amusement. It came when panelist Roger Mudd of CBS asked Goldwater just how far he would go in trimming back the size and scope of government.

"For instance," Mudd asked, "you've said you'd like to sell the Tennessee Valley Authority to a private utility. What else do you have in mind?"

"I think some smart entrepreneur could give the post office a real run for its money," he said, "which is, of course, the taxpayers' money."

Two days later, a Herblock cartoon appeared in the *Washington Post* showing Goldwater as a used-car salesman in front of a post office advertising: "This Week Only—Try Our 'Express Mail'— Just $5 Each!"

There was no second debate; Kennedy's negotiators made sure of that. And in the closing days of the campaign, events from far away played directly to the President's core argument. On October 14, Soviet premier Khrushchev, buoyed by the public support for his economic reforms and his arms talks with Kennedy, successfully turned back an attempt by Leonid Brezhnev and others to remove him from power. Two days later China exploded its first atomic weapon in the remote Central Asian province of Sinkiang.

Wrote columnist Roscoe Drummond, "History may record that the President's visit last spring to the Soviet Union may have been the first time that a state visit helped keep the world's two most powerful men in their jobs."

"The polls have said for months," added James Reston of the *New York Times*, "that America, having almost lost its president to a madman's bullet, was not eager to lose him at the ballot box. Now whatever slim chance Senator Goldwater might have had to convince the American voter that they could risk a change in the Oval Office disappeared somewhere between the bowels of the Kremlin and the radioactive atmosphere over the Takla Makan Desert in China."

By the time the polls in the East and Midwest closed, Larry O'Brien's forecast had been confirmed. It was going to be an early night.

Kennedy had taken all of once solidly Republican New England; only New Hampshire wound up in Goldwater's column. ("Well, it's the only state in the region with a right-wing Republican senator," Kennedy said. "All the others—Smith, Aiken, Saltonstall—they're farther away from Barry than I am.") The Middle Atlantic states were all in the Democratic column, though Richard Scammon—moonlighting from his job as Census Bureau director to help the campaign analyze the vote—noted a measurable fall-off among the white ethnic city and inner-suburban votes. And Californians threw out the state's open-housing law by a 2–1 margin.

"New York, Newark, Buffalo, Philadelphia, Pittsburgh, Milwaukee, California—it's backlash, it's widespread, and it's something to worry about down the road."

"Tell it to Bobby or Teddy or Hubert or Stu," Kennedy said. "Don't bother this elder statesman with these grubby political matters. And speaking of worries: the South—"

"Pretty much gone," Scammon said. "Maybe for a generation."

The same Deep South states that had voted for Strom Thurmond's States' Rights Democratic Party in 1948—South Carolina, Alabama, Mississippi, and Louisiana—had been joined by virtually every state in the old Confederacy, including Texas.

"Lyndon's revenge," O'Donnell said, with a nod toward Bobby. "He always blamed you for driving him off the ticket."

"Not that I wouldn't take the credit," Robert Kennedy said, "but I see the fine hand of Governor Connally in this."

"No," the President said. "You wouldn't see his fine hand—

because he sat on them all fall. I hope he and his country club friends will be happy when we cut the oil depletion allowance to zero."

The one consolation from the South came from Florida, where an overwhelming Jewish vote, unsettled by some of Goldwater's more militant right-wing supporters, and seniors, unnerved by Goldwater's hostility toward Social Security and Kennedy's Medicare proposal, delivered the state to Kennedy by a narrow margin.

As it happened, the President would not need Florida's votes to win a second term. In the industrial Midwest, four years of a Catholic president had eased the fears of Ohio Protestants, and the state he'd lost by a wide margin in 1960 turned Democratic; so did Wisconsin. In Illinois, there was no talk of Mayor Daley's vote-counting skills; they weren't needed this time. The state went to Kennedy by eight points. Senator Symington's presence on the ticket was enough to win Missouri again. And with the Pacific Coast states in his column—Kennedy had spent the last two days of the election up and down the West Coast—the President wound up with 332 electoral votes and 54 percent of the popular vote. There'd be no repeat of the Did-he-steal-it? Does-he-have-a-mandate? arguments that clouded the post-campaign atmosphere in 1960.

However, Kennedy's reelection did not come with coattails. Democrats picked up five seats in the House and held their majority in the Senate, which meant that the coalition of Southern conservative Democrats and Republicans still had the power to stall much of Kennedy's agenda. The one Democratic Senate loss was painful: with Governor Connally's all-but-open help, Ralph Yarborough lost his Senate seat to a transplanted New Englander, George Herbert Walker Bush. By contrast, the one Senate pickup gave Kennedy a special sense of satisfaction. All during the run-up to the Cuban missile crisis, New York Republican senator Kenneth Keating had been warning of a Soviet missile buildup on the island; in ten speeches on the Senate floor, he urged the President to take action, and when the presence of the missiles was revealed, Keating's warnings were a source of embarrassment to the White House. So when New York City mayor Robert Wagner Jr. won the Democratic nomination to oppose Keating, the Kennedy campaign funneled cash, campaign aides, and personal campaigning by the President across New York. On Election Night, Wagner defeated Keating by a 700,000-vote margin.

(Wagner's victory had a decisive impact on New York City politics: when he resigned the mayoralty to take his Senate seat, Wagner was replaced by city council president Paul Screvane, who had enough support from the reform wing of the Democratic Party that he was able to defeat liberal Republican congressman John Lindsay a year later in a close race for mayor.)

Just after 11:00 p.m., Barry Goldwater called Kennedy to offer a gracious concession, and the two men agreed to meet at the White House in two weeks' time. When the call ended, Kennedy and a half dozen aides and friends spent a few quiet moments over a bottle of fifty-year-old brandy and H. Upmann cigars (some of the 1,200 cigars Kennedy had sent Pierre Salinger out to buy just before announcing an embargo in 1961).

"He never had a chance, did he?" LeMoyne Billings asked.

"No, not Barry, not this year," the President said. "But don't forget: this is a conservative country at heart. It took a Republican Party split in half to put Wilson in the White House; it took a Depression to get FDR in and keep us there. But what happens if there are race riots not in three or four cities but thirty or forty? What happens if there's another 'little war' like Korea where our boys are dying and no one really knows why? What happens if the economy stalls on our watch, which Heller thinks might happen if we can't get that damn tax cut passed." He shook his head. "Why can't these damn conservatives understand: a tax cut will give us so much growth, we'll actually have *more* revenue. It's so obvious.

"And what happens if somebody can make Barry's arguments without scaring the country half to death? You all saw Ronald Reagan's fund-raising pitch for Barry, didn't you? Pat Brown tells me there are a bunch of millionaires in California already talking about running him for governor. Pat's praying for his nomination, thinks he'd slaughter him, but I'm not so sure."

As a president focused, if not obsessed, with his place in history, there was another concern: one he'd raised with Arthur Schlesinger the week before the election.

"You're his historian, so you tell me," he'd said, sitting in his rocking chair in the Oval Office. "Second terms haven't exactly been raging successes, have they?"

"Lincoln and McKinley were shot . . ."

"I took care of that one in my *first* term," Kennedy said.

"Grant left in scandal," Schlesinger continued. "Wilson was paralyzed by a stroke, FDR lost his Congressional majority, Truman left with all-time low ratings, Ike had a stroke, Sputnik, and a recession. Of course, there *is* Teddy Roosevelt—he could have won another term if he hadn't said he wouldn't run; he spent the rest of his life trying to get back."

"Well," Kennedy said, "it's too late to demand a recount, and I doubt we can get the twenty-second Amendment repealed. Still, there are a couple of close relatives of mine who might have an interest in seeing that the Kennedy name does not become an epithet."

As he left the Kennedy compound for the short trip to the Hyannis National Guard Armory and his victory speech, he could be forgiven for a sense of satisfaction. He had survived an attempt on his life; he had won a victory big enough to justify an ambitious second term. Yes, there were minefields to navigate. He was going to have to face the question of race head-on without stirring more resentment in the middle class. That meant working for two things: the vote and jobs. Lyndon had been right: a white may not want to share a lunch counter or a pool with a Negro, but not letting someone vote because of skin color? He could win that fight, and once he did, as Johnson had put it, "Strom Thurmond will be kissing every black ass in South Carolina." And, yes, welfare drove taxpayers crazy, but getting people off the dole and into a job? Sure—as long as it's not *their* job.

And he'd have to steer a careful course abroad. There was a real chance to move away from the cold war, but not if the country thought he was letting its guard down. He'd have to find a way to untangle the mess in Vietnam—a mess in good part of his own creation—without setting off a new round of recriminations and fears that the dominoes were falling. It wouldn't be easy, he knew, but he was determined to avoid the wounds that had afflicted his predecessors in their second terms.

Had he thought more deeply into history, he might have remembered that some of the worst wounds inflicted on even the most gifted of leaders are *self*-inflicted.

CHAPTER FIVE

THE OTHER CAMPAIGN: RESOLVING THE VIETNAM DILEMMA

There was no blizzard this time to paralyze Washington on the eve of the inauguration, and predictions of a freezing cold January 20 proved happily off the mark. It was 38 degrees and the sky was all but cloudless when President Kennedy, clad in a formal morning coat and a top hat, walked down the Capitol's east front steps to take the oath of office. (The hats were a concession to politics: he rarely wore one, but the hatters' union vice president, Alex Rose, was the boss of New York's powerful Liberal Party.) He'd been up late the night before, at an inaugural gala that was already provoking controversy. Along with the more traditional performers—Louis Armstrong, Barbra Streisand, Perry Como—the Gala featured for the first time stars from rock and roll, the now decade-old dominant American music that still stirred fears among some of the old that it fed rebellion and licentiousness among the young.

The Beach Boys sang "Fun, Fun, Fun (in a Second Term with JFK)"; Roy Orbison sang "Oh, Pretty Woman"—introducing it by

saying, "This one's for you, Jackie!"—and the Supremes offered a
version of Mary Wells's hit "My Guy" with lyrics tailored for the
occasion:

> *Here's to JFK*
> *On Inauguration Day,*
> *He's our guy,*
> *Leader of the land,*
> *With our future in his hand,*
> *He's our guy.*
> *Three cheers from sea to shining sea*
> *For John Fitzgerald Kennedy,*
> *It's genuinely great*
> *That you're still the head of state,*
> *You're our guy.*

(The next day, *New York Times* columnist Arthur Krock decried
the "unappetizing spectacle of a celebration once steeped in tradition and grandeur sullied by an exercise in vulgarity. What next?
Shall we have a hip-shaking 'pop star' sing the National Anthem?")

"Four years ago," Kennedy said in his second inaugural, "I offered a series of challenges to the American people, and said, 'Let us
begin.' Today we can say to ourselves and to each other, 'We have
begun.' The horror of nuclear holocaust has receded; the prospects
for cooperation with our adversaries are brighter. Nuclear weapons
no longer threaten to poison our atmosphere. Here at home, our
economy has enriched not just the well-being of this generation but
the possibilities for the next.

"And yet, that very progress shines a harsh light on those left
behind: those who are denied the most basic of rights because of the
color of their skin, those—of every color—condemned to a life of

poverty generation unto generation. Even as we join others in an effort to combat the tyranny of poverty and hopelessness around the globe, we must face the hard fact that, in this wealthiest of all nations, poverty still tyrannizes millions of our own.

"I have spoken often of the need for a 'New Patriotism.' Nothing more demonstrates a genuine love of country than the desire to see its blessings reach every one of our citizens—and the willingness to invest 'our lives, our fortunes and our sacred honor' to make that hope real."

The inaugural parade had been designed to his specifications; it was much shorter than the first, and featured no military hardware. He noted with satisfaction the two Negroes marching with the Coast Guard Academy honor guard. Four years ago he had been startled by the all-white honor guard and told aide Dick Goodwin to follow up. Within a year the first black member of the academy had been admitted. After a long night of five inaugural balls, with Jackie's silver Givenchy gown the center of attention, he'd ended the evening at 2:00 a.m. as he had four years ago, dropping by the Georgetown home of columnist Joseph Alsop, the wellborn WASP who sat at the center of the capital's aristocracy. After a brief retreat upstairs for a private engagement, he lingered over champagne and terrapin soup. Alsop, however, had something else on the menu.

"You've been dithering for four years, Jack," Alsop said. (He was the only person, other than family members and the closest of friends, not to call him "Mr. President," and thought nothing of lecturing the Chief Executive as though he were a wayward student.) "I was in Vietnam two months ago, and I can tell you without an ounce of doubt that if we do not commit combat forces into Vietnam—at least two hundred thousand of them—it will be in Communist hands within a year, and every nation in the region will be in mortal peril."

"It's not that simple, Joe," Kennedy said, then held up his hand defensively. "But could I ask, as a matter of personal presidential privilege, that I might be spared such weighty matters of state at least until sunrise?"

It did not take that long—only until he was back in the limousine headed home to the White House—for him to reflect again on what the start of his second term would mean. For four years he had been feeling his way along a narrow path between a disastrous military folly 10,000 miles away and political disaster right here at home. For four years he had been telling friends and colleagues that he could not do what he wanted to do about Vietnam unless and until he was reelected.

Now, in winning that second term, he had found what just might be a path out of the Vietnam trap—a trap that had, in good measure, been of his own creation.

He had run for and won the presidency calling for a more offensive stance against America's Communist adversaries from Havana to Moscow: "They have taken the lead in space, they are building bigger bombs and missiles, they are fomenting insurgencies in Latin America, Africa, Asia."

As president, he had pressed the military for a more assertive strategy in Vietnam. If the Communists could infiltrate the South, he demanded, why couldn't anti-Communist forces infiltrate the North? If insurgency was the big threat to Saigon, why couldn't that threat be defeated with counterinsurgency? Kennedy had authorized $19 million for a 3,000-man special forces group to provide that capability. The "Green Berets," they were dubbed, and they held special appeal for John and Bobby Kennedy's faith in freelance, unbureaucratic, James Bond–like initiative.

In his inclination to take the offensive, Kennedy was reflecting a long-standing national consensus that the loss of any territory to a Communist insurgency was a threat to every other nation in the region. His top foreign policy and defense aides believed it. At the end of 1961, Rusk and McNamara captured that consensus perfectly when they concluded: "The fall of South Vietnam to communism would lead to the fairly rapid extension of Communist control, or complete accommodation to communism, in the rest of mainland Southeast Asia and in Indonesia. The strategic implications world-wide, particularly in the Orient, would be extremely dangerous."

The major journals of opinion believed it too. When Kennedy shunned military force in Laos in favor of a neutral government, *Time* called it "a cold war defeat" and warned that "if South Vietnam falls, the fall of all of Southeast Asia would only be a matter of time. If the U.S. is to save South Vietnam, it must be willing to get far more deeply involved—to the point of fighting if necessary." It was a consensus that was embraced, at least rhetorically, by Kennedy in his 1960 campaign.

There was, however, another side of John Kennedy, one that had long doubted the wisdom or the effect of combating an insurgent threat with a massive injection of combat troops. He and his family had visited the region in 1951, and he'd come away convinced it would be folly to "ally ourselves to the desperate efforts of a French regime to hang on to the remnants of empire." In 1956 he'd spoken on the Senate floor in favor of independence for Algeria, which at that time was fighting a bloody war against its French colonial rulers. (The speech drew scorn both from the Eisenhower administration and from voices in the Democratic foreign policy establishment, like former secretary of state Dean Acheson.) And a year later he'd argued that "the single most important test of American foreign policy today is how we meet the test of imperialism," and decried America's "failure to appreciate how the forces of nationalism are rewriting the geopolitical map of the world."

Yet, in a striking irony, Kennedy's very skepticism about the use of military force pulled him into an expanded U.S. role in South Vietnam. By the fall of 1961 he had refused to support the collapsing Bay of Pigs invasion with American forces; refused to follow the advice of Ike and the Joint Chiefs to send the U.S. military into Laos; suffered a psychological defeat at the hands of a bellicose Premier Khrushchev at the Vienna Summit; and stood by as the East Germans built a wall to trap their citizens in East Berlin. The politics of the moment demanded that he draw a line somewhere—and that "somewhere" was in South Vietnam, where he dispatched "advisors" to support the struggling army. By late 1963 there were 16,000 of them; more than 100 had been killed.

And it wasn't enough. The National Liberation Front—the "Viet Cong"—supported and supplied by the North, was striking with impunity across the South. American journalists, like the *New York Times*' David Halberstam and *Time* magazine's Charlie Mohr, were writing almost daily dispatches undercutting the optimistic assessments of American officials. (Kennedy had tried to talk *Times* publisher Arthur Sulzberger into pulling Halberstam out—which ensured that he would remain.) And more and more, the government of Ngo Dinh Diem, once celebrated as "the George Washington of Vietnam" by stalwart liberals like Hubert Humphrey and Supreme Court justice William O. Douglas, was losing the support of the people with his crackdowns on the Buddhist majority. Some of the monks were dramatizing their disaffection by setting themselves on fire; the images of their self-immolations filled the front pages and the evening newscasts. It had reached the breaking point just before Kennedy went to Dallas in November 1963. After a frac-

tious dispute among his advisors, Kennedy authorized a coup against
Diem and his brother Ngo Dinh Nhu; both men were quickly murdered, and Kennedy recorded a tape chastising himself for a hasty,
ill-informed decision. More than once, he found himself shaking his
head over a lost opportunity. One of the reasons for wanting Diem
and Nhu out was that they were reportedly looking to cut a deal
with Hanoi. When those rumors surfaced at a press conference,
Kennedy said acidly, "The day after it was suggested, we would have
some troops on the way home." *Maybe,* he'd thought more than
once, *we should have just left them to their own devices, let them cut
that deal, and leave.*

Indeed, that was part of the dilemma he faced. From the beginning, just about every member of his national security and defense
team had been telling him he needed to put American combat
troops—lots of them—into South Vietnam. But there were other
voices telling him the whole idea was crazy.

When he'd visited Charles de Gaulle on his way to Vienna in
1961, de Gaulle told him that putting troops in Vietnam would be
"a bottomless military and political quagmire."

George Ball, the number three man at State, had warned him
back then of the dangers of introducing even combat support
troops.

"Within five years," he said, "we'll have three hundred thousand men in the paddies and jungles and never find them again . . .
Vietnam is the worst possible terrain from a physical and political
point of view."

"George, I always thought you were one of the brightest guys
around here," Kennedy replied sharply. "But you're crazier than hell.
That just isn't going to happen."

John Kenneth Galbraith, from his perch as ambassador to India,
cautioned that it would be folly to "spend our billions in those dis-

tant jungles," and asked, almost heretically, "What is so important
about real estate in the space age?" He urged Kennedy to find a way
toward a neutral coalition government.

Senator Mike Mansfield, who had spent years in Southeast Asia
and who had been a friend and supporter of Diem, came to Palm
Beach to visit with the vacationing President after a tour of Vietnam;
he brought with him a warning that the United States could find itself drawn into "a truly massive commitment of American military . . . in short, going to war and the establishment of some form of
neo-colonialist role in South Vietnam." Kennedy was angry at Mansfield—"This isn't what my people are telling me," he countered—
but his anger stemmed from frustration. All through his first term,
he was balancing his impulse to find a way out of Vietnam with his
conviction that it would be politically fatal to do so.

Maybe that's why the President kept pushing back, sometimes
almost single-handedly refusing to put combat troops in Vietnam,
persistently pushing his advisors to consider the dangers of any involvement. As early as November of 1961, at a National Security
Council meeting, the President "questioned the wisdom of involvement in Vietnam . . . [H]e suggested he could make a strong case
against intervening in an area 10,000 miles away against 26,000
guerrillas with a native army of 200,000, where millions have been
spent for years with no success." And by the time he left for Texas
two years later, his administration announced that 1,000 U.S. forces
would be heading back home, and that most of the rest would likely
be home by the end of 1965. There was, however, nothing firm
about that date. "If things are going bad in Vietnam," he'd said,
"we'd look very foolish pulling those men out."

It was just part of the growing Vietnam mess that he left behind
as he headed for Texas on November 21, 1963, when he told Mike

Forrestal to organize a top-to-bottom review of "every option we've got, including how we get out of there."

When he returned from Dallas, that mess was waiting for him.

That decision to return 1,000 men from Vietnam was based on a premise that the effort was succeeding; that the South Vietnamese would have the capacity and the will to fight off the guerrillas and their North Vietnamese allies. But now, after the coup, there was a military regime in power that lacked even the diminishing support Diem Nhu had achieved. Moreover, his advisors were deeply divided: Defense Secretary McNamara—quite possibly with the quiet encouragement of the President—was pushing for the withdrawal timetable with the blunt assertion that "we need a way to get out of Vietnam, and this is a way of doing it." Mac Bundy, his national security advisor, and Maxwell Taylor, chairman of the Joint Chiefs of Staff, were saying that without a huge step-up in American involvement—including troops—South Vietnam's government would fall to the Communists.

So in early 1964 the President gathered his advisors once again and tried to make it clear what he wanted—and did *not* want—as he campaigned for a second term.

They gathered in the Laurel Lodge on a Saturday morning in mid-February, wearing sport jackets, corduroy slacks, sweater vests: the semiofficial uniforms of Powerful Men Summoned to Weekend Work. A midwinter snow blanketed Catoctin Mountain and covered the grounds of Camp David. Not a good day for the horseback riding that Jacqueline and the children enjoyed at the presidential retreat, but they had gone to Glen Ora, the Virginia horse farm the Kennedys had rented as a private family retreat. This weekend was strictly business—apart from a few breaks for the President to enjoy rest, recuperation, and recreation. Most of the faces were familiar— Rush, McNamara, Bundy, Taylor, Averell Harriman, Bobby, CIA chief McCone—but there were others in attendance whose presence came as an unwelcome surprise to some.

"What are you doing here?" Rusk snapped to a middle-aged man with a scholarly demeanor.

"He invited me," the man said, pointing to Michael Forrestal.

"And he invited him," President Kennedy said as he walked slowly into the room on crutches, "because I asked him to."

Paul Kattenburg was a forty-year-old State Department Foreign Service officer with a deep immersion in the history, culture, and politics of Vietnam. That was why he had chaired the Department's Vietnam Working Group—until he had made the mistake of speaking his mind. Back on August 31, 1963, he'd been invited to sit in on a National Security Council meeting, where he found himself appalled at what he was hearing.

"There was not a single person there who knew what he was talking about," he said to a colleague. "They didn't know Vietnam. They didn't know the past. The more this meeting went on, the more I sat there and thought, 'My God, we're walking into a major disaster.'"

Finally, unable to contain himself, Kattenburg blurted out that perhaps it was time to review the whole mission, that they might want to consider the possibility of an honorable withdrawal—in other words, that the emperor might not be fully clothed. For his pains, he was abruptly cut off by Rusk—and within a few weeks was removed as head of the Vietnam Working Group. When Forrestal mentioned this to the President, Kennedy said, "I'd like him at that review—and tell him to speak his mind. What the hell, they've broken it off with him already; what has he got to lose?

And make sure Mansfield and Galbraith are there. I've got to have other voices. If Tommy Thompson and Bobby hadn't been in those ExComm meetings during the missile crisis, I don't know if I'd have been able to stop the push for a strike."

The President said little during the first hour or so of discussion, which was as blunt and heated as Kennedy could have hoped for. From Rusk, Bundy, and Taylor came the case for a full military commitment. "We gave the signal for the coup; the new government cannot hold out indefinitely in the face of new Communist offensives; the fall of Saigon imperils Laos, Cambodia, Thailand, Indonesia; Chinese influence in the region will grow."

From Paul Kattenburg, freed from career constraints, came a different view: "I do not recognize the country you're talking about. Ho Chi Minh has been waging his fight for decades—and he may be the only Communist leader besides Fidel Castro who could win a free election. Our military says it would take a million men and five years to end the threat—and God knows how many bombs. And you know what would happen when those five years are up? They'd start all over again. And about China? The Vietnamese have hated China for a thousand years. They'd rather see the U.S. Chamber of Commerce in Saigon than a Chinese embassy."

Rusk shook his head.

"So you're saying what? That Ho Chi Minh is another 'agrarian reformer' like Mao and Fidel? That there won't be reeducation camps, drumhead executions, no police state?"

"No," Ken Galbraith interjected. "It'd be the kind of government we'd find intolerable. It might even be worse than what's there now. But it won't be East Germany; it won't be a Soviet satellite . . . more like Tito, I think; and the last time I looked, we were doing a lot of business with Yugoslavia."

"And what about our standing in the world?" Bundy asked.

"What does it say to our allies when a friendly government is faced with an external threat to its survival and we walk away?"

"From what they've told me," Kennedy said, "it looks very much like a civil war to them. But I take your point, Mac. It seems to me that the heart of the issue is that we need to find a way out without just 'walking away.' It's remarkable if you think about it: one of the reasons for getting rid of Diem and Nhu was that we'd heard that Nhu was talking to the North—complaining there were too many Americans. Why in hell didn't we take them up on that?

"But here's the point. I've said it to you, Mike." He nodded to Mansfield. "I've said it to Kenny O'Donnell. I've said it to Charlie Bartlett. We don't have a prayer of staying in Vietnam. Those people hate us. They are going to throw our asses out of there at almost any point. But I can't give up a piece of territory to the Communists and then get reelected. If I tried that, we'd have another McCarthy scare on our hands. But I *can* do it *after* I'm reelected, even if I become a very unpopular president. So," he said with a grin, "we better make damn sure I'm reelected. General, I'm obviously not including you in that mission," he said to Taylor.

"So what I'm talking about for the rest of the year," he said, "is a four-corners offense."

"I haven't the vaguest idea what you're talking about," Averell Harriman said.

"Apologies," Kennedy said. "In college basketball, you can take as long as you want to shoot a basket; no twenty-four-second rule like in the pros. So a team with the lead late in the game will just hold the ball—pass it from one corner to the other—to try to run out the clock. That's what I want in Vietnam: a 'four corners' offense. Let's bring those thousand men home, but as quietly and routinely as possible. No bands; no parades. No declarations of 'victory' or 'mission accomplished' bullshit."

He reached for a piece of paper.

"And I want the language of this action memorandum as non-committal as possible. No 'win the fight' . . . no 'commitment.' Nothing that looks like a pledge." He got up slowly, painfully, and reached for the crutches, and as the group filed out he motioned for Forrestal and Kattenburg to stay behind.

"Michael," Kennedy said, "you think there's room for one more body on the NSC staff?"

"It'll be tight, but if Paul's not too particular about office space . . ."

"You know where they're planning to put me?" Kattenburg said. "On the *Guyana* desk. A broom closet will be fine."

"You help me get out of this goddamn mess and you'll be in that corner office on the seventh floor at State," Kennedy said.

All through the 1964 campaign, the Kennedy administration and the Kennedy campaign (which was more or less the same thing) had one goal: keep Vietnam as far away from the spotlight as possible, offering no provocations to the enemy. For instance, when the CIA came to Kennedy with an "Operational Plan—34A" to step up covert actions against North Vietnam—naval sabotage operations, aerial reconnaissance, incursions across the 17th parallel—Kennedy said no. When he learned that South Vietnamese patrol boats had likely triggered reprisal hits in the Gulf of Tonkin, his suspicions grew that the CIA just might be encouraging such provocations on the sly. When a series of coups turned the Saigon government into a revolving door—Minh replaced by Khanh, who brought back Minh, who was dumped by Khanh, Thieu, and Ky—Washington issued bland pronouncements of tepid support for South Vietnam's independence.

He shaped his campaign rhetoric toward another goal: a cautious, politically sensitive attempt to nudge public opinion away from a cold war frame.

In the spring, he'd called in Ted Sorensen and Arthur Schlesinger and asked the historian about Franklin Roosevelt and the 1940 campaign—when a president looking to help Great Britain stave off a Nazi conquest was running in a deeply isolationist country.

"It was a terrible challenge," Schlesinger told them. "It took all of his skills to frame an argument for helping Britain that the country would accept, like 'lending a garden hose to your neighbor if his house was on fire.' And there were times when he just flat-out dissembled—as when he said 'Our boys will not be sent to fight any foreign wars' when he knew damn well that sooner or later they would be. But, Mr. President, your job will be just as hard. For one thing, everyone—you included—has spent twenty years telling us that if one nation falls, the whole world collapses. And how many times in these last three and a half years have you talked about how 'not one inch of free territory has fallen to the Communists on Kennedy's watch'? And then there are all those speeches from the *last* campaign . . ."

"Well," Kennedy said, "it's not as though I can go on television and talk about what happened to the Russians in Finland, Britain in the Boer War, France in Indochina—no one will know what the hell I'm talking about. And if I say: 'Sorry, America, I'd like to save Vietnam from a Communist takeover, but they don't want to save themselves, and we can't do it without killing thousands of our men and God knows how many of theirs—so we're throwing in the towel.' Reelected? Hell, I'd be impeached."

So Kennedy and Sorensen took a more elliptical track, using in his stump speech the same formulation he'd used late in 1961 in Seattle, and in other venues, warning:

"We must face problems which do not lend themselves to easy or quick or permanent solutions. And we must face the fact that the United States is neither omnipotent nor omniscient—that we are only 6 percent of the world's population; that we cannot impose our will upon the other 94 percent of mankind; that we cannot right every wrong or reverse each adversity—and that therefore there cannot be an American solution to every problem."

There was another, less traditional approach that Kennedy took to bending public opinion on matters of war and peace, one that yielded an unexpected, powerful benefit. He was intrigued by the success of *Seven Days in May*, a novel about an attempted military coup against a peace-minded president, and encouraged Hollywood to turn it into a movie; he even scheduled travels to Hyannis Port on weekends when director John Frankenheimer needed to film in and around the White House. Before that film was released in the summer, another politically charged movie debuted: *Dr. Strangelove or: How I Learned to Stop Worrying and Love the Bomb*, Stanley Kubrick's black comedy about a rogue Air Force general who launches a nuclear attack on the Soviet Union. Did Kennedy know the details of the movie when he arranged for a White House screening of the movie? Did he know that one of the characters, Buck Turgidson (played by George C. Scott), a red-faced, cigar-chomping general with a Let's-get-it-over-with approach to nuclear war, bore an uncanny resemblance to a real-life red-faced, cigar-chomping high-ranking general with a Let's-get-it-over-with approach to nuclear war? What became very clear—and very public—was that during the final scene, as a "doomsday device" destroys the world with an endless explosion of hydrogen bombs, Bobby Kennedy was heard to crack: "This public service announcement was brought to you by General Curtis LeMay."

When the *Washington Star*'s Mary McGrory wrote of the screening, and of Bobby's remark, LeMay resigned his post as Air Force chief of staff with a stinging attack on the "ill-conceived, weak-kneed policies of a president whose incompetence poses a threat to our national security." Within a month, LeMay had signed on as national security advisor to Barry Goldwater's presidential campaign. That caused real concern in the Kennedy campaign—an Air Force chief of staff could lend credibility to Goldwater's claims of weakness and unpreparedness—until LeMay began speaking to the public, happy to use the bully pulpit to ease the public's fears about the atomic age.

"We seem to have a phobia about nuclear weapons," he said in answer to a question from Jack Nelson of the *Atlanta Constitution.* "I think there are many times when it would be most efficient to use nuclear weapons. However, public opinion in this country and throughout the world just throws up its hands in horror when you mention nuclear weapons because of a lot of propaganda that's been fed to them." A few moments later he was waxing nostalgic about a time when the United States had a monopoly on atomic weapons:

"That was the era when we might have destroyed Russia completely and not even skinned our elbows doing it," he said, all but echoing the line from *Dr. Strangelove* when General Turgidson says of World War III, "I'm not sayin' we wouldn't get our hair mussed . . ." (For the rest of the campaign, General LeMay's remarks were confined to four Deep South states and small towns in rural Wyoming, Idaho, and Montana.)

Watching the evening news, Kennedy called in Pierre Salinger and said, "I want you to send a box of our best Havanas to LeMay, and sign it, 'With deep appreciation for all you are doing for the cause of peace.'" It was an accurate if puckish notion. The more important point, though, was that LeMay's comments were a more pungent version of arguments that Goldwater himself had made when he argued that nukes were "just another weapon," suggesting, for example, that foliage protecting Viet Cong guerrillas could be cleared away with the use of such devices. In a populace where the distinction between a twenty-megaton H-bomb and a nuclear-tipped artillery shell was not always clear—and that still remembered a close brush with all-out nuclear war—loose nukes talk sent a chill through millions. In that sense, Barry Goldwater became one of John Kennedy's best arguments for a new approach to the cold war that would strengthen the case against combat in Vietnam.

He had another ally as well, one even less likely. Ever since the Moscow summit, where grain sales and trade agreements had put more bread, meat, and consumer goods in Russian stores and sent Khrushchev's popularity rising, he and Kennedy had formed something of a backdoor mutual assistance society. The Soviet leader's promise/threat that "we will bury you" had been replaced by more talk about "peaceful coexistence" (or, as he put it to a highly discomfited Averell Harriman once, "Just because two men want to fuck the same girl, it doesn't mean they have to kill each other. She can pick whoever brings the most flowers, or has the biggest . . . ").

For his part, Kennedy reworked Woodrow Wilson's famous phrase and challenged Khrushchev to join him "in making the world safe for diversity. Mr. Chairman, we will neither fear nor threaten any nation that freely chooses your path; you should neither fear nor threaten any nation that freely chooses liberty."

The more important dialogue took place far from the public spotlight, and once again the Kennedys reached out to their long-time back-channel conduit, Colonel Georgi Bolshakov. Back in 1962, when the fragile coalition in Laos threatened to explode into full-scale warfare, Kennedy received from Bolshakov assurances from Khrushchev that Moscow would not support any "large-scale actions" by the Communist Pathet Lao in the region. Now Kennedy sent Bobby to meet with Bolshakov while the attorney general was attending an international law conference in New Delhi.

Bobby had always spoken in unusually candid terms with the Russian, and did so again in an "unofficial" meeting at the Swedish embassy.

"The President is going to withdraw from South Vietnam," Bobby said, "but he will do it slowly, more slowly than your government might like. In fact, it would be helpful to him if the Chairman would attack the President for supporting the Saigon government. But the Chairman must know that the more the insurgency attacks U.S. positions in South Vietnam, the harder it will be for us to leave. And the more we can talk about a neutral coalition government that will set the stage for reunification, the better."

"Surely you cannot be under any illusions about what the outcome of that unification will be," Bolshakov said.

"My brother has his faults, but laboring under illusions is not one of them," said Bobby.

Ten days later, word came to the Kennedys from Bolshakov: *The National Liberation Front makes its own decisions. The People's Republic of Vietnam is a sovereign nation. But the Chairman wishes you to know that he intends nothing that would lessen the possibility for a peaceful unification of Vietnam . . . and, based on the conversations in New Delhi, can provide the same assurances as he did to resolve the situation in Laos.*

Left uncommunicated were the words Khrushchev had spoken to a skeptical Presidium:

"If the Americans put their armies into Vietnam, it will take a decade for them to realize their folly. Before they follow the French out, before Ho Chi Minh enters Saigon, millions may die. If Kennedy can save face with a coalition, Vietnam will fall like a ripe fruit into Ho's hands in, what, three years, five years? And we save billions in the arms we would be sending."

"You place a lot of trust in Mr. Kennedy," Leonid Brezhnev said.

"Trust? Only that I trust him to want to avoid catastrophe."

The historian in President Kennedy no doubt appreciated the irony that two of his most important assets in his approach to Vietnam were the man running against him for president and the ruler of his country's longtime adversary. There was one more potential ally, equally unlikely—one whose support would come with a heavy price tag. And even as he asked Evelyn Lincoln to place the phone call, he was hoping that the price would be worth paying.

There was no more powerful member of the United States Senate than Richard Brevard Russell Jr. of Georgia. He'd mastered its arcane rules and procedures almost thirty years earlier, as a newly elected thirty-five-year-old senator. Now, thirty years later, he was the courtly, unfailingly polite chief strategist and tactician of the coalition of Southern Democrats and Republicans that had effectively ruled the Senate since the days of FDR. For Russell, two issues dominated his concern:

First, the protection of "the Southern way of life," which meant resisting any efforts by the federal government to stop racial segregation and outright racial subjugation, which ranged from intimidating prospective voters to lynchings. Unlike Southern colleagues like Mississippi's Bilbo and South Carolina's "Cotton Ed" Smith,

Russell never resorted to outright race baiting, never uttered the word "nigger" on the Senate floor, always spoke in terms of high-minded constitutional principles. (Rarely did he let his true feelings emerge, as when he told the Senate: "Any white man who wants to take the position that he is no better than a Negro is entitled to his opinion of himself. I do not think much of him, but he can think it.")

Second, the worldwide struggle between the United States and the Soviet Union, which required a never-ending commitment to massive defense spending—a commitment he protected as chair of the Senate Armed Services Committee. He'd been one of only nine-teen senators to vote against the Limited Nuclear Test Ban Treaty, warning his colleagues that the Soviets were not to be trusted, that they would use the treaty to strengthen their nuclear arsenal, and that the treaty was a step on the road to some form of world government.

There was, however, one other dimension to Richard Russell: he was uncommonly clear-eyed about strategy and tactics, whether on the Senate floor or in the international arena. He demonstrated that in the opening moments of the call, when the President asked him to share his thoughts about Vietnam.

"Well, frankly, Mr. President," Russell said, "it's the damn worst mess that I ever saw, and I don't like to brag and I never have been right many times in my life, but I knew that we were going to get into this sort of mess when we went in there. And I don't see how we're ever going to get out of it without fighting a major war with the Chinese and all of them down there in those rice paddies and jungles. I just don't see it. I just don't know what to do."

"How important do you think Vietnam is to us?" Kennedy asked.

"It isn't important a damn," Russell said. "It's a hell of a situa-

tion. It is a mess, and it's going to get worse, and I don't know how
or what to do. If it came down to an option of just sending the
Americans in there to do the fighting—which will, of course, even-
tually end in a ground war and a conventional war with China—or
just pulling out, I'd get out. But then, I don't know. There is un-
doubtedly some middle ground somewhere."

"And how do we do that without . . . You know, Rusk and
Bundy keep telling me it would be a devastating humiliation, shake
the confidence of our allies . . ."

"Well," Russell said, "I'd get the same crowd that got rid of old
Diem to get rid of these people that are in power now—get some
fellow in there that said, 'We wish to hell you Americans would get
out.' That would give us a good excuse for getting out. But then, I
can just see the Russians going to town about the weak Americans,
threatening us . . ."

"I think I can give you some assurances on that, Dick. Khrushchev fears what *we* might do a lot more than I fear what he might
do. There's a weapon we could deploy that must be giving him the
night sweats every time he thinks about it."

"You have a weapon I haven't been told about?" Russell asked
sharply.

"No," the President said. "I mean we can simply spend them
into bankruptcy . . . as long as your committee gives us the go-
ahead."

"You'll never get a fight from me on that score," Russell chuckled.

"I thought not," Kennedy said. "But, Dick, if I'm determined to
find a way out—and I am—you know how important it will be to
have you with me. I know the Republicans will be all over me, but
I can't afford to have Dodd and Scoop Jackson and Carl Vinson
talking about 'retreat, defeat, surrender, national dishonor . . .'"

"From what I can see," Russell said, "getting in there would be like Korea only on a much bigger scale, with a terrain that's just right for a guerrilla army. Hell, the French lost two hundred fifty thousand men and spent a couple billion of their money and two billion of ours down in there. Just got the hell whipped out of them. And you know, Mr. President"—here Russell paused for a moment—"as I see it, it's *never* a good idea for a large outside force to try to move in and tell another people how to live their lives."

And John Kennedy understood clearly the price he would have to pay if he wanted Dick Russell to help him out of Vietnam.

He made the case to Sorensen on a flight back from a campaign swing through Ohio.

"If I go all in on civil rights, I'll almost surely lose anyway—and I'll have Russell on my ass every time we pull another five hundred men out of Vietnam."

"And if we turn and run on civil rights, what do we say to those Negroes who risked their lives to sit in at Woolworth's and ride those buses?" Sorensen asked.

"You really think I'll lose a lot of Negro votes to Barry Goldwater? But, Ted, you tell me what's worse for that young Negro sitting at an Alabama lunch counter: not being able to order a hamburger and a Coke, or getting his ass shot off in a jungle ten thousand miles away? There'll be time once he gets the vote to change those stupid laws. But right now there's a different fight I have to win."

"And if you win it," Sorensen said, "not one of those Negroes—not one of our liberal friends—is going to know what they were saved from."

"Like I've said before, Ted, life is unfair. Although not entirely, and not always," he added, ringing for a steward to bring him a bowl of chowder and a beer.

"You know," Kennedy said, "anyone who calls the presidency the toughest job in the world has never flown on Air Force One."

It was past 3:00 a.m. when Kennedy reached the White House at the end of his long inauguration day and night. He'd made it to his second term with more than half of the 16,000 "advisors" home from South Vietnam, with 12,000 more due home by the end of 1965. Averell Harriman was in Geneva, working with his Soviet counterparts on a possible treaty to limit strategic arms, while highly private, highly informal negotiations were going on with the State Department's Roger Hilsman and *his* Soviet counterparts over the shape of a neutral coalition government in Saigon—with representatives from Hanoi and Saigon. *Maybe something will come of them, maybe not,* he thought. *But it buys us time.*

More significant, in his new foreign policy and defense team, he finally had a group in place that would be allies rather than adversaries. Dean Rusk was gone at State, replaced by Robert McNamara—who, Kennedy had come to realize, was a world-class courtier, determined to support with absolute certainty whatever the President favored. *If Lyndon were in charge, Mac would be telling him we had to go to war.* George Ball, who had warned Kennedy early on of the danger of Vietnam escalation, was installed as McNamara's deputy.

At Defense, Kennedy had made his most controversial of moves, installing his brother Bobby, who had lobbied hard for a role on the domestic side.

"I can't do it, Bobby," the President said. "If we're serious about these negotiations, if there's any opening to China, I need someone at Defense who has the absolute confidence of the President, so there's no room for end runs or passive insubordination. And that's you."

It was a contentious confirmation fight: the *New York Times* editorially chastised the President for "once again appointing his brother to a job for which he has no qualifications. On-the-job training may have worked at the Justice Department, but is nothing short of dangerous at Defense." Several Southern senators sarcastically "endorsed" the nomination. (North Carolina's Sam Ervin said, "If Bobby Kennedy can annoy and harass the Russians as much as he did the American South, victory in the Cold War is assured.")

If all went well, Vietnam would be in Kennedy's rearview mirror by year's end. And then? There were no guarantees. If Ho Chi Minh's more militant colleagues grew impatient—if the South Vietnamese government collapsed and the red flag were raised over Saigon—Kennedy would take a political hit. ("I'm likely to become a very, very unpopular president," he'd said to O'Donnell.) Some of his critics were not waiting for that outcome.

"Each American fighting man, each advisor, that returns from Vietnam is a symbol of presidential failure," *Time* magazine wrote. "Among seasoned geopolitical observers, there is a growing fear that the United States will be paying the costs of Kennedy's fecklessness for years, even decades to come."

Nor was there any guarantee that the cost would be worth it. He had fences to mend with a disappointed civil rights community; he had to do something about the poverty that afflicted tens of millions beyond a few nice words in a speech.

As he slipped into bed, Kennedy thought of one of his favorite stories about risk, a story told by the Irish writer Frank O'Connor that Kennedy himself related:

"As a boy, he and his friends would make their way across the countryside, and when they came to an orchard wall that seemed too high and too doubtful to try and too difficult to permit their voyage to continue, they took off their hats and tossed them over the wall—and then they had no choice but to follow them."

He had thrown his cap over the wall. There would be no war in Vietnam.

CHAPTER SIX

A DIFFERENT COUNTRY—
BUT HOW DIFFERENT?

It was March 8, 1965, and the President of the United States was in a lousy mood.

Some of it could be chalked up to the weather. It was a gray, drizzly day, and the evening promised to be no better . . . which meant that the Potomac cruise on the *Honey Fitz* with a few close friends would be a chill, gloomy affair, even if the weather didn't turn foul enough to call the whole thing off.

Some of it was a matter of health and well-being. The ills that had plagued him all his life were back with a vengeance; when he wasn't in pain, he was still weakened by the afflictions of his body. Even worse, his wife and his brother had effectively walled him off from Dr. Max Jacobson, whose injections had been a source of instant energy. As for well-being, for more than a year and a half, since the death of his infant son Patrick and the shooting at Dallas, he'd completely curbed the impulses of a lifetime . . . well, *almost* totally . . . but he could sense those impulses returning. He'd once told Harold Macmillan that three days without a woman left him with headaches. *By now I should be suffering from terminal migraines,* he thought. And that brought him thoughts of Mary Meyer . . .

She had not been a casual, quick romp, nor even a long-term lover. She was that, but she was also a friend, an intimate of the family—along with her sister, Toni Bradlee, and Toni's husband, Ben, Mary was a frequent guest at White House dinners, cruises on the *Honey Fitz* down the Potomac, weekends at the Cape. She was that rare woman Kennedy could find intellectual as well as sexual pleasure with . . . one of the few women whose company he sought back in the fall of '63, after the death of Patrick. And then, last year, she'd been murdered during a walk along the canal towpath in Georgetown, most likely by a would-be robber or rapist. Her brother-in-law Ben had mentioned something about a diary, but as with all such matters, Kennedy trusted his friends to keep his secrets. Still, he missed her greatly.

More than personal discontent, President Kennedy's foul mood was the product of a painful political dilemma. There was in John Kennedy's makeup an acute sense of timing: he would temporize, delay, avoid making a decision unless he absolutely had to. And then he would act. He pushed back against the urgings of his advisors to strike the missiles in Cuba, even held back when a U-2 was shot down, waiting until Khrushchev found the running room to end the standoff. He'd split the difference in South Vietnam, telling his military, *Okay, there'll be support troops and we'll see if they're willing to help themselves, but we are* not *putting combat troops in there; it's a recipe for disaster.* And now the Americans were on their way out.

He had brought that same innate sense of caution to the civil rights issue. He'd readily bought support among powerful Southern congressmen for his economic program by appointing racist judges to the federal bench. He'd repeatedly delayed the executive order he'd promised to sign that would "end discrimination with a stroke of the pen." Then, in June of 1963, after the Birmingham cops had turned police dogs and fire hoses on demonstrators, his sense of timing had told him to go on national television and proclaim civil rights "primarily a moral question," then ask the question of white America in a way no president had ever done: "Who among us would willingly trade places with a Negro?"

Now, in March of 1965, he had decided it was once again time to act.

But he was damned if he could figure out *how*.

Just a day earlier, on Sunday, March 7, a crowd of peaceful marchers on their way from Selma to Montgomery, Alabama, to demand the right to vote were set upon by club-wielding cops on the Edmund Pettus Bridge. Television beamed the images—bloodied heads, clouds of tear gas, black marchers beaten by white police and state troopers—into millions of American homes. The calls on the White House for action were loud and tinged with more than a touch of disappointment. When the Civil Rights Act died in the Congress in 1964, a suspicion rippled through the liberal community that Kennedy might actually be relieved to be rid of so divisive an issue in the midst of his reelection fight. One of his few black advisors, Louis Martin had once said to him, "You care more about Germany than Alabama," and that sentiment was echoed by other disappointed liberals.

Walter Lippmann, the dean of Washington columnists, wrote with unusual acidity: "Mr. Kennedy once spoke—inaccurately, to put it mildly—of a 'missile gap' between the United States and the Soviet Union. Now he faces a real gap between the reach of his proclaimed intentions and the timidity with which he has sought to bring life to those intentions. It is nothing less than a 'credibility gap,' and one he must close if his second term is to be anything close to a success."

It was a stern judgment, but one that Kennedy could not dismiss. Losing the fight to desegregate coffee shops and hotels had been a blow, but if it had been the price for Senator Russell's silent assent on his stealth Vietnam plan, it had been a price worth paying. *This* fight, however, was about the right to vote: the issue Kennedy himself had argued was the key to racial progress. Besides, there were new voices out there that made the nonviolent civil disobedience of Martin Luther King seem the mildest of provocations. There was Stokely Carmichael, who talked of vindicating civil rights "by any means necessary" and who had engineered a significant change in the name of the organization he led: the Student *Nonviolent* Coordinating Committee had become the Student *National* Coordinating Committee. There was Carmichael's SNCC colleague James Foreman, who had said publicly, "If we can't sit at the table, let's knock the fucking legs off." There was Malcolm X, the onetime Black Muslim spokesman, who had talked of "white devils." (True, he had disavowed his more incendiary anti-white rhetoric before he was murdered, but those earlier, harsher sentiments were resonating across black America.)

So, yes, he *had* to get a voting rights bill through the Congress, but the 1964 election had left it a Congress where, despite the big Democratic majorities, that conservative coalition of Republicans and Southern Democrats still held the whip hand, tying his own team in knots.

There *had* to be some answer.

And there was . . . even if it did come in the form of a telephone call from the unlikeliest imaginable source.

———

"How are you, Lyndon? Or should I say, 'Mr. President.'"

"Doing the Lord's work down here," the president of Southwest Texas State Teachers College said. "We've got plans for eighteen buildings now, aiming for close to sixteen thousand students, and I'm squeezing some of my oil friends to join me in doing serious penance for their evil ways with some serious donations. In a year or two I'm gonna have a few thousand young coloreds and Mexicans here who wouldn't have dreamed they'd ever set foot on a college campus except as maids and porters. I've got to tell you, Jack—Mr. President—I've never been happier."

When Lyndon Johnson resigned the vice presidency in early 1964 and retreated to Texas, the investigations into his finances ended. Most of those who knew Johnson, and who knew his primal fear of humiliation, assumed he would end his days in seclusion and that his end might come swiftly. It was a shock to almost everyone when he stepped into the presidency of his old alma mater and turned his ferocious energy into a massive fund-raising and expansion program.

"Give me five years," Johnson said to a skeptical board of trustees, "and we'll be the envy of the Longhorns."

"I never thought of you as the college president type," Kennedy said to Johnson.

"Well," Johnson said, "I looked at what happened over in England when that cabinet man—Profumo?—had to quit because he'd been caught in that sex scandal. Brought down poor Macmillan. You know what he's been doing? Cleaning toilets for a charity. Not exactly my style, but there's other good work to be done and it's better than eating and drinking and smoking myself to death."

"Admirable," said the President, who had paid very close attention to the Profumo affair. "And I'm glad to talk with you. But I gather you have something specific on your mind."

"I do," Johnson said. "I've been thinking about the fix you're in on civil rights, with Selma and all . . . You know, two years ago I tried to explain to Sorensen about the timing . . . but that's water over the dam. But you have just *got* to get that vote through the Congress this spring, or those bulls over there are going to be treating you like a cut dog. And I know you don't need my advice"— *Never did ask for it,* he thought briefly—"but since you don't really have a way around the Russells and the Byrds"—*as I would have*— "you've *got* to get your Republicans up there on board with you . . ."

"Yes, we're thinking that perhaps I should call a joint session of Congress and give a speech—"

"You'll pardon me, Mr. President, but I'd recommend against it. I'm not sure the ones you need will listen to you. You're a Massachusetts liberal and they're not gonna give your words all that much weight"—*I could have talked to them as a Southerner*—"and the Congress was never really your home." *It was mine.* "But there is one weapon that might do the trick."

"Which is . . . ?"

"Shame."

"You need to explain that," Kennedy said.

So Lyndon Johnson did.

They gathered in the shadow of the Lincoln Memorial, where 200,000 had marched for "jobs and freedom" nineteen months before. The crowd was smaller this time, no more than 50,000, but it had a unique characteristic: almost all were dressed in the uniforms they had worn as members of the U.S. armed forces. They were middle-aged veterans of World War II, when troops were segregated by race; they were younger men (and a few women) from Korea, when official segregation ended but de facto discrimination was the reality. A few, some in wheelchairs, wore the olive drab garb— wool garrison cap, wool trousers, wool shirt, and wool four-button tunic—from their World War I days.

Overhead, a series of overflights by reconditioned Bell P-39 Airacobras and Republic P-47 Thunderbolts brought cheers from the crowd, which recognized the planes of the 332nd Fighter Group—the Tuskegee Airmen, the first black military airmen in the U.S. military. The planes had been lent to the ex-Airmen by a special directive from Secretary of Defense Robert Kennedy.

On the stage just below the statue of Lincoln were people un- known to most Americans but celebrated among blacks as iconic figures.

There was First Lieutenant Vernon Baker, who had taken out a German machine-gun nest in Viareggio, Italy, in the Second World War, and who would have won the Congressional Medal of Honor had he been white. There were men from the Montford Point Ma- rines, who had endured brutal hardships in a segregated facility at Camp Lejeune, North Carolina. There was Lieutenant Colonel Harriet West Waddy, who had become one of the highest-ranking black officers in the Women's Army Corps and had made radio broadcasts urging Negro women to join the ranks. Behind the stage stretched a red, white, and blue banner reading: VETS FOR THE VOTE.

They listened to stories from men who had come home from combat with scars on their flesh and shrapnel in their bodies, and who had been met with contempt, economic reprisal, and violence when they tried to vote. They heard music carefully selected to strike patriotic chords, like Woody Guthrie's "This Land Is Your

Land," sung by Odetta and Harry Belafonte. When the speeches
and the singing were done, a balding, portly middle-aged Negro
stepped to the microphones.

"Good day," he began. "My name is Carl Rowan, deputy assistant secretary of state. Twenty years ago, I was one of the first Negroes to serve as a commissioned officer in the United States
Navy . . . at a time when racial segregation was the official policy of
the United States government. I joined, as so many of us did, because I believed that the land of the free and the home of the brave
was free enough to speak openly about its wrongs, and brave enough
to right those wrongs. So now let us walk down Constitution Avenue and ask the men in the halls of Congress to redeem the promise
of that Constitution."

Down the avenue they marched, singing "America the Beautiful" and "My Country, 'Tis of Thee." (A few struck up the racier
versions of "Mademoiselle from Armentières" and "Colonel Bogey
March," before the parade marshals reminded them of the cameras
and microphones.) At the Capitol, the marchers dispersed into the
Senate Office Buildings to lobby the senators from their home
states. For all but the die-hard segregationists, the visit of men and
women dressed in the uniforms of the military was a photo opportunity not to be missed, especially when the visitors were accompanied by wire-service photographers.

The reaction was precisely what Lyndon Johnson had
counted on.

"You take your housewife in Milwaukee, your steelworker in
Pittsburgh," he'd said to Kennedy. "Maybe they don't want the coloreds in their neighborhoods, in their daughter's school. But you
show them a man with the scars of battle on his body who wants to
vote, that's not a threat to them, not a threat to their kids . . . There's
no backlash about standing next to a colored man in a voting booth,

except in the states you couldn't have won with Jesus doing your advance. And for the Republicans? You put those men in uniform and it's not a 'demonstration'—it's Flag Day."

It was that stroke—making black veterans the symbol of the issue—that gave President Kennedy the strategic high ground. As the Senate debated whether to end debate, he remained offstage as much as possible. When aide Richard Goodwin drafted a speech that adopted familiar words from a civil rights anthem, Kennedy shook his head.

"Give that speech to one of our Southern friends in the Senate: it will have a lot more clout coming from one of them."

So it was Tennessee's Al Gore, freshly reelected, who stood on the Senate floor, with dozens of uniformed Negro veterans in the gallery, and proclaimed, "It isn't just the Negro but all of us who must overcome the crippling legacy of bigotry and injustice. And we shall overcome." (From Tennessee and other Southern states came letters, phone calls, and telegrams denouncing him as a traitor. From newspapers across the country came editorials suggesting that a serious Southern contender for the 1968 presidency may have emerged.) And when Republican Senate leader Ev Dirksen rounded up twenty-three votes—standing on the Senate floor, urging his Republican colleagues to "stand with the men who stood watch on lonely nights, shivered in the cold, sweltered in the heat, heard the thunder of guns, saw the lightning of the bombs, and now ask for no special privilege but for the sacred right for which they risked their lives"— the debate ended. On August 6, Kennedy signed the Voting Rights Act into law at the foot of the Lincoln Memorial.

"Two years ago," Kennedy said, "Martin Luther King Jr. stood before two hundred thousand Americans of all races and creeds, and said: 'We refuse to believe that the bank of justice is bankrupt. We refuse to believe that there are insufficient funds in the great vaults of opportunity of this nation.' Today, that faith in our nation and its people has been redeemed."

There was in that statement an implicit optimism about the way America worked. It was an unsurprising sentiment: America's national leaders are *supposed* to be upbeat about the country they lead. What was notable is that the same sense of optimism infused much of the political engagement of the early 1960s, including the emergence of the "protest" movement: sit-ins to protest segregated lunch counters in the South; Freedom Rides to protest "white and colored" seating on bus lines; pickets outside the White House to protest nuclear testing. "Protests" they may have been, but they were, with few exceptions, devoid of anything that could remotely be called "radical" in philosophy or tactics. The students at the sit-ins wore coats and ties and studied their textbooks while white thugs threw ketchup and mustard at them. During the anti–nuclear testing demonstration in 1961, the White House invited some of the protesters in to talk to administration officials; during the 1962 demonstration, as a snowstorm fell on Washington, the White House sent out coffee. A folk singer like Phil Ochs could write protest songs about racial injustice and war ("I Ain't Marching Any More"), but he could also write a song that called America "a land full of power and glory, beauty that words cannot recall."

When a new organization called Students for a Democratic Society issued its manifesto in 1962, there were no "demands," nonnegotiable or otherwise. As cofounder Tom Hayden later said, "The model was peaceful transition, reformism; there was no thought of violence as a tactic." During the 1964 campaign, SDS endorsed the President with the slogan "Part of the way with JFK" while chiding him for temporizing on civil rights and economic justice. Unlike their counterparts in other nations, where flags were burned and stones were thrown, these participants formed the core of what *Washington Star* reporter Mary McGrory called "a kinder, gentler dissent . . . the sit-ins, the Freedom Rides, the picketing, the rallies—reflect discontent, but do *not* reflect disillusion. Far from being 'anti-American,' they embrace the same faith that led Martin Luther King Jr. to begin his already classic March on Washington speech with a lengthy quotation from the Declaration of Independence."

What was emerging in the early years of the 1960s, then, was a movement rooted in an optimism that seemed justified by the recent past. In less than thirty years, the rights of labor had been written into federal law; Social Security had brought older Americans a sense of security; public power had brought electricity into millions of homes; the depredations of Wall Street predators had been brought under a measure of control; racial segregation in schools had been struck down; and it was only a matter of time before the next steps in the progressive agenda were reached: health care for the old, federal aid to education, Negro emancipation. While there was a growing sense of *cultural* disaffection among a segment of the young, its targets were the corporate mentality of men in gray flannel suits, the stifling conformism of the suburbs, the mendacity of TV commercials and crooked quiz shows—not the root premises of the American system. In that optimism, the politically engaged progressives were reflecting something of a national consensus: three-fourths of Americans, Gallup was reporting in 1964, trusted the government to do what was right all or most of the time.

The real, wholesale distrust of government was found predominantly on the fringes of the political right, where voices from Father Coughlin to Joe McCarthy to John Birch Society founder Robert Welch taught that Jews held the levers of power; or that FDR had caused Pearl Harbor and sold out the cause of freedom to Stalin at

Yalta; or that the government was infested with traitors, and that
President Eisenhower himself was a "dedicated, conscious agent of
the Communist conspiracy"; or that unseen forces were intent on
putting fluoride into our drinking water to weaken our resistance to
a Communist takeover. One distinguished historian, Richard Hof-
stadter, had a phrase for it: "the paranoid style in American politics." (That kind of irrationality was what Kennedy had gone to
Dallas to talk about at the Trade Mart on November 22, 1963.)

The question for the rest of the 1960s, then, was as simple as it
was crucial: How much of that optimism, how much of that implicit respect for boundaries, would hold? What few grasped at the
time was how much the answer to that question rested on the fact
that John Kennedy did not die on the streets of Dallas . . . and on
the decisions he made once he returned to the White House.

When John Kennedy's first term began, at the start of the decade,
America was perched on a cusp. By mid-decade, a different culture
had emerged, one that divided the country in a way it never had
been before.

And John Kennedy straddled that divide.

You could see that divide in the country's popular entertainment,
where unsettling voices, sounds, and images had emerged in that
grossly misnamed "silent decade" of the 1950s: James Dean's time
bomb of sullen alienation; Marlon Brando's leather-jacketed motor-
cycle rider who, when asked: "What are you rebelling against?" answered: "Whadda you got?" On the radio, the soothing melodies of
Patti Page, the Four Lads, the Four Aces, Vic Damon, and company
had given way by the mid-1950s to rock and roll, to Little Richard,
Fats Domino, Elvis, Chuck Berry, music that was a pulsating, visceral incubator of teenage lust that dozens of communities had tried

to ban, much as King Canute had sought to order back the tides. On bookshelves, after the courts effectively neutered censorship laws, grown-ups could buy *Lady Chatterley's Lover* while their kids could pick up *MAD* magazine, which mercilessly mocked conventional pieties, on the candy store racks (Riverdale High School's beloved Archie as a drug dealer?). Comedy had a new bite for adults as well, from Stan Freberg's send-ups to Mort Sahl's jabs at the Eisenhower administration to Lenny Bruce's excursions into the further shores of race, drugs, and sex.

Yet, clear boundaries were still in place. In most states, films still had to be licensed by censorship boards, and Hollywood's Production Code still forbade nudity, obscenity, most profanity, and any portrayal of illicit sexuality that did not lead to retribution. Rock and roll's bawdier lyrics were never heard on radio; so Little Richard's "Tutti Frutti good booty" became "Tutti Frutti au rutti" and Hank Ballard's "Work with Me Annie (All Night Long)" became Georgia Gibbs's "Dance with Me Henry." On television, which by the mid-sixties was nestled in more than nine out of ten American homes, the culture was frozen in amber: free of profanity and premarital, extramarital, and even marital sex. On numberless TV shows, cheerful Negroes cooked and cleaned, and women labored in the home or in clearly defined and limited workplace roles.

And in a sense, what Americans saw on their television screens was an accurate reflection of the dominant culture. The Supreme Court might be striking down segregation laws, Betty Friedan might have written a best-selling book about the social and legal limitations on women, but as John Kennedy began his second term, no Negro had ever sat in the Supreme Court, in the cabinet, or (save for Reconstruction) in the United States Senate; of the hundred senators, two were women. None had ever served on the High Court, nor in any of the key cabinet posts. If the major media insti-

tutions did not spend much time examining these facts, it may
have been that they were themselves firmly anchored in traditional
ways. No black or woman had ever anchored a network broadcast
or served as a key editor at any major newspaper or magazine; at
Time magazine, women could aspire to be researchers, not correspondents.

As for mores: in 1960, the FDA had approved the sale of an oral
contraceptive—the Pill—to women, uncoupling sex from preg-
nancy, raising the specter of unbridled coupling. At the same time,
on a typical college campus, women were required to be in their dor-
mitories by 10:00 or 11:00 p.m. on weeknights; abortion was illegal
everywhere; homosexuality (defined in some states as "the abomi-
nable and detestable crime against nature") was a criminal offense,
and so was adultery; divorce could derail a political career, as Nelson
Rockefeller discovered in 1964.

John Kennedy was, in many ways, solidly implanted in the older
culture. While the Twist was danced at the White House on occasion, the President's taste in music ran to show tunes: composer
Frederick Loewe had performed on several occasions, playing songs
from his hit shows *My Fair Lady* and *Camelot*. While Kennedy enjoyed the company of women (to put it mildly), there was not a single woman in any position of influence in his administration; the
only Negro he knew with any familiarity was George Thomas, his
butler. His politics were characterized by a sense of caution, a suspicion of political passion, that seemed at odds with his bold rhetoric.

"We stand today at the edge of a New Frontier," he'd proclaimed
in his 1960 acceptance speech. "We must climb the mountaintop,"
he'd urged the readers of *Life* magazine. And then there was the
image, the persona, of this strikingly young man with an even more
strikingly young wife, constantly in motion, so different from his
sedentary predecessors. When he governed, however, he seemed to

follow one of his favorite pieces of political wisdom: "When it is not
necessary to change, it is necessary not to change." In a much-
discussed commencement speech at Yale in 1962, Kennedy seemed
to shun the notion of a clear choice between right and wrong in one
key arena.

"What is at stake in our economic decisions today," he said, "is
not some grand warfare of rival ideologies which will sweep the
country with passion but the practical management of a modern
economy. What we need is not labels and clichés but more basic
discussion of the sophisticated and technical questions involved in
keeping a great economic machinery moving ahead."

It was that caution, that careful calculation of political costs,
that had fed doubts in the liberal community from his first days as
a potential president. Columnist Karl E. Meyer had labeled Kennedy an emblematic politician for "the Age of the Smooth Deal":

"Too obsessed by the problems of his 'image' to explore the controversial issues of his time . . . too impressed by opinion polls and
lacking in inner conviction . . . too prone to conceive of electoral
survival as an end in itself; his nose is so implanted in the middle of
the road that his eyes lose sight of the horizon." That sense of artifi-
ciality inspired songwriter Malvina Reynolds to add an additional
verse to her 1962 hit, "Little Boxes":

> There's a white house in the capital
> And inside are the Kennedys,
> And they're all made out of ticky-tacky
> And they all sound just the same.
> There's Bobby, and Teddy,
> And Jacqueline and the President,
> And they're all made out of ticky-tacky
> And they all sound just the same.

What that dismissive view missed was how Kennedy's *political* caution was offset by a *stylistic* boldness. In his youth, his good looks,
his use of language, in the frank embrace of the arts, high fashion,
and physical exertion, Kennedy was demonstrating a presidential
energy not seen since the days of Theodore Roosevelt; in an age of
mass media, that energy was reaching millions. Back in 1960, novelist Norman Mailer had written about the potential impact of a
Kennedy presidency this way:

"If one had a profound criticism of Kennedy, it was that his
public mind was too conventional, but that seemed to matter less
than the fact of such a man in office because the law of political life
had become so dreary that only a conventional mind could win an
election. Indeed there could be no politics which gave warmth to
one's body until the country had recovered its imagination, its pio-
neer lust for the unexpected and incalculable. It was the changes
that might come afterward on which one could put one's hope.
With such a man in office the myth of the nation would again be
engaged . . ."

Kennedy's aide Richard Goodwin put it this way: "He seemed
to embody the idea of America . . . [I]t had to be constantly renewed, always contemporary . . . JFK expressed, in words, in action,
in manners, his own belief in America's possibilities; that we were a
nation with a large purpose, a mission."

Five years later, that myth had taken hold, especially among
younger Americans. Even before Dallas, there was something attractive, even cool, about the idea of their country being governed by a
young, handsome, apparently physically robust man with a younger,
undeniably hot wife. When a photo of a grinning, dripping-wet
President on a public beach in Los Angeles surrounded by admiring

onlookers appeared, one editor said, "Can you *imagine* seeing Ike or Harry Truman like that? And would you want to?"

And it wasn't even that surprising when, in February of 1964, four young men from Britain found themselves invited to the White House after their concert at the Washington Coliseum. In a surprise event, kept off the public schedule, Kennedy introduced them to an audience of 200 at the White House East Room with a mocking complaint.

"Not since the British burned the White House in 1812," Kennedy said, "has a foreign invader conquered our land as swiftly and thoroughly as have John, Paul, George, and Ringo. And not since the Volkswagen," he added, "has there been a greater threat to the U.S. trade balance than the emergence of the Beatles." In the days that followed their brief performance, newspapers and magazines had a field day with composite photos showing what Kennedy's hair would look like on the foursome—and what JFK would look like with a moptop.

It was, of course, impossible to measure what the impact on the national mood would have been had that all been lost in Dallas. Dean Acheson had tried to capture it when he wrote to a British friend, observing that "if this young and vibrant man had become a corpse within an hour, the vast factor of chance and insecurity in all our separate lives as well as in our collective life would have become oppressive and paralyzingly terrifying."

Kennedy himself pursued that line of thought in a conversation with Arthur Schlesinger on an early June evening in 1965 when he scoffed at the notion that great sweeping forces make history inevitable.

"Do any of your colleagues," he asked, "really believe that if Zangara had killed Roosevelt in Miami that John Nance Garner would have led us out of the Depression? Or that if Halifax had been chosen as prime minister instead of Churchill the British would have survived the Blitz? Or, not to compare myself with those giants—"

"Of course not, Mr. President—"

"—if that nut outside my home in Palm Beach had blown me up, do you think it might possibly have made a difference if Lyndon had been president during the missile crisis?"

"As long as you're being morbid," said Schlesinger, "if it had stopped raining in Dallas, and the bubble top wasn't on your car, it *has* occurred to me to wonder where we'd be in Vietnam . . ."

But the rain hadn't stopped; the bubble top had stayed on. And John Kennedy was still president, a figure with a force of personality that resonated far more than did his cautious politics. For example, if he was the symbol of the government, then there was something attractive, even cool, about signing up out of college for something more than immediate lifetime employment. It wasn't as if anyone with a college education was going to find trouble getting a job— not in this economy, with steady growth, low unemployment, and no inflation. You could hardly walk across a campus without stumbling across a recruiter for GM or IBM or GE or U.S. Steel or any of the other corporate behemoths that were promising twenty-one-year-olds generous salaries, health care, and retirement benefits. Signing up for two years with the Peace Corps even came with a draft deferment—not that anyone was worried about the prospect of being drafted for a nonexistent war.

Now, after Kennedy survived an attempt on his life, the power of his image had grown far more powerful. Norman Mailer himself had captured the power of that survival in an *Esquire* essay, "Lazarus in the Oval Office," when he wrote, "To the myth of the Outsider was now added the myth of the Invincible; Superman had come not to the supermarket, but to the streets of an inhospitable city at high noon, and had returned to us whole. Led by a man with such powers, who would not follow?"

So when in early 1965 the Congress authorized AmeriCorps, Kennedy's domestic version of the Peace Corps, the response was overwhelming. AmeriCorps recruiters saw lines at Columbia University snaking out of Low Library, doubling back over the length of College Walk. At the University of Wisconsin, a line of more than a thousand students stretched down the steps of the Memorial Union, down Langdon Street for three blocks; and at Berkeley, where a university ban on off-campus political activity on campus had led to an explosive confrontation a year earlier, another near riot ensued, this time when the AmeriCorps recruiters ran out of applications. SDS, while expressing "clearly warranted skepticism," encouraged its members "to test the ability or willingness of a government agency to challenge the injustices." In Newark, SDS cofounder Tom Hayden left the Community Union Project to sign on as the regional deputy director of AmeriCorps.

(Not everyone followed Hayden's example. A twenty-seven-year-old Berkeley graduate student named Jerry Rubin left his studies to work as a high school organizer for Junior Achievement, which taught teenagers how to start a company, sell stock, and produce and sell a product. "I've found the New Frontier and its address is Wall Street," said Rubin, who would go on to build a hugely successful penny-stock company before his youthful treasurer fled the country with his fortune. "I never should have trusted an accountant under thirty," he said to the sentencing judge.)

Even as the youth culture was setting hands to wringing and stomachs to churning, even as young men's hair began to grow longer and young women's skirts began to grow shorter, even as the lyrics of the music grew racier, there was an absence of darkness, of rage. Elders might be dense, clueless, intolerant, but it wasn't as if there were a *war* raging; it wasn't as if there were a chance that the young men pursuing lingerie or protesting racial discrimination might be plucked off a campus to face combat and possible death 10,000 miles away; it wasn't as if their television screens were filled with pictures of carnage at the hands of their own countrymen.

In fact, the news seemed to be of a very different kind: from the 1963 Test Ban Treaty, to the 1964 JFK-Khrushchev Moscow Summit, to the negotiations on a coalition government in Vietnam, to the Harriman-Dobrynin Geneva negotiations on the Strategic Arms Limitation Treaty, there was tangible evidence that the superpowers were slowly, steadily stepping away from the cold war precipice.

Even more newsworthy was what *wasn't* being reported in the news. More and more, Kennedy was tapping the journalists he had turned to before as a way to opening channels that could not be tapped through regular sources. Former *Look* magazine editor William Attwood, now a special representative to the United Nations, was in regular contact with Cuban diplomats, probing for possible openings toward renewed diplomacy. (This had led to a rare, sharp argument between the President and his brother, who still looked for ways to topple Fidel Castro. "Give it up, Bobby," the President finally said. "This isn't some grudge match.") Norman Cousins, the *Saturday Review* editor who had played a crucial role in the Test Ban Treaty negotiations, had left the magazine to devote himself and his considerable family fortune to lobbying work, hiring director John Frankenheimer to create a "Promise of Peace" series of television commercials.

Most remarkable was the role about to be played by one of the country's best-known journalists.

Theodore H. White—"Teddy" to everyone who knew him—was the author of *The Making of the President 1960*, a groundbreaking look at the election that took readers behind the scenes, and turned the Nixon-Kennedy contest into a romanticized battle, with Kennedy clearly wearing the white hat. Long before this success, Teddy White's beat had been China. He graduated summa cum laude from Harvard with a degree in Chinese studies; he'd spent years in the country and had written a book, *Thunder Out of China,* that noted the corruption of the Nationalist pro-American government led by Chiang Kai-shek, and chronicled the power and popularity of Mao's Communist force. That viewpoint had forced White to leave the employ of *Time* owner Henry Luce, whose devotion to Chiang bordered on the messianic.

Kennedy and White had talked about China often, White chiding Kennedy for his "Who lost China?" demagoguery as a young congressman, Kennedy asking White early in his presidency whether he thought there'd be any point in pursuing a meeting with Mao in Asia.

Now, in July of 1965, Kennedy invited White up to Hyannis for a strictly off-the-record chat. "I think it's time," Kennedy said, "for Americans to get a long, inside look at China from someone who knows the country well. Someone like you."

"Well," White said, "there is that small matter of a travel ban on U.S. citizens traveling to the mainland. I've grown quite fond of my passport."

"Travel regulations are not writ in stone," the President said, and pressed the issue. "We're talking about the most populous nation on earth, an atomic power. I read the speeches of some of their leaders, and they seem perfectly happy with a war that leaves three billion dead, as long as the survivors are Communists. You know those leaders; they'll talk with you. And when they do, I want you to deliver a message from me. I want them to know we're open to the idea of a different relationship with them."

Teddy White chuckled.

"I'm missing the joke," Kennedy said.

"I'm just imagining what Richard Nixon is going to say when he learns the President is interested in opening the door to Red China. I think he's going to throw a fit . . . and then he's going to see how much trouble he can cause you."

Neither White nor the President could imagine it, but it wasn't Richard Nixon who posed potentially fatal political trouble for President Kennedy. That would come from a few men who had occupied some of the most powerful positions in America's public and private power centers. Two years before, they had seen Kennedy as a potential threat to the nation's long-term security. Now, for a handful of them, the threat was no longer potential. It was clear and present. In 1964 they had stayed their hand for fear that the alternative, Senator Barry Goldwater, was too hot-tempered, too impetuous, to occupy the Oval Office. Now, in Vice President Stuart Symington, they saw a serious, levelheaded statesman with a commitment to a strong defense and a tough-minded approach to the Soviets.

And so, they decided, the time had come to render President Kennedy politically impotent, with the one weapon against which he had no real defense: himself.

CHAPTER SEVEN

THE THREAT

"Mistah Speak-ah . . . the President of the United States . . . and one *very* sexy brother-in-law!"

The sixteen guests gathered around the dining room table stood and applauded in a semi-serious salute as Ethel Kennedy sat down. The President raised his champagne glass and gestured to his younger brother, then began his toast by mocking his most famous speech.

"Let the word go forth, from this time and place, that the torch must soon be passed from an officially middle-aged, increasingly frail Secretary of Defense . . . a man who, to paraphrase my good friend and former adversary, has always believed that ruthlessness in defense of the President is no vice—and moderation in pursuit of our common enemies is no virtue. To my older younger brother: May your next forty be as tranquil, as peaceful, as trouble-free as your first forty. Happy birthday, Bobby."

Bobby Kennedy stood and acknowledged the raucous cheers with a tongue-in-cheek response of his own.

"My thanks, Mr. President—for all you have given me over the period of the last two decades: every gray hair, every wrinkle in my forehead, as well as every terror that awakens me at three o'clock in the morning. If there is anyone who seeks to know what torment an older brother can inflict on his helpless younger sibling, *let them come to Hickory Hill!*"

The men and women at the table on this late November evening in 1965 were among the closest of Kennedy confidants: Ben and Toni Bradlee, Red Fay, David Hackett, LeMoyne Billings, Charlie Bartlett. It is doubtful that any of them, no matter how close, fully grasped the truth behind Robert Kennedy's remarks. They all knew that from the moment John Kennedy entered public life, Bobby's life had been spent in the service of his brother. They all knew of the endless hours he'd spent organizing the campaigns, using the power of persuasion and threat to extract support. What none of them knew was just how much energy Bobby had spent in protecting his brother from mortal threats to his political life—none more dangerous than the threats that had emerged just before the President had gone to Texas exactly two years ago. As he concluded his brief thank-you and sat down, he was again struck by a thought he could not share with any of them: the bullet that had almost taken John Kennedy's life may well have spared him from an end to his presidency.

Where did it stem from, this compulsive, careless, reckless pursuit of women, this apparent indifference to the risk to his political career, this behavior that had continued—even accelerated—*after* he'd won the White House?

Maybe it came from the example his father had set. Joe Sr. would bring his mistresses home, invite them to dinner with his wife and children; he'd enter the guest rooms where friends of his daughters were staying; his sons would warn their dates to be careful. His children not only knew of Joe's philandering, they would sometimes look for female companionship for him during his travels.

Maybe it came from his many brushes with early death, in hospital beds, on operating tables, and in the waters of the South Pacific, which taught him that his life would likely end early, and that pleasure was to be taken whenever and wherever he could find it.

Maybe it came from the medication he'd been taking since youth; the corticosteroids he'd been ingesting to deal with his many intestinal maladies were thought to spark the libido.

Maybe it came from a sense of entitlement as the handsome, charming son of one of the richest men in the United States. He'd never had to pay a bill, wait on line, or defer any desire, so why deny himself a woman he fancied? The fact of his marriage was of no matter; when he was escorting his youngest brother, Ted, down the aisle, he'd whispered, "Just because you're getting married doesn't mean you can't have other women." As for Jackie . . . of course he loved her, but that was another part of his life, far removed from the diversions of the moment.

And if he thought himself invulnerable to exposure—if it was true that he'd once said, "They can't touch me while I'm alive, and when I'm dead, who cares?"—he had good reason for his confidence. The press culture of the time drew clear lines between a man's public and private behavior, in part, no doubt, because of the people-who-live-in-glass-houses rule: How many reporters, editors, or news executives could survive scrutiny of *their* behavior? When there were hints that a story might surface, the power of the Kennedy family or its money could usually compel or purchase silence. Whatever the reasons, from the time he'd entered public life, his compulsive, reckless sexual behavior had never become a matter of public knowledge, save for the occasional rumor, even when there

was a determined effort to make his conduct a public scandal—
even when there was proof of a sort . . . as Leonard and Florence
Kater had learned.

One night in 1958, the Katers were awakened at 1:00 a.m. by the
sound of someone throwing pebbles at the upstairs window of a
room they had rented out to a young Senate aide named Pamela Turnure. It was her employer, Senator Kennedy, who was demanding—
and got—entrance to her room. The Katers, straitlaced folks, were
sufficiently outraged to rig up a tape recorder in the air vent that led
to Turnure's room and recorded what went on during Kennedy's
next visit.

The Katers threw Turnure out—but Florence Kater didn't stop
there.

"I was so outraged that this Irish Catholic senator, who pretended
to be such a good family man, might run for president, that I decided to do something about it," she said. That was an understatement; what she launched was something of a crusade. She and her
husband staked out Turnure's new residence and snapped a picture
of Kennedy when he next visited her. They called his father. They
drove to his Georgetown home and waited for him—provoking
Kennedy to warn: "If you ever bother me or my father again, I'll see
to it that you never work in Washington as long as you live." They
picketed Kennedy's campaign appearances with homemade signs,
and inundated more than thirty reporters at newspapers and magazines. Only the *Washington Star* began looking into the story, then
dropped it for unknown reasons. And the one source that *did* publish that photograph helped undermine the story. It was the *Thun-
derbolt*, a neo-Nazi white supremacist newsletter. (It wasn't even that
clear a picture—Kennedy had covered his face with a handkerchief,
and besides, it could have been taken anywhere.)

So John Kennedy's indifference to the dangers of his behavior might be understandable, but Robert Kennedy knew it was badly misplaced. For one thing, the administration had been paying a heavy political price for silence almost from the beginning. For another, on the eve of his departure for Texas, some of the details about John Kennedy's private life were in danger of public exposure.

The FBI's files on John Kennedy's liaisons reached back to the early 1940s, when he'd had an affair with a Danish-born expatriate named Inga Arvad, who was suspected of being a Nazi agent. They were as recent as his affair, while president, with Judith Exner, who was also the mistress of Chicago Mafia boss Sam Giancana. (Frank Sinatra had introduced her to both men, before Robert Kennedy forced his brother to cut off all ties with the singer out of concern for Sinatra's gangland friendships.) More to the point, FBI director J. Edgar Hoover was at pains to let the President and his brother know what he knew about the link between Exner, Giancana, and Kennedy; it was nothing less than a gold-standard job-security guarantee. (Hoover would turn the mandatory retirement age of seventy in 1965 and was determined to stay in the job he'd held for more than forty years.) There was a "mutually assured destruction" tinge to all this—given what the Kennedys knew about Hoover's own private life, they had protection against Hoover spreading secrets—but Lyndon Johnson had been right, if inelegant, when he observed that "Hoover has Kennedy by the balls."

It was bad enough for Bobby that he had to yield to Hoover's imperious demands: signing off on the bugging of Martin Luther King Jr.'s hotel rooms and offices, enduring Hoover's obsession with a virtually nonexistent U.S. Communist Party and his indifference to organized crime. But in October of 1963 he'd been forced to beg for Hoover's help in containing a potential public scandal. It arose from the stories coming out of one of Capitol Hill's most influential figures: Senate Democratic secretary Bobby Baker, the thirty-four-

year-old protégé of Lyndon Johnson. When Baker's financial deal-
ings became the focus of official and press inquiries—how did a
young man on the government payroll accumulate a net worth of
$2 million?—investigators learned that Baker was a source not only
of limitless campaign cash but of women—"party girls" as they
were called—courtesy of the Quorum Club, which he'd run out of
a Capitol Hill hotel. The problem for Bobby was that one of the
prostitutes, twenty-seven-year-old Ellen Rometsch, had been a frequent visitor to the White House. And because Rometsch had fled
East Germany and now worked at the West German embassy,
Hoover was convinced that she was a Communist spy.

Bobby Kennedy thought he'd contained the Rometsch problem
back in July, when he'd had her summarily deported to West Germany in the company of her boyfriend—who happened to be one
of Kennedy's old investigators from his Senate Rackets Committee
days. Now, however, with the Bobby Baker story exploding, her
name had come to the attention of one of the most fearless investi-
gative reporters in Washington: Clark Mollenhoff of the *Des Moines
Register*. On October 26, Mollenhoff reported, "Evidence is likely to
include identification of several high executive branch officials"
who Rometsch had partied with.

The story sent the White House into a frenzy of urgent telephone calls. And Bobby had been forced to turn for help to the man
he most despised, begging Hoover to meet with Senate leaders from
both parties, assure them that Ellen Rometsch was *not* a spy, that
there was *no* evidence that she'd had sex with *any* White House
official . . . but that the trail from Baker's prostitutes to any number
of *senators* was clear and crowded. ("Boy," President Kennedy had
said with no apparent irony to his friend Ben Bradlee, "the dirt
[Hoover's] got on those senators, you wouldn't believe it.")

That effort by Hoover did little to ease Bobby's mind. What if the press kept following the story of the President's extracurricular behavior? Back in June, he'd had to confront two reporters from the *New York Journal-American* for publishing a story linking a British prostitute to a "high elected American official"—by which, they said, they meant the President. That kind of pressure was just not going to work with Mollenhoff, who'd had run-ins with Bobby Kennedy in the past and who was already driving the administration crazy with his investigations into a huge defense contract. What if Ellen Rometsch, furious at her deportation, went public? What if Mollenhoff put her in touch with Senator John Williams, the Delaware Republican who often acted as his own Sergeant Friday, and whose zeal in exposing corruption had put more than one official miscreant in prison? What if Williams brought her back from Germany? He wouldn't be diverted by pleas from the leadership. And what of all those people privy to the President's behavior—a rogue Secret Service agent, say, or one of the partygoers at those highly private social gatherings?

And then the President went to Texas . . .

No one—not Mollenhoff, not anyone—was going to write about the President's sexual behavior while he lay in a hospital bed, fighting for his life, any more than they would have written about LBJ's financial behavior had he succeeded to the White House if Kennedy had not survived his wounds. In a moment of national trauma, there was simply no appetite for such a story. Even the best-selling book in America, a highly critical, non-salacious account of the President called *JFK: The Man and the Myth*, disappeared from bookshelves within hours of his shooting. Mollenhoff put it bluntly in his diary a week after Dallas: "Any reporter who wrote about where the President might have been putting his penis would have been ridden out of town on a rail . . . if he was lucky."

The expected revelations about Bobby Baker, the "party girls," and "high executive branch officials" never developed; in an ironic twist, it was Baker's mentor, Lyndon Johnson, who was the victim when the stories about financial kickbacks and his rise to great wealth forced him from office. Even among those who knew of Kennedy's behavior, there was a belief that he had changed—that the loss of his infant son and the shooting that had happened with his wife at his side had curbed his appetites—at least for now.

So by the time the President was raising his glass to celebrate Robert's fortieth birthday, his brother could relax, more or less confident that John Kennedy's private life would remain just that . . .

Unless, of course, there were powerful people with a powerful motive to make it public.

By late 1965, John Kennedy's determination to move out of the cold war framework of the last two decades had become steadily more apparent. His long-held belief that nationalism was the dominant force in the developing world was now more or less official policy. Back in May, for example, he had refused the urgent requests of his military and hard-line elements in the State Department to send Marines into the Dominican Republic to prevent a leftist politician from assuming the presidency.

"If our boys set foot on that island," his aide Dick Goodwin had argued, "it will give Fidel ten years' worth of speeches denouncing 'gunboat diplomacy.' Juan Bosch may make some of our multinationals unhappy, but he's certainly no threat to us."

At the United Nations, special representative William Attwood was in the second year of intermittent conversations with Cuban diplomats, testing the possibilities of a thaw between Washington and Havana. Sometime over the summer, Cuban official Carlos Lechuda brought with him a gift for the President: a box of one hundred of the finest Havanas. They were H. Upmanns, Hoyo de Monterreys, and two dozen Cohiba Robustos cigars that would not be formally introduced in Cuba until the next year, for the exclusive enjoyment of Fidel Castro and the inner circle of his government and the Communist Party.

When the Secret Service said the cigars needed to be tested for possible contamination, Kennedy refused.

"No," he said, "only *our* intelligence people would be stupid enough to try something like that."

As for the central players in the cold war, the Harriman-Dobrynin talks in Geneva had yielded a framework for negotiations on strategic arms limitations . . . although the President himself was dubious about the real significance of such agreements.

"I think the idea that we're closer to peace if we each have five hundred missiles instead of a thousand is an illusion," he said in an off-the-record conversation with half a dozen columnists. "We don't distrust each other because we're armed; we're armed because we distrust each other. But I suppose, as a symbol, it has its uses, and it'll make the folksingers happy. You know that song by Joan Baez that says 'The paper they were signing said they'd never fight again'? They actually *did* sign a piece of paper back in 1928. It was called the Kellogg-Briand Pact. Didn't quite work, did it?"

In fact, the symbolism was more powerful than Kennedy had imagined. When U.S. and Soviet diplomats met to draft the specifics of a treaty, the *Bulletin of the Atomic Scientists* "Doomsday Clock," which had been set at seven minutes to midnight in 1960, and twelve minutes to midnight after the Nuclear Test Ban Treaty, was moved back to twenty minutes to midnight. The thaw between the two powers led to more openness on the cultural front. CBS broadcast a two-hour special from the Bolshoi Ballet, while Soviet TV carried a two-hour pop and jazz festival from Lincoln Center's newly opened New York State Theater, although one band had to be cut because Soviet officials made it clear that they would not broadcast the "degenerate music" of the Beach Boys. ("Apparently," Kennedy said at a press conference, "KGB agents discovered that if you play 'Little Deuce Coupe' backwards, it says 'Marx was wrong.'")

No piece of symbolism was more powerful and controversial than the issue of *Life* magazine that hit the newsstands on September 17, 1965, with its striking cover headline: INSIDE RED CHINA TODAY. To the surprise of its readers—and the smoldering resentment of its competitors—*Life* carried a 25,000-word report from Theodore H. White, accompanied by photographs from the magazine's most celebrated photographer, Alfred Eisenstaedt. (Time-Life owner Henry Luce had signed off on the project, insisting only that a flattering profile of Chiang Kai-shek be included in the issue.) White was unsparing in his portrayal of a ruthlessly authoritarian regime, and also wrote of "a potential schism within the Communist leadership that could propel a cadre of fanatics into positions of authority—fanatics who seem determined to launch a new revolution, to wipe out every trace of traditional culture."

By contrast, his portrait of Premier Chou En-lai, whom White had met decades ago during his years in China, was benign—as were some of Chou's words.

"Ten years ago," Chou said, "your secretary of state, Mr. Dulles, refused to shake my hand at the Geneva summit. It was the clearest signal imaginable that your government was determined to impose the puppet Chiang regime on the people who had thrown him out—as you yourself, Mr. White, witnessed and reported. Your political leaders call us an 'outlaw nation.' So how is it that we have normal, civil diplomatic relations with virtually all of your allies—

Britain, Canada, France? We trade with each of these nations . . . none of which have anything in common, nor any admiration, for our social system (as we have little admiration for yours). So, perhaps it is time for you Americans to ask yourselves two questions: First, which of us is the truly 'isolated' one? Second, if you are so proud, so confident of your way of life, what is it about us that you fear?"

When asked about the *Life* spread at his next press conference, Kennedy at first said only: "I read it with interest." Then, in an answer that seemed clearly crafted in advance, he added:

"If we were to have diplomatic relations only with those countries whose principles we approved of, we would have relations with very few countries in a very short time. We recognize and trade with the Soviet Union; does anyone seriously argue that this means we endorse communism? We recognize and trade with Spain and Portugal. Does that mean we endorse dictatorships? I've said many times that we have neither the ability nor the intention to impose our will on any nation; our test is whether a nation abides by the norms of international diplomacy and respects the integrity of its fellow members of the world community." He ignored the shouted follow-up question: "Do you believe Red China meets those standards?"

DID JFK HINT AT RED CHINA RECOGNITION? the *Washington Post* headline asked the next morning. For some of the President's political foes, the answer was clear.

"An ill-conceived, naive, dangerous notion," Richard Nixon said in a last-minute addition to his speech at the Chicago Commonwealth Club. "Mao and Chou lead a totalitarian regime that has openly welcomed the idea of a nuclear war that would kill billions as long as it ended in a Communist conquest. They have called the

United States 'a paper tiger,' and the President's remarks will only confirm their belief." Connecticut senator Tom Dodd, a prominent Democratic hawk, took to the Senate floor to denounce "this latest demonstration of a profound weakness of will." At the White House, 600 members of the conservative Young Americans for Freedom marched with picket signs and an oversize white flag, chanting: "Hey! Hey! JFK! How many Reds did you hug today?"

And *Time* reported that "from Tokyo to Manila to Jakarta, from Singapore to Bangkok to Melbourne, a sense of unease has fallen across the Asian continent: Was Uncle Sam preparing to abandon its commitment to its free world allies, to usher in Red China as the ruler of a new Greater East Asia Co-Prosperity Sphere?

"'It took war to free us from the Japanese tyrant,' remarked a frowning cabdriver in Kuala Lumpur. 'Does Mr. Kennedy not understand that we will fight another to save us from a Red one?'"

Despite its harsh words, *Time* was one of dozens of magazines and newspapers to apply for permission to report from mainland China. When the requests were granted, *New York Herald Tribune* columnist Roscoe Drummond wrote, "This is another signal—cryptic though it may be—that the Kennedy administration is preparing the nation for a new relationship with Communist China . . . and a broader change to the two-decade-old core of U.S. foreign policy."

To many of those who had shaped and executed that policy, and who still believed in it to their core, there was nothing cryptic about the signal. They would turn to their allies in Congress and in the media to resist what they saw as President Kennedy's dangerous views. For a few of these men, however, the matter was far more urgent; in fact, it was nothing less than an emergency. The President was pursuing a course that threatened the United States . . . and he had to be stopped.

———

This was no group of conspirators that had set out to plot against a president. Many had voted for Kennedy in 1960; some had gone to work in his administration, and still held key posts inside the national security-defense-intelligence complex, while others occupied corner offices in law firms or held tenured posts at prestigious universities. Within that group was a much smaller circle: men who believed that John Kennedy's course would weaken the nation irreparably. They had watched him flinch from decisive force at the Bay of Pigs and during the missile crisis . . . stage a furtive retreat from South Vietnam . . . begin to bargain away the country's military superiority over Moscow . . . permit a leftist to assume power in the Dominican Republic . . . and open the door to legitimizing the most militant Communist power on the planet. Their years-long doubts about his ability and character—"a weak leader," "a coward," "a degenerate"—had hardened into a blend of contempt and fear: contempt for his judgment and character, fear over where he would leave America when his term ended in 1968.

Look at what he'd done with his staff in his second term. Dean Rusk was out at State, exiled back to the Rockefeller Foundation. Walt Rostow was packing up at his State Department post, from which his stream of memos to the White House had gone largely unread. Now McNamara, that numbers-obsessed technocrat, was at State, with George Ball his chief deputy. And Bobby Kennedy, of all people, was at Defense, driving the Joint Chiefs crazy with his assaults on "waste" and his edicts about racial discrimination.

In their most private of conversations, some of these men pointed to an unhappy accident of fate that had left John Kennedy in the Oval Office. Were it not for the weather in Dallas, Lyndon Johnson would very likely have become president, with instincts and judgments very different from Kennedy's. He was, they believed, far more traditional in his approach to America's adversaries—"You have to treat them like any bully," he'd long argued, "show them you're willing to fight and they'll back down"—far more deferential to the recommendations of the military and the wise men of the Democratic Party, the Achesons and Nitzes and Cliffords. During the missile crisis, Johnson had sat virtually silent during the Ex-Comm meetings, but he let it be known later that he would have gone with the Chiefs and taken those missiles out promptly.

Now Johnson was gone, but in Vice President Stuart Symington they saw something of a kindred spirit, with a mind-set firmly anchored in cold war assumptions; one who would never have set out on the path Kennedy was following, and who would not continue on that path should he be in charge.

If Symington was unhappy at Kennedy's policies, he made it certain that no one but a few intimates knew of it. (He'd be sixty-seven in 1968, but that did not mean he couldn't try once more for the White House.) Had he known there was a determined effort under way to undermine Kennedy's hold on the presidency, he would have been appalled. But he didn't know, and none of those behind the effort had any intention of telling him . . . especially considering the weapon they intended to use.

Looking back at it, it is nothing short of astounding to realize how many people most hostile to John Kennedy were in possession of damning facts about him—and how limited they were in their willingness or capacity to use that information.

There were Secret Service agents who were dismayed by Kennedy's behavior, and who felt their own mission compromised by it.

Who were those women coming into the presidential suites on campaign trips, cleared into the White House by Kenny O'Donnell or David Powers or Evelyn Lincoln when Mrs. Kennedy was away? What if the President had a health crisis during those pool parties with young press-office girls while the agents were outside? For all they knew, however, they were bound by a strict code of silence.

J. Edgar Hoover knew *all* the secrets: the affair with a mobster's mistress; the White House visits by a German embassy employee who moonlighted as a prostitute; the encounters with Hollywood stars. Much as he reviled Kennedy for his conduct, Hoover's goal was not exposure but the retention of power. There were also long-standing hints that the Kennedys had information about the director that would prove fatal to his own career. It was Dallas, however, where Bobby Kennedy found his ace in the hole: a statement from the Dallas bureau chief that Hoover had personally ordered him to destroy a threatening letter he'd received from Oswald before the shooting. Bobby had made it clear to Hoover that this information would remain secret just as long as Hoover continued to absolve the President of any improper behavior.

Some of the most powerful press barons were deeply conservative, passionately anti-Communist: Henry Luce's Time-Life empire, the *Reader's Digest* of the Wallaces, Ben Hibbs's *Saturday Evening Post*, among others. They were also among the least likely to publish accounts of a public figure's sexual exploits, at least not openly. (*Time* had an innuendo code: A man's mistress was "his great and good friend." A gay man was "a confirmed bachelor.") Luce himself had his own reasons for discretion: he'd had a string of lovers, and his wife, Clare Boothe Luce, had had a long-term affair with the President's father. As for the *Post* and the *Digest*, they were firmly anchored in a bucolic, bygone pastoral; no hint of extramarital sex ever stained their pages.

In a later era, none of this would have kept these secrets out of
the public eye; but in the mid-1960s, the idea of an interconnected
population able to distribute and receive information in an instant,
able to send audio and video from their homes out into the wider
world, was something out of a science fiction fantasy. Communica-
tion was a one-way street. If the Katers wanted America to hear
what was on the tapes they'd made of John Kennedy and his press
aide in her bedroom, they would have to find a radio or TV station
to broadcast them, or a record company to put out a recording, or a
newspaper to print the transcripts. If a British prostitute claimed to
have slept with Kennedy, she'd have to find a publication willing to
print that allegation; and (as the *New York Journal-American* reporters had learned) even a veiled reference could provoke the wrath of
the extended First Family. Moreover, there were *gatekeepers* in the
mid-1960s: newspapers, magazines, and television stations that had
a sharply defined and limited sense of what was news, especially if
there was no clear proof of misbehavior. If they chose to exclude a
public official's private life, that pretty much confined such stories
to rumors and whispers that stayed underground. Sure, there was
an appetite for scandal. *Confidential* magazine had proved that in
the fifties, when its diet of outing adulterers and homosexuals made
it one of the largest-selling magazines in America. Its target was
Hollywood celebrities, though, not politicians, and by 1960 a string
of lawsuits had effectively neutered it.

For the men who wished to strike a fatal blow at Kennedy's stature, then, two things were necessary: first, a story so damaging that
it would break through the private-life/public-life barrier; second, a
willingness on the part of some respectable journalistic force to
publish it.

On the first count, they had no doubt at all . . .

"So," Clark Mollenhoff said to his dinner companion over brandy and cigars, "let me understand how I'm going to justify a fifty-dollar dinner expense to my editor." They'd spent the last two hours at La Niçoise, one of the more fashionable Georgetown restaurants.

"Well, let me tell you a story," the man across the table said. "You have a woman from a prominent family—blond, beautiful, brilliant—marries and divorces a high official in the Central Intelligence Agency. She's related by marriage to a Washington player, and she's a regular at White House dinners, on the presidential yacht . . . and maybe those weren't the only times she was seeing the President."

"You don't need to brief me on Mary Pinchot Meyer," Mollenhoff said. "Cord's ex-wife, Ben Bradlee's sister-in-law . . . She was murdered a year or two back. Is that what you've got on your mind?"

"No," the man said. "Looks like the cops got the right guy and the jury got it wrong; probably a botched robbery or rape. It's about who *else* she was seeing besides the President."

"I think you may be confused with the *National Enquirer* stringer."

"No, Clark, not 'seeing' that way. Look, when Mary divorced Cord, she went bohemian—took up painting, along with a painter or two. She also got it into her head that she and some of her women friends could change the world if they could change the mind-sets of the men who held the levers of power. And the way to that change, she thought, was . . . drugs."

"I'm starting to think I'm going to be on the hook for this bill," Mollenhoff said.

"Hold on, Clark. Mary Meyer spent a lot of time up at Harvard . . . and the professor she was seeing was Timothy Leary."

"Huh," Mollenhoff said, and leaned a little closer to his dinner guest. Leary had spent years at Harvard experimenting with LSD and other hallucinogenic drugs before being fired in 1963. His enthusiasm for the drugs had made him a national figure; public figures like poet Allen Ginsberg and author Aldous Huxley had used it and celebrated the experience. "So what are you pitching here?" the reporter asked. "You telling me that Meyer turned on the President of the United States?"

There was a lengthy silence.

"I was skeptical too," said the man, "until I heard the tapes."

"Have another brandy," Mollenhoff said. "Have two. I don't think the expense account is going to be a problem."

For James Jesus Angleton, the CIA's chief counterintelligence officer, conspiracies were everywhere. Every Soviet defector, he believed, was a double agent sent to throw U.S. intelligence off the scent; moles were at work at every level of the agency. In his office, he worked in semidarkness with blinds drawn, to insulate himself from his enemies. For Angleton, whose wife had been a close friend of Mary Meyer, the knowledge that the ex-wife of a high CIA official was a lover and confidant of the President, and an enthusiastic participant in the emerging drug culture, was more than enough for him to take defensive measures . . . by tapping her telephones and putting listening devices into Meyer's town house. And when Kennedy began veering sharply away from the cold war consensus—when he began moving toward a kind of reconciliation with the Communist world—Angleton drew what was for him the obvious, unmistakable conclusion: Kennedy had listened to Mary Meyer, shared his closest thoughts with her. And now, Meyer was succeeding in the goal she had talked about with her closest friends:

through the use of sex and drugs, she had turned the President of the United States. This was beyond the reckless, notorious sexual behavior, beyond the dangers of a president using amphetamines to ease his chronic pain. *This* was a threat to everything Angleton and the intelligence community was sworn to protect, and it was a story that *had* to be told. In the America of the mid-1960s, the idea of a president surviving a public revelation of adultery was highly unlikely. ("What's Kennedy going to do?" an Angleton colleague asked sarcastically. "Go on TV and ask for forgiveness?") The idea of a president surviving a story of drug use—a tiny fraction of Americans had tried marijuana in 1965, and nine out of ten thought it should be treated as a crime—was out of the question.

In Clark Mollenhoff, Angleton and his colleagues knew they had reached out to the most determined, most fearless reporter in Washington. They knew he had been at odds with the Kennedys for years—triggered by some petty bullying by Bobby at a Hickory Hill party—and they knew he had come close to breaking the Ellen Rometsch story just before the President was shot in Dallas. He was apparently immune to persuasion or intimidation. So it was no surprise that, two weeks after that dinner at La Niçoise, word began circulating through Washington that "Clark is onto something big." It was still below the radar: whispers at dinner parties, a casual question or two to press secretary Salinger, more pointed comments to the Kennedy brothers by loyalist friends in the press like Charlie Bartlett. For that handful of men, there was a powerful sense of anticipation: it was only a matter of time before the story went public, and John Kennedy would be finished.

Except . . . John and Robert Kennedy lived by one philosophy: when it came to their political fortunes, the ends justified the means . . . *any* means.

The President was as furious as anyone had ever seen him.

"We've been fucked," he said. "They've kicked us in the balls."

It was April 10, 1962, and the chairman of U.S. Steel, Roger Blough, had just left the Oval Office after informing Kennedy that the company was going to raise its prices in the face of an apparent labor industry agreement to hold down wages and prices. To the President, the price hike was more than an inflationary danger; it was a personal betrayal, one that would make him look weak, ineffectual. He was determined to force U.S. Steel and its competitors to roll back the price hike. In the days that followed, every weapon of the federal government was pressed into service, no matter how questionable its use.

The Defense Department began moving contracts away from the major steel companies to smaller competitors who had held the price line. The Justice Department began preparing antitrust suits; it seemed highly suspicious that the companies matched the price rise to the penny. Reporters were called and visited by the FBI in the middle of the night, to be grilled about conversations they might have had with steel executives. Attorney General Robert Kennedy made the stakes clear to his Justice Department aides.

"We're going for broke," he said. "Their expense accounts and where they'd been and what they were doing . . . I told the FBI to interview them all—march into their offices . . . subpoenaed for their personal records . . . subpoenaed for their company records. We can't lose this . . ."

No one was immune from the Kennedys' fury. When the President saw a report on NBC's *Nightly News*, he was incensed by what he perceived as anchorman Chet Huntley's kindness to the steel industry. He called Newton Minow, chair of the Federal Communications Commission, and snapped: "Did you see that goddamn thing on Huntley-Brinkley? I thought they were supposed to be our friends. I want you to do something about that—you do something about that."

The President himself explained the deployment of another potential weapon—one of Washington's best-placed lawyers.

"If any one person deserves the credit," he said to his old friend Red Fay, after the steel companies backed down, "it's that damned Clark Clifford [who represented some of the companies] . . . Can't you just see Clifford outlining the possible courses of action the government could take . . . ? Do you know what you're doing when you start bucking the power of the President of the United States? I don't think U.S. Steel or any of the other major steel companies wants to have Internal Revenue agents checking the expense accounts of the top executives. Do you want the government to go back to hotel bills that time you were in Schenectady, to find out who was with you? Too many hotel bills and nightclub expenses would be hard to get by the weekly wives' bridge group out at the country club."

The Kennedys took some heat from the press for their abuse of power, but at a family dinner the President seemed unconcerned, joking about his conversation with a steel company president: "He asked me, 'Why are all the income tax returns of all the steel executives in all the country being scrutinized?' And I told him the Attorney General would never do any such thing, and of course he was right!"

"They were mean to my brother!" Bobby interjected. "They can't do that to my brother."

The President left out of his jocular remarks another fact: Bobby Kennedy had ordered the FBI and the CIA to bug the phones and offices of steel executives as well.

And if that's what the Kennedys did to win a policy dispute . . . what might they do if the presidency itself was at stake?

"John, we've got a problem—actually, we've got a *lot* of problems."

From his office in downtown Minneapolis, John Cowles heard his Washington attorney with a sense of disbelief.

"Where?" he asked.

"Everywhere, it seems. Three days ago, we got a notice of inquiry from the FCC about our TV stations in Memphis and Daytona. Apparently something to do with record keeping. Yesterday, the IRS decided to order up an audit on *Look*. Then an hour ago we got *another* inquiry about our Des Moines station from the Justice Department's antitrust division; they say they're looking at 'cross-ownership.' Christ, we've had that station for a decade! I'm not a great believer in coincidences, so . . . what have you folks been doing that's got the government so wound up?"

"I haven't got a clue," Cowles said. "Let me do some checking."

The Cowles Media Company was hardly an enemy of the Kennedy administration. The family was Republican, but its ties were to the Progressive Republicans of Teddy Roosevelt. Yes, the *Des Moines Register* had backed Nixon in '60, but they'd swung to Kennedy over Goldwater in '64. So had the *Star Tribune* in Minneapolis. And *Look* magazine had run so many flattering photo spreads of the Kennedy family that some Republicans were suggesting it change its name to *Look at JFK*.

It took three phone calls for Cowles to locate the all-but-certain source of the problem.

"We were about to call you, John," said the chief of the *Register*'s Washington bureau. "We're working on something that's way above my pay grade. Whether we run it is going to be your call."

An hour later Cowles and three executives were on their way to the airport. By early evening they were in a suite at the Mayflower Hotel, meeting with Clark Mollenhoff. At 11:00 p.m., Mollenhoff stormed out of the suite, cabbed back to the bureau, and announced his immediate resignation.

"I didn't see that we had any choice," Cowles said later to a small group of executives. "The story looked solid, but you could just imagine the reaction. Clark said the tapes sure *sounded* like Kennedy but how many people can imitate that voice—hell, Vaughn Meader's still making a living at it. Then there's the question of how we got to hear the tape. Were we criminally liable for communicating the fruits of an illegal wiretap? We hear that heads have already started to roll at the CIA. And when you look at the potential cost to the company . . ." He shook his head.

"But I'll tell you this," he added. "It'll be a cold day in hell before our papers have another good word to say about the Kennedys."

The story didn't disappear, not completely. It survived in that twilight region of rumors and urban legends, like the stories about John Kennedy's first marriage and his fling with Marilyn Monroe. The *Realist*, an "underground" publication with a bent for dark satire, published a "celebration" of John Kennedy's "Dionysian Appetites," saluting his "buoyant departure from the Victorian strictures of earlier times," under the title: "Hail to His Briefs." A twenty-four-year-old playwright named Barbara Garson wrote a lengthy parody of the famous Lord Byron poem she called "Don John."

"Ask not," he said, "what I can do for you."
For what he asked, no maiden could resist.

And when his trumpet summoned her again
'Twas not his trumpet she was pleased to kiss.

Among the more sophisticated news readers, the understanding
grew that John Kennedy did not live by the traditional standards of
morality. Given how radically those standards were under siege in
the later half of the 1960s, this understanding did not prove politically fatal.

The real fallout, however, was within the journalistic community. The Kennedys' view of the press had always been "instru-
mental": there were friends, there were foes. There was money to be
spent when necessary: the family had loaned the *Boston Post* owner
$500,000 in 1952 as the price of a senatorial endorsement, and had
put a muckraking New York journalist on the family payroll for
$1,000 a week to buy his loyalty. There were sanctions for apostasy:
Kennedy had angrily canceled White House subscriptions to the
New York Herald Tribune for its critical coverage, and had exiled
Washington Post editor Ben Bradlee from his inner circle for months.

Now, however, the press had seen another side of the Kennedys:
a blunt use of political power directed not at some rogue corporations but at *them*. It would color their approach to the President for
the rest of his term, arm them with the motivation to recast his record in more skeptical, critical terms. It was just what Kennedy did
not need as he turned to the challenge of building his legacy.

CHAPTER EIGHT

THE LAST CHAPTER

Welcome home, Mr. President."

"Not my home for much longer, J.B."

Chief usher J. B. West chuckled as he took the crutches from Kennedy and guided him toward the wheelchair. Over the course of his second term, the President's steadily weakening back had all but collapsed. For his first years in the White House, a regimen of hot baths, exercise, and drugs had kept him reasonably mobile; only occasionally did the public get a glimpse of the crutches Kennedy used to maneuver, or the way he gingerly rose and sat. By the end of 1967, the years—and the corticosteroids he had taken for most of his life—had turned his lumbar region into what one physician called "a disaster area." Now, on this early November morning in 1968, the wheelchair had become a commonplace sight in and around the White House, and Jerry Bruno's advance team found itself spending most of its time staging events that would limit Kennedy to the shortest possible number of steps. More than once, Kennedy had found himself remembering what he'd said when he was asked why he was going for the presidency back in 1960: "I just don't know that I'll be healthy enough in eight years."

The last three days had been grueling for the President: he'd been in seven states—New Jersey, Pennsylvania, Ohio, Wisconsin, Illinois, Missouri, and then out to California and the overnight flight back across the country. The crowds were huge: 30,000 at Liberty Park, with the Statue of Liberty in the background; 45,000 in Madison's Camp Randall Stadium; a million lining State Street for Chicago's traditional torchlight parade, led by Mayor Daley, the President, and the Democratic nominee. But crowds could be deceiving. ("There is no place," Kennedy once said in Ohio after losing badly in 1960, "where I get a warmer welcome and fewer votes than this great state.") This was, by every measure, going to be close, and not just because the polling showed a dead heat nationally and in a dozen key states.

"America has rarely witnessed an election," wrote Johnny Apple of the *New York Times*, "where the two major candidates not only represent such utterly contrasting beliefs and policies, but represent utterly contrasting strengths and weaknesses. And rarely has a campaign hinged—possibly decisively—on how a deeply divided nation feels about its departing leader."

As Kennedy wheeled himself to the East Wing elevator for a bath, breakfast, and a rest, J. B. West held up a finger.

"Mr. President, Mrs. Kennedy said she'd like a moment with you after your nap. Said to tell you it's important."

Curious, he thought for a moment, then found his mind drifting back to the election, now only two days away. Apple was right, he thought. This election was at heart a referendum on his stewardship. And however much he had succeeded by the traditional rules of politics, he knew better than almost anyone how much those rules had changed.

"I've got one question for you," a frustrated Kenny O'Donnell had asked pollster Lou Harris shortly after the 1966 midterms, which saw Democrats lose twenty-eight seats in the House and two in the Senate. "Just what the hell is it about peace and prosperity that Americans don't like?"

There was no question that the American economy was in fine shape. Seven years of uninterrupted, steady growth had helped drive the jobless rate under 5 percent. So had the aggressive jobs program that had begun in 1965 and had expanded every year since. "A rising tide lifts all the boats," Kennedy had said in the early sixties as he pushed for his tax cuts—to which Pat Moynihan, then an assistant secretary of labor, said, "With respect Mr. President, some of the boats have holes in the bottom." For the last three years a welfare-to-work effort in big cities and rural communities had finally begun to move the once-intractable numbers in black neighborhoods and Appalachian hollows. Robert Kennedy, who had wandered the inner city streets of Washington as attorney general and visited ghettos in a dozen cities when he'd moved to Defense, said to his brother, "I remember going to a job fair in Oakland a few years ago, with ten thousand people waiting on line for seventy-five jobs. Last week I was in St. Louis, and there were two thousand people waiting for five hundred jobs. That's something, but . . ."

"Bobby," the President said, "just once before I leave this job, could you just say, 'Jack, I have really good news!'?"

As for inflation, "It's the dog that didn't bark in the night," Walter Heller remarked as he was leaving the chair of the Council of Economic Advisers for a tenured post at the University of Minnesota.

"Yes," said Ken Galbraith. "Just absolutely remarkable what can happen to the economy when you're not fighting a war on the other side of the world . . . You don't need to raise taxes . . . you don't need to print money . . . you can even spend a little extra on frills like education and transportation. If the President can buy off those rural congressmen with a bigger farm subsidy, we may able to celebrate the Bicentennial with a high-speed rail system."

Why, then, was the President's job approval rating hovering at 50 percent? Why was the public telling pollsters by a significant margin that "America was on the wrong track"?

"It's pretty fundamental," pollster Harris had said to O'Donnell. "When the economy's bad, people vote on the economy. When a war's going badly, they vote on the war. And when there's 'peace and prosperity,' they sometimes think about other things. And they're not very happy about those 'other things.'"

One of those "other things" had long been at the heart of Kennedy's political concerns. In March of 1966, shortly after the Tet holidays, South Vietnam's fragile coalition government collapsed in the face of an attack by National Liberation Front and North Vietnamese forces, which raised the red flag with the yellow star over Saigon's Independence Palace and proclaimed the birth of the unified "People's Republic of Vietnam." There were bipartisan denunciations of what Richard Nixon called "an inexcusable failure of will in the face of naked Communist aggression" and what Democratic senator Russell Long labeled a day of "retreat, defeat, surrender, and national dishonor." In response, the President dispatched the Sixth Fleet to the South China Sea and staged hastily organized military exercises with the armed forces of Thailand and the Philippines. In a press conference, Kennedy read a statement warning that "no potential aggressor should misread the events in Saigon: the United States will honor every binding commitment it has anywhere those nations are threatened." He also reminded the reporters of what he had told CBS's Walter Cronkite in the fall of 1963: "In the final analysis, it's their war," adding, "There is no clearer example of a country that could not be saved unless it had decided to save itself."

The collapse of South Vietnam was a blow to the Kennedy administration, but in political terms it was a flesh wound. For more than two years American forces had been leaving the country. With American men no longer in harm's way, major news organizations had also departed, shuttering bureaus, redeploying frontline correspondents. Because the United States had never made a serious military commitment to South Vietnam, even Kennedy's most zealous opponents could not charge that "American boys died in vain."

"Whatever prestige the United States may have lost," wrote the *Washington Post*'s Stanley Karnow, "is nothing compared to what would have happened had the world's mightiest nation committed its blood and treasure and *then* failed to prevail. No maimed veterans crowd our VA hospitals; no memorials on Washington's mall or on small-town squares to remind us of who and what we would have lost."

So the fall of Vietnam was not the fatal political blow that had haunted the President's fears in his first term. What *did* afflict his second term were three other powerful forces. One was thoroughly predictable, so much so that its impact was mitigated; another was utterly unforeseen; a third came in the form of a once-friendly force that had turned hostile in the wake of the Kennedys' desperate fight to save the presidency from scandal.

John Kennedy and his allies had approached the 1964 campaign with one central fear: that the tinderbox of race would rip apart the Democratic Party coalition formed more than three decades earlier. It could be found in the collapse of the once-solid Democratic

South and the flight of South Carolina's Strom Thurmond to the ranks of the Republican Party when Barry Goldwater won that party's presidential nomination. With Kennedy at the head of the ticket, without Texan Lyndon Johnson as his running mate, other Southerners defected to the Republicans, including Virginia senator A. Willis Robertson. "I made my decision," he explained, "after an evening of prayerful contemplation guided by my son and spiritual guide, Pat, whose Christian Broadcasting Network is bringing His word to millions."

The issue of war and peace had overwhelmed the race issue in 1964 and propelled Kennedy into a solid reelection triumph. Still, as his second term began, Kennedy had no illusions about the political dangers posed by racial conflict. It was why, just before his Dallas trip, he'd coupled his intention to move on the poverty front with an admonition to the liberal Walter Heller that "I also think it's important to make clear that we're doing something for the middle-income man in the suburbs." It was why his 1964 campaign pledge to put jobs at the center of his domestic campaign theme had been linked to his promise to "end welfare as we know it." His Voting Rights Act victory in 1965 was in large measure the product of Lyndon Johnson's advice to frame the issue as a matter of patriotism, where white middle-class racial animus would be at a minimum.

None of that could seriously diminish the power of race in dozens of American cities, where the familiar ethnic clashes over political and economic power had taken on a toxic quality when intermingled with the visceral issues of black and white. *Who would run the schools? Who would police the police? What would be built, and where? Who would control the jobs? Who would get the jobs? Where would public money be spent, and on whom . . . and who would bear the burden of paying for that money?* When confrontations between white police and black citizens ignited violence and looting in Newark and half a

dozen other cities in the summer of 1965, the traditional black working class–white Democratic coalition had begun to crack wide open.

Indeed, by 1966, Teddy White's warning that Kennedy had
cited back in 1964 had proven prescient: Northern politicians had
begun to tap into white resentments over black demands. New York
Republican congressman Paul Fino took to the House floor, warning that Kennedy's community development program was "a tool of
black power . . . [D]raw the line and stand up to black power." In
Chicago, Mayor Richard Daley was positioning himself as the protector of neighborhoods, in the face of Martin Luther King's campaign for open housing. In Boston, School Committee chair Louise
Day Hicks was leveraging her resistance to court-ordered busing of
schoolchildren into a likely bid for mayor in two years. In Newark,
another busing foe, an ex-Marine named Anthony Imperiale, was
leading armed patrols to guide white residents through city streets
and planning a run for city council. As for California, that state had
provided an early warning back in 1964 when the same voters who
gave Kennedy a million-vote margin over Goldwater had voted a
ban on open-housing laws by a 2–1 margin and sent former song-
and-dance man George Murphy to the U.S. Senate over state con-
troller Alan Cranston.

The President's convictions and his unparalleled political instincts led him to a continuing search for insulation from the full
force of racial backlash. When he traveled to big cities in 1965 and
'66, it was to visit job centers and the local development corporations that were channeling public and private money into housing
repair and small businesses—and to remind audiences of the moral
bankruptcy of welfare. He'd stop by police precincts to shake hands
and be photographed in front of what the press corps was calling
"the wall of blue"—rows of uniformed police—and argue that
"crime is a civil rights issue no less than the right to equal treatment

at a coffee shop or hotel or public park. For what good is the right
to a public accommodation if a citizen fears to walk the public
streets that will take them there? The hard fact is that fear of random violence imprisons too many of our citizens as surely as does
any Berlin Wall." (The *New York Times* editorially scolded the President for "echoing the repressive rhetoric of George Wallace and
Barry Goldwater." By contrast, some black voices, like Claude
Brown, who'd written an affecting memoir called *Manchild in the
Promised Land*, praised the President. "Who do the editors of
the *Times*, safe behind their doormen suburban enclaves, think are
the principal victims of break-ins, muggings, shootings?" Brown
wrote scornfully, "A significant drop in violent crime would be as
big a boon to blacks in the North as the Voting Rights Act was to
blacks in the South.")

And unlikely as it seems, race was at the heart of his travels to
the heart of white America. In the fall of 1965 he'd gone to Appalachia. He revisited West Virginia, where his primary victory in 1960
had provided crucial evidence to the Democratic power brokers that
a Catholic could win an overwhelmingly Protestant state. He went
back to the mines of Mullens, Beckley, Logan, and Welch, and then
traveled to southeastern Kentucky, to Vortex, Barwick, Hazard. He
spoke at the Letcher County Courthouse in Whitesburg, where he
announced a program to put the jobless miners of the region to
work on the roads and bridges of the region, and where the theme
of his speech was framed by a recent, celebrated book on the plight
of Appalachia.

"Let this be heard loud and clear," Kennedy said. "The long
night of the Cumberlands is ending."

The real message of the speech was clear only to the most politically sophisticated: *When you hear about poverty*, the President was
saying, *do not think of race. Remember these white men who want and*

need work, these white women who struggle to feed and clothe their white children.

For all the determination of Kennedy not to be trapped by rising racial conflicts and resentments, there was simply no way to avoid the political fallout. The busing of schoolchildren that was ordered by federal courts; the lawsuits to force craft unions to open their ranks to blacks; the crime rate that continued to rise year after year (and how could you prove it would have risen much faster without those jobs programs?); the struggle for control of city halls in a dozen cities—all drove white working and blacks further and further apart . . . and politicians from both parties knew it. Alabama's George Wallace, barred from another term as governor, was installing his wife, Lurleen, as a figurehead chief executive while promising to enter presidential primaries across the country.

"Now that they're sufferin' just like we in the South have been, now that they're seein' their little children forced onto buses to take them into crime-ridden schools, now that they see their millionaire President drivin' down their property values and their neighborhoods," Wallace said on *Face the Nation*, "I think the folks up North are ready to stand up. Remember, the Tea Party didn't happen in Mobile or Biloxi—it happened right in Kennedy's backyard. Could be time for another one."

Race, however, was only one reason why Kennedy's job approval ratings had turned anemic. Another powerful force came not from the mean streets of the inner cities but from the pastoral groves of academe.

"Maybe you should count your blessings, Clark," Kennedy said to the president of the University of California in the early spring of 1966. "The students in Hue just burned down our library and cultural center. They're throwing stones at the police in Barcelona. They're using clubs in Yokosuka and Tokyo. Berkeley looks like a walk in the park."

"It *is* a walk in the park, Mr. President," Clark Kerr said. "A walk where a few hundred young men and women have left their clothes off, and what they're smoking isn't sold in any stores. As far as some of my regents are concerned, they might as well be setting fire to the library or . . . I don't know, burning an American flag . . . and with respect, Mr. President, you do *not* need to remind me that I made the world's worst prediction."

It was at a 1959 conference about the coming generation of college students that Kerr had offered this prophecy: "The employers will love this generation, they are not going to press very many grievances, there won't be much trouble, they are going to do their jobs, they are going to be easy to handle. There aren't going to be riots. There aren't going to be revolutions. There aren't going to be many strikes."

Within a few years Clark's prediction—actually an observation offered less as an endorsement than as an assessment—had been thoroughly undermined by a combination of forces. The sheer number of young men and women crowding college campuses, combined with the power of hormones, could spark chaos even when nothing of consequence was involved. In May of 1963, students at Princeton, Brown, and Yale went on a series of rampages in search of women's underwear—so-called panty raids. It could be chalked up to harmless if offbeat fun . . . except that the raids turned violent, with police clubbing students and both sides throwing punches. Another was the example that had been set back in 1960, when Negro college students sat in at segregated lunch counters and boarded segregated buses in the South; it was, in fact, the decision of Berkeley officials to seal off its property from off-campus causes that had led to the massive protests of late 1964. Moreover, the students who had traveled south in the "Freedom Summer" of 1964 had come back to their campus armed with the skills to organize on a whole series of issues:

Why were women required to be in their dorms by 10:00 p.m. on a school night? For that matter, why was it any of the university's business if young adults chose to have sex with each other, whether or not they were married?

Why were no students on the boards of trustees, which set policy for the universities and colleges?

Why was birth control not available at student health centers?

Why was marijuana a criminal offense while the government subsidized the tobacco that killed tens of thousands every year?

Why were men compelled to serve in the Reserve Officers Training Corps in order to graduate?

Why were so many college courses a series of lectures, to hundreds of students at a time, with little chance for face-to-face learning?

There was, above all, a sense of disaffection, or revolt, born less out of any specific grievance than a broader, more diffuse sense of estrangement. There were pieces of it in books that appeared before the 1960s really began, like Jack Kerouac's *On the Road* or Paul Goodman's *Growing Up Absurd* or Sloan Wilson's *The Man in the Gray Flannel Suit*. It could be found in the mockery of television programs and commercials found in *MAD* magazine; in the political jabs of comedian Mort Sahl and the acerbic commentaries about race, drugs, and sex from Lenny Bruce. It could be found in the way the music they had grown up with, the three- and four-chord music of rock and roll, had grown more complex, with lyrics that spoke of sex and drugs—or seemed to. A Peter, Paul and Mary song, "Puff (The Magic Dragon)," about a little boy, was turned into an anthem about marijuana, over the strong objections of its author; and college students heard blatant sexual images in the Kingsmen's "Louie, Louie." (An FBI agent, tasked with deciphering the song, reported that it was "incomprehensible at any speed.")

As hair grew longer, as skirts got shorter, as the air grew more pungent, a T-shirt began appearing on campuses bearing the warning found on an IBM punch card: "I am a student. Do not fold, bend, or mutilate"; and at Berkeley, graduate students sang a mocking "anthem" to the melody of Beethoven's Ninth Symphony:

> Keep the students safe for knowledge
> Keep them loyal, keep them clean,
> This is why we have a college
> Hail to the IBM machine!

Journalists and academics might spend hours debating the source of this behavior; there was no debate about its impact. Among the broad middle class, the specter of young men and women massing in San Francisco's Golden Gate Park, getting high on illegal drugs, shedding their clothes, was appalling. And especially among those without the money to send their children to college, the idea of privileged children—on a track for a far more affluent life than their children would ever know—shutting down their campuses for the "right" to help run the place was somewhere between laughable and contemptible. And at least one increasingly visible California public figure expressed that emotion with perfect pitch—especially after Kerr crafted a compromise that kept protesting students from expulsion.

"Let me read to you what the star of *Bedtime for Bonzo* said about me—*and* you," Kerr was saying to President Kennedy. "I'm quoting here.

"'There is no better example of a failure of leadership than what has been perpetrated at Berkeley, when a small minority of beatniks, radicals, and filthy speech advocates have brought such shame on a great university,' Ronald Reagan declared. 'And the silence of Governor Brown—and, for that matter, the President—is deafening. Mr. Kennedy, it should not take a "profile in courage" to call to account those who break the law and defile fundamental moral standards.'"

"Actually," Kennedy said, "I'm thinking it *is* time I said something about this. I know I spoke at Charter Day four years ago, but your commencement—"

"Consider yourself invited," Kerr said.

"I am painfully aware," Kennedy said to the tens of thousands gathered at Berkeley's Memorial Stadium, "that many of you regard the commencement speech as that endless interlude between celebrations where you are compelled to hear earnest advice that is as forgettable as it is well-intentioned. Yet, there *have* been events like this one when the words that were spoken had lasting impact. Winston Churchill proclaimed the descent of an 'Iron Curtain' at Westminster College in Fulton, Missouri; George Marshall announced the postwar European recovery plan at Harvard; and there are those who trace the origins of the Nuclear Test Ban Treaty to a commencement speech I gave at American University. And at another campus, the University of Michigan"—here he waited for the good-natured boos aimed at Cal's frequent Rose Bowl rival to subside—"I proposed an idea that became the Peace Corps and then AmeriCorps, which have seen tens of thousands of young people spend two years of their lives to make a better country and a better world.

"Only a few years ago, the competition for your time would have been the lure of affluence—well-paying, comfortable jobs at our major corporations and industries. Now there is another temptation: what we might call the temptation of Dionysus, the god of celebration, of excess."

(There were knowing grins among the White House Press Corps at that line.)

"It is," Kennedy said, "noteworthy that the troubadour of your generation, who once sang of changes that were 'blowin' in the wind,' now beckons you to 'dance beneath the diamond sky, with one hand waving free' and to 'forget about today until tomorrow.' But it is also troublesome. Because we dare *not* forget about today until tomorrow. When the music stops, when the dancing ends, when tomorrow morning comes, the challenges of today remain. And to confront those challenges, the temptations of Dionysus are shallow diversions. What is needed, rather, is the challenge of Sisyphus, the king of Corinth condemned for his sins to roll a stone endlessly up a hill, only to see it roll down again . . . forever.

"There are times when the labors of justice seem endless; but the good news is, they are not. In your own short lifetimes, you have seen the evils of discrimination begin to end; you have seen the threat of nuclear catastrophe replaced by an era of negotiations, and the poison of radiation cleared from the skies. Now new tasks await: there are still the hungry to be fed, the homeless to be sheltered, the young to be taught, the old to be succored. There is work to fill a hundred lifetimes. Each of you has one. If you do not help in the work we have, who will? And if not now, when?"

The speech won praise from editorial pages, while *Time* magazine offered faint praise for the President's "belated but well-earned verbal spanking he delivered to the bearded and bra-less brats of Berkeley." From Ken Kesey, the author and psychedelic drug champion, traveling with his Merry Pranksters across the southern United States, came the cryptic comment: "Since Mr. Kennedy is clearly off the bus, we invite him, and Jackie, if she is so inclined, to join us *on* the bus for further journeys."

The President's words, however, did little to lessen the consequences of the cultural upheaval, at least in California. The mix of disorder, dissent, and excesses at Berkeley and other campuses was a key reason why Ronald Reagan defeated Governor Pat Brown by more than 700,000 votes—and instantly became a potential presidential candidate. His victory in a state that was a microcosm of America was, in pollster Harris's memo to the White House, "a clear warning that millions of Americans believe 'the guard rails have come off,' that their beliefs and values are under assault. Mr. President, your most urgent political task over the rest of your term is to convince the nation that you are the guardian of those beliefs and values."

Unfortunately for Kennedy, he was learning that he could no longer count on one of his most reliable resources in carrying his message to the public.

"You can think of it as the 'six-year itch,'" Arthur Schlesinger had warned the President as they sat with a clutch of advisors a few weeks after the midterms with the morning papers spread out on a coffee table in the Oval Office. "It's not just the voters that punish every president in his sixth year; in fact, you got off relatively lightly. The press has seen and heard your act by now. You've been on their front pages and on their evening news just about every single day. You can count on them looking for the next chapter."

Even if historically predictable, that change in the press's affections would have unsettled the President. He and his family had befriended the press, shared secrets, sometimes bought their assistance or loyalty or silence, sometimes enlisted them as allies, even as go-betweens, as when ABC's John Scali carried significant messages to Soviet officials during the Cuban missile crisis. Newspapers, magazines, and television had celebrated the Kennedys' tastes and glamour; what could have been an unflattering portrayal of wealth and privilege instead became a celebration of American royalty. And in his first White House years, John Kennedy could count on the discretion of the press to ignore the details of his private life.

When the story of what happened to Clark Mollenhoff and the *Des Moines Register* began to circulate—as it inevitably did—something changed. Now the use—or misuse—of official power was not being directed at greedy steel companies, or thuggish labor unions, or corrupt politicians, or the bosses of organized crime. Now that power had been used to threaten one of their own: a newspaper that was investigating a serious charge against the sitting president of the United States. Maybe the story wasn't conclusive enough to print; maybe it was a mix of rumor and innuendo that wouldn't stand up under scrutiny. But that wasn't the point. The President had unleashed the full might of his office to threaten the newspaper's parent company with financial ruin.

Maybe the press couldn't follow up on that story; maybe it crossed the line into the personal at a time when no serious journalist would have argued that "the personal is political." But there was nothing to keep America's newspapers, magazines, and television networks from casting a much more jaundiced eye on the *public* record of the administration, to illustrate the kind of pressure that had been applied to one of their own.

And that's what many of them began to do.

HOW JFK SILENCED HIS CRITICS, a *Wall Street Journal* headline read, introducing a story that detailed how the White

House and the Democratic Party funded sham "citizens' groups" that filed complaints against right-wing radio broadcasters as the 1964 campaign began. With the FCC applying the "Fairness Doctrine" rule that required radio stations to broadcast contrasting viewpoints, dozens of the Kennedys' severest critics simply left the airwaves. An accompanying story reported that Robert Kennedy, then attorney general, had urged the IRS to aggressively audit conservative organizations and individuals. ("If true," Richard Nixon argued in a speech to Illinois auto dealers, "it is an unconscionable, indefensible, if not impeachable abuse of power. Just because a president does it does *not* mean it's legal.")

A month later another newspaper ran a three-part excerpt from a new book by Clark Mollenhoff. The title alone conveyed the thrust of the book: *The Imperial Presidency: John Kennedy and the Abuse of Power*. Even more eye-opening was the venue in which it appeared: the *Washington Post*, whose late publisher Phil Graham had been one of the President's closest friends and supporters in the press. ("Publisher's ink is thicker than water," his widow, Katharine Graham, explained to friends. "What they did to John Cowles is simply unacceptable.") The excerpts went back to the 1962 fight over the steel price hikes, and spelled out in detail the threats of income tax audits and expense account scrutiny, as well as the use of FBI agents to interrogate reporters. Mollenhoff also included a cryptic reference to "the summary deportation of a witness, an attractive 'party girl' named Ellen Rometsch, who may have had crucial information about financial and personal transgressions on both ends of Pennsylvania Avenue."

There were even stories about White House "image making"—a relatively new term that was becoming familiar to news readers and viewers, as reporters tried to lift the curtain that once shielded manipulation from public view. An *Esquire* magazine reporter named

Tom Wolfe managed to ingratiate himself with a White House advance team long enough to write an eye-opening piece—"If There's Room for Everybody, the Room's Too Damn Small!"—detailing the search for a venue small enough to ensure that the President spoke before a full house. An essay by *New York* magazine's Gloria Steinem explored the uncritical, even fawning profiles of Jacqueline Kennedy in women's magazines.

"The distance from Eleanor Roosevelt's crusade for the poor to Jacqueline Kennedy's 'crusade' for designer gowns and White House furnishings is a long, disheartening one," Steinem wrote. "One can hope that in the future, a First Lady will embody less of the feminine mystique and more of a feminist one—not to mention the hope that at some point, we might take seriously the concept of a woman occupying the West Wing of the White House."

Standing alone, none of these afflictions—racial division, generational division, a less deferential press—would have been enough to seriously damage President Kennedy's standing in the face of a buoyant economy and a more or less peaceful world. Together, they led to a polarized electorate, one that was almost evenly divided in its assessment of his presidency.

And by the time the 1968 campaign hit its final stage, the choice faced by the country fully reflected that wide and deep division.

If the 1968 campaign had been fought on the terrain of the previous three decades . . . had someone other than John Kennedy been occupying the White House . . . Richard Nixon would have been the all but inevitable candidate of the Republican Party.

Ever since FDR battled to a third term in the shadow of a second world war, events beyond America's borders had dominated presidential campaigns: the United States was immersed in that war

in 1944; then came the cold war, communism, Korea, nuclear testing, the missile gap, peace in a nuclear age, all of which had been
decisive issues in the campaigns that followed. For Nixon—who
had come to prominence exposing the Soviet espionage of Alger
Hiss; who had debated Nikita Khrushchev in the model kitchen of
a U.S. cultural exhibit in Moscow; who had traveled the world since
his narrow 1960 defeat—the international stage was his natural
habitat. (That was why his 1962 run for governorship of California
was so misbegotten, he realized after he'd lost: his vision was focused on the future of Asia, the relevance of NATO. Highway
construction plans and school budgets put him to sleep.)

Nixon had spent his years in the wilderness wisely, endorsing
Goldwater in 1964, speaking for every GOP nominee who'd have
him in the 1966 midterms, challenging John Kennedy's foreign policies in speeches and magazine articles. He'd stayed silent as his most
formidable potential ally, Michigan governor George Romney, self-
destructed in a single disastrous television interview. (When asked
by WKBD's Lou Gordon why the Republican Party had chosen
Goldwater despite his unsettling views, Romney replied, "Because
we had a convention of delegates who'd been brainwashed by the
far right." In a last-minute effort to recover, Governor Romney appeared on the debut episode of *Rowan & Martin's Laugh-In*, a new
topical comedy show, repeatedly putting an oversize foot in his
mouth, to no avail.) By the time 1968 began, only the potential
entry of New York governor Nelson Rockefeller seemed to stand
between Nixon and the nomination; and for the increasingly Southern and Western base of the party, Rockefeller embodied everything
they'd been fighting against for almost thirty years.

Except . . . the country wasn't thinking all that much about the
outside world.

There were no American boys fighting and dying in a faraway

war, as there had been in 1952 when he'd run with Ike the first time. There was no dangerous standoff in Berlin, or a cold war that periodically threatened to turn hot, as there had been in 1960, when "Experience Counts" was his theme. The U.S. and China were opening embassies in each other's capitals, and the Cuban embargo had been suspended since early 1967. Now America was turning inward. For the rank and file of the Republican Party, the concerns were *here*: crime on the city streets, outbursts of disorder and violence, a younger generation at war with traditional morals. Their fears may have been overwrought—writer Jimmy Breslin noted that "most of these Republicans live in places where the muggers couldn't afford the bus fare to get to them"—but they were real enough as far as motivating their votes went.

It wasn't that Nixon didn't *understand* these impulses. Hell, he'd pretty much *invented* the "forgotten American" theme in his very first congressional campaign back in 1946 and saved his political life with it in his "Checkers" speech in 1952: the returning vet with the wife, kids, dog, mortgage; the man who lived a simple, unglamorous life; the man who promised to restore clean language to the White House. It was just that there was someone else who could speak to the disaffections of his party in a way that Richard Nixon couldn't . . . and who could bring to a campaign something that John Kennedy had shown to be of enormous value: a candidate who was also a *star*.

It was very easy to underestimate Ronald Reagan. It was also proving politically fatal.

When he'd announced in 1966 that he was running for governor of California, the actor jokes began. ("Ronald Reagan for governor?"

studio chief Jack Warner supposedly said. "No, no, Jimmy Stewart for governor, Reagan for Stewart's best friend.") When he had faced off against San Francisco mayor George Christopher in the Republican primary, all the smart money was on the moderate mayor. When Reagan won the primary by a 2–1 margin, Governor Pat Brown's staff all but threw a party. Their man had beaten Richard Nixon four years earlier, for God's sake. This actor would be a pushover. When Reagan won with a 700,000-vote plurality, the joking was replaced by a blend of speculation and disbelief: *Could this guy actually try for the presidency?*

By the time his first year in office was over, the answer to that question was: *Well, yeah.* Three weeks after taking office, he'd gotten the board of regents to fire Clark Kerr as university president; within six months he'd worked out a budget with his Democratic legislature and also signed the nation's most liberal abortion bill. The only setback to Reagan's presidential bid was a charge by columnist Drew Pearson that a "homosexual ring" existed inside the Governor's inner staff. And by the spring, that issue had faded. Now the question was how openly to pursue a campaign, and it turned out that the current occupant of the White House was the key to their strategy.

"When we looked at the terrain," Reagan advisor Lyn Nofziger recalled, "we saw that we were in the same place Kennedy was in back in '60. We knew we'd take a big hit on 'experience.' Kennedy did, and he'd been in office for fourteen years, not one. But the big mountain he had to climb was to prove he could win. That's what West Virginia was all about. For us, Nebraska and Oregon would be our West Virginias . . . and JFK in the White House was one of our best arguments: *'That's* the kind of candidate we need!'"

Reagan never set foot in either state; he was on the ballots because state officials could list candidates whether or not they'd declared for president. What voters in both states saw—over and over again—was a five-minute television film produced by a group called Republicans for Victory.

"Six years ago, in the nation's second biggest state, a weak Democratic incumbent soundly defeated the nation's best-known Republican," the film began, with clips of a victorious Governor Brown and an embittered Richard Nixon announcing "my last press conference."

"Four years ago," the film continued, "a new voice arose in the West, a new champion for American values." And there was a minute-long clip from Reagan's 1964 TV speech for Goldwater, "A Time for Choosing," including its most famous line:

"You and I have a rendezvous with destiny. We'll preserve for our children this, the last best hope of man on earth, or we will sentence them to take the last step into a thousand years of darkness."

"Two years ago," the film went on, "that new voice—that new leader—won a landslide victory over that same Democratic governor."

Then, over a split-screen image—a buoyant, smiling Reagan; a dour, defeated Nixon—the film concluded: "Now, as the campaign to take back the White House begins, ask yourself: Who embodies our values, shares our convictions, and can win in November?"

When Reagan won 41 percent of the Nebraska primary vote on May 14, finishing just six points behind Nixon, ABC's Bill Laurence observed that "to paraphrase this network's famous sports show, Mr. Reagan is enjoying the joy of a close defeat, while Mr. Nixon is suffering the agony of a Pyrrhic victory." Two weeks later in Oregon, where liberal Republicans like Senator Mark Hatfield and Governor Tom McCall thrived, Reagan won 35 percent of the vote.

"There is now no doubt," said NBC's Sander Vanocur, "that Ronald Reagan is a viable contender. The question is: Will he formally enter the race? And if he does, can he overcome the formidable phalanx of supporters that Mr. Nixon has in his corner . . . and can he shake loose the delegates that have declared their allegiance to the former vice president?"

Five days later Reagan came close to answering the first question when he set out on a five-day, 7,000-mile "non-campaign" speaking tour that took him to New Orleans, Charlotte, Fort Lauderdale, Miami Beach, Chicago, Columbus, and Cleveland. "Welfare cheats" and "lawbreakers" were his special targets. A week later, after he had won all of California's delegates in the state's uncontested primary, Governor Reagan answered the question directly. "Yes," he said, "the voters have made this decision for me. I'm a candidate for the Republican presidential nomination."

"The timing was critical," chief delegate hunter F. Clifton White said later. "Had he waited until the convention was about to open, Nixon's big guns—Goldwater, Thurmond, John Tower—might have gotten commitments from enough delegates to win. Ron's announcement kept just enough of them in play."

As it turned out, what actually determined the Republican presidential nominee was . . . the flip of a coin.

The tactic had been suggested not by any of his aides but by the candidate himself in a meeting in his Fontainebleau hotel suite two days before the convention began.

"I don't think I'm being cocky about this," Reagan said, "but if I could get in front of these delegates and speak to them, I think we could pull enough of them away from Dick to stop a first-ballot nomination. And then . . ."

"And then you'd win it," Stu Spencer said. "The question is how to do it. They're not about to let you have that audience all to itself."

Reagan grinned at Spencer and shook his head.

"Of course not, Stu," he said. "But what if the delegates *demand* it?"

On Saturday, Nevada governor Paul Laxalt and two dozen conservative Republicans stood in front of a press conference and announced their intention to back a new convention rule: every candidate seeking the nomination would be invited to give a ten-minute speech to the delegates just before the balloting began.

"With debates now a permanent part of our political landscape," Laxalt said, "it is a logical next step for the men and women choosing our nominee to hear them make their case before casting their ballots. We have seen," he said in a clear reference to Nixon, "how critical it is for our nominee to be able to make our case in the public arena."

The Nixon campaign pushed back hard. Speechwriter William Safire drafted a statement labeling the rule "a cheap cynical contrivance to turn the campaign into a carnival." Their campaign, however, was caught in a whipsaw. Governor Nelson Rockefeller's one slim chance at the nomination was the same as Reagan's—to push the fight to a second ballot. His campaign chief, Leonard Hall, urged the Rockefeller delegates to support the rule. Across the ideological divide, dozens of conservative delegates had been prodded into supporting Nixon by party heavyweights like Strom Thurmond and John Tower—but their hearts were with Reagan.

"Nixon has my vote on the first ballot," a South Carolinian said to Thurmond, "but I'm voting to hear these men speak. If we learned anything from Kennedy, it's that good ideas don't matter much if you can't communicate them." With telephone calls and telegrams deluging the convention, with "Let them speak!" chants disrupting convention business for minutes at a time, the delegates adopted the rule change by a 100-vote margin. And when the flip of a coin determined that Reagan would speak last, "that's when we knew we had it," Nofziger said.

The delegates listened in sullen silence to Rockefeller's speech . . . those that showed up for it. They'd been urged by the convention chair not to repeat the 1964 moment when delegates booed and hissed Rockefeller's remarks.

They dutifully cheered Richard Nixon's talk, which charged the Kennedy White House with "a systematic abuse of power directed at its political enemies and a systematic weakness in dealing with our Communist enemies abroad and the enemy of crime and disorder at home."

And then Reagan came to the rostrum. Speaking without a teleprompter, without a text, he spoke of a letter he had been asked to write for a time capsule, to be opened in a hundred years. He spoke of writing about "the erosion of freedom taking place under Democratic rule in this country, the invasion of private rights, the controls and restrictions on the vitality of the great free economy that we enjoy."

And as he reached the climax of his speech, the hall grew still.

"And suddenly it dawned on me: those who would read this letter a hundred years from now will know whether we met our challenge . . . Whether they will have the freedom that we have known up until now will depend on what we do here. Will they look back with appreciation and say, 'Thank God for those people in 1968 who headed off that loss of freedom, who kept us now a hundred years later free'? And if we fail, they probably won't get to read the letter at all because it spoke of individual freedom and they won't be allowed to talk of that or read of it.

"This is our challenge and this is why we're here in this hall tonight. Better than we've ever done before, we've got to go out and communicate to the world that we carry the message they're waiting for."

It took twenty minutes for the cheers to stop. From their glassed-in booths, the network anchors and analysts could see furious arguments breaking out in a dozen state delegations as individual delegates demanded permission to change their votes.

Before the candidates spoke, Richard Nixon's private count showed that he would have twenty-five votes more than he needed for the nomination. When the first ballot ended, he was seventy-five votes short, as his support in the South and mountain West had eroded. On the third ballot, Ronald Reagan won with a sixty-five vote margin.

His choice of running mate was as unprecedented as his own victory.

"Representative Gerald Ford was the right choice four years ago," Reagan said, "and four more years of experience makes him an even better choice today."

At a post-convention dinner, Governor Reagan interrupted the celebration to raise a champagne glass.

"First, I propose a toast to the Soviet Union, for its exquisite sense of timing. If they'd invaded Czechoslovakia a month *before* our convention, instead of a month after, Dick Nixon would be doing the celebrating tonight; it would have played right to his strength. And I also propose a toast to the man without whom this would not have happened," he said. "To the man who convinced our party to care about *how* we say *what* we say: to John Fitzgerald Kennedy."

A few weeks later, the Democratic nominee would have reason to toast that same man.

———

It was eight o'clock in the evening in mid-October 1967 when Senator Hubert Humphrey sat down next to an intense, bespectacled thirty-eight-year-old man in the inner office of his suite on the second floor of the Beaux Arts Old Senate Office Building.

"All right, Al," he said. "Suppose you tell me why this conversation is so confidential it couldn't be listed on my schedule and had to wait till my staff cleared out. When I told Gartner and Connell I was staying late, they decided I was having a *very* private meeting with that secretary on the Education Committee."

"I want to offer you your best chance to be president," the man said. "It's just that I want to offer it to you before all those tested pros around you start telling you that I'm crazy."

"I don't think anyone around me thinks you're crazy, Al. Driven, obsessed, a royal pain in the backside, sure. But as far as I'm concerned, you've earned the right to a hearing."

Al Lowenstein was, by conventional measurements, a college teacher and administrator, a lawyer, a former congressional staffer—he'd worked for Humphrey a decade earlier as a foreign policy specialist—and an advocate for liberal causes, most specifically civil rights. To hundreds if not thousands of people, he was a force of nature, a Pied Piper, a man who could sweep through a city, gathering an eclectic mix of people to his side for hours-long meals, day-long conversations, all in the service of whatever cause Lowenstein was embracing. He'd sneaked into Southwest Africa in 1959, uncovering brutalities committed by the racist South African government administering that territory; he'd spent a year crusading to bring that story to public attention; he'd recruited foot soldiers for Mississippi's Freedom Summer in 1964, pushed to get the Freedom

Democratic Party seated at the convention that year. When President Kennedy disengaged from Vietnam, he'd organized student government presidents and student newspaper editors to support Kennedy's policy, and did the same when the President opened diplomatic relations with China and ended the Cuban trade embargo. There was something about his persistence, his earnestness, his apparent guilelessness, that endeared him to an astonishing breadth of people; he counted Eleanor Roosevelt and William F. Buckley Jr. as friends and admirers.

"I'll begin by conceding a point: if you run for president the conventional way, you have a perfectly decent chance for the nomination. You'll have solid black support; the liberal reformers will be on your side; and you'll have half of labor on your side, although it'll likely be the much smaller half."

"No argument there," Humphrey said. "Meany as much as told me he'd be going all in with Scoop. He pretty much called the President an appeaser the last time we spoke. 'Apple doesn't fall far from the tree,' George said. 'Joe caved in to Hitler; Jack's caving in to the Kremlin.'"

"Which still leaves you Reuther's auto workers, some of the other industrials—"

"Except for all those folks who make the bombers, the fighter jets, the missiles . . . Scoop never met a weapon system he didn't love."

"Understood," Lowenstein said. "So what about the political leaders—the 'bosses,' as we Manhattan folks say."

Humphrey shrugged. "Daley, Lawrence, Unruh, Green—some of 'em think I'm too close to the blacks, some of them wish I spent a little less time on campuses . . . and all of them probably have the same question the press does, which is—"

"Which is: 'Can he win?' Which is why I am here. The only way you're going to win the nomination is to do what Kennedy did eight years ago: prove you can win by *winning*. And the way to do that, Senator, is to run as John Kennedy's third term."

Humphrey smiled.

"You may have noticed that there's an ambitious young secretary of defense who I'm sure is thinking pretty much the same thing," he said, "and Bobby would be a *real* third Kennedy term."

"Not a chance, and you know it," Lowenstein said. "In the first place, you don't get to run for president in your first election unless you've won a world war, like Ike did. Exceptions to the rule? Sure: William Howard Taft and Herbert Hoover. How'd they workout? Bobby has to start somewhere else, to get the rough edges off. Besides, it's just too soon. You saw what that Texas senator said on *Meet the Press*, didn't you? 'This is America, not some foreign emirate: we don't do dynasties.' George Bush is right. It's just not possible for Bobby, and Teddy's not even thirty-six yet. So give me five, okay, ten minutes to tell you why and how you run and win as the rightful heir."

It took longer than that—no one ever said Al Lowenstein was concise—but the argument was clear. First, while the country was evenly divided about Kennedy's record, Democrats were not; the President's approval rating was at 64 percent within his party, and the number was artificially deflated because of his staggering unpopularity among Southerners, most of whom still called themselves Democrats.

"Those folks will be solidly for Wallace, but there aren't any Southern primaries; he did okay in Indiana in '64, and he might get votes in Ohio and California if he decides to spend money and run there, but he won't matter because those segregated Southern delegations will never be seated—not after the rule changes at the last convention. Who *will* be seated? Biracial delegations, with strong feelings about Kennedy.

"Now look at the terrain on which you'll be fighting," Lowenstein continued. "Except for California, none of the major states have primaries—or if they do, they're in name only. Some of those state organizations picked their convention delegates months ago. One of these days we're going to have real primaries, where the people choose the delegates, but that's not this year's fight. As far as the Vice President is concerned, it's still 1960—or 1940, or whatever year Symington is living in. He still thinks he can wait for the convention to settle on everybody's second choice. So you might ask: Where are the real primaries? That's not the real question," Lowenstein said. "The real question is: Where are the *first* real primaries, where Humphrey victories can answer the Can-he-win? question before the spring arrives. New Hampshire and Wisconsin."

"Wisconsin is my backyard, Al—I was the Democrats' 'third senator' before the party finally won a Senate seat there in '62. But New Hampshire? They don't like government, they don't like 'big spenders'—"

"And they don't like foreign wars, and they don't have mandatory voting," Lowenstein added. "The way to win—there and in Wisconsin—is with something that's never been seen before . . . a guerrilla army.

"You've got a whole slice of the younger generation that's spent the last decade engaged in political work," Lowenstein pointed out. "Not party politics, but politics in the broadest sense. Kennedy brought them into the Peace Corps; they've lived in villages in Asia and Africa, where they've organized food co-ops and schools. He pulled them into AmeriCorps projects from Watts to Harlan County. They've risked their lives to run voter registration drives in

Lowndes County, and helped Cesar Chavez organize farmworkers in Delano. They may not all know it, but some of them—maybe a lot of them—believe they might have been drafted into a war in Vietnam or Cuba or God knows where, and they want a president who'll keep the peace. If they could, they'd vote JFK in for a third term. You read the polls: Kennedy's fifteen to twenty points higher with young people than with the general public. And they know what I know: there's been no stronger fighter for peace than Hubert Humphrey. They're smart, fearless, and they live off the land. We can put five hundred of them in New Hampshire for the cost of one full-page ad in the *New York Times*."

"Just what I need, Al: five hundred people with beards, beads, jeans, and tie-dyed shirts parading through those bucolic New England towns."

"Senator," Lowenstein said with a broad smile, "I'm way ahead of you."

On December 4, 1967, Hubert Humphrey announced his second run for the presidency in front of the Humphrey Drug Store in Huron, South Dakota, where he had once worked as a pharmacist for his father. He was joined by George McGovern, the state's junior senator and a member with Humphrey of the informal Senate Peace Caucus, who endorsed him with the assertion that "no one in Washington has done more in the cause of a less dangerous world than this 'Happy Warrior' for peace."

On that same day, four dozen young men and women from colleges and universities across the country set up a "Youth for Humphrey" office on the second floor of a building on Elm and Granite Streets in Manchester, New Hampshire, just across from Veteran's Memorial Park. The men wore button-down shirts and sport jackets; their hair was trimmed to fall above their ears. The women wore medium-length skirts and blouses with appropriate underclothing. (LOSE THE GREASE, WIN THE PEACE, read one banner stretched across the headquarters' wall.)

Not all the volunteers were of college age. AmeriCorps official Tom Hayden took a leave of absence from his post to relocate to New Hampshire, where he led workshops on how to approach voters—and answered scornful charges of "Co-option!" from his former SDS colleagues. From his faculty post at Wesleyan University in Connecticut, former White House aide Richard Goodwin signed up as an all-purpose speechwriter/media hand. His presence might have raised eyebrows among the political press—was the Kennedy White House taking sides?—had any political reporter bothered to look into the Youth for Humphrey movement. Their time was spent at the official Humphrey headquarters eight blocks away, or at the bar of the Sheraton-Wayfarer Hotel, where reporters and aides from every campaign traded gossip and old war stories.

It wasn't until ten days before the primary that the dimensions of Al Lowenstein's "guerrilla army" became evident. Hundreds, maybe a thousand or more, mostly young recruits were sleeping in the basements of churches, invited in by ministers who took the gospel of peace literally; they were crashing in the guest rooms and garages of like-minded voters.

("I live every day with the memory of the Cuban missile crisis," one grocer told a Humphrey volunteer who had knocked on his door. "If Scoop Jackson had been president, I don't know if any of us would be around today. So if you and your friends are looking for a place to sleep, I've got a large pantry and a spare room upstairs.")

With Vice President Symington staying out of the primaries, and George Wallace shunning a state where racial and cultural disorder appeared only on television screens, New Hampshire came down to a two-man fight . . . although there were a few moments when a more dramatic possibility appeared. Paul Corbin had a checkered connection to the Kennedy family that went back to the 1960 Wisconsin primary. He was distrusted by almost everyone around the President . . . except his brother Bobby, whose children called Corbin "Uncle Paul." One indication of his tangled background and beliefs was that he had once been a card-carrying member of the Communist Party . . . and a business partner of Senator Joseph McCarthy. Now a *Boston Globe* reporter found him at a telephone bank just across the state line in Haverhill, Massachusetts, where he was organizing a write-in campaign for Robert Kennedy. It took a personal phone call from Bobby—after prodding by the President—to persuade Corbin to fold his tents.

Scoop Jackson, with the backing of the state's AFL-CIO chapters, worked the textile and shoe factories that lined Manchester's Merrimack River. He had praise for President Kennedy's domestic agenda, but on defense matters he made his differences clear.

"To those who say we must take risks for peace by cutting the meat from our military muscle, I say you are unwittingly risking war. I'm not a hawk and I'm not a dove. I just don't want my country to be a pigeon."

"Who is it," Humphrey answered in a speech at Saint Anselm College, "who risks war? Did John Kennedy 'risk war' when he stood up to Soviet aggression with firmness and flexibility? When the two great nuclear superpowers began to move from confrontation to negotiation, did that risk war? Do we really want to return to a world where one miscalculation can mean the deaths of millions?"

This was the message that Humphrey's young volunteers were carrying to the increasingly suburban southern towns of Nashua and Brattleboro, up to Berlin in the north. ("For God's sake," one New Hampshire native said to a group of volunteers. "It's BER-lin . . .

not the city in Germany!") In the last week of the campaign, that message appeared in a new venue, in the form of a one-minute commercial that ran on every Boston television station (WMUR, the state's only VHF TV station, was so insignificant that it was still broadcasting only in black-and-white). Reporters soon labeled the commercial "the *Dr. Strangelove* ad," because it opened with a montage of nuclear explosions before dissolving into pictures of Kennedy.

"This did *not* happen," the voice of actor Gregory Peck intoned, "because the right man was president. On March 12," he added, as the image of Humphrey appeared, "the people of New Hampshire can make sure it will *never* happen . . . by choosing the right man again." The ad ended with a quick black-and-white shot of Kennedy's 1961 inaugural—"Let Us Begin!"—dissolving to a full-color shot of Humphrey—"Let Us Continue!"

The lavish ad buy surprised many in the political world, given that the Humphrey campaign had complained consistently about being strapped for cash. They would have been even more surprised had they learned the source of the money: a satchel filled with $100 bills—$25,000 worth—that had been supplied by the reclusive Las Vegas billionaire Howard Hughes. His obsessive fear of germs was only surpassed by his fear of atmospheric nuclear testing, and among the candidates for president, he saw Humphrey as the one least likely to resume them.

Whether it was the advertising, the swarm of volunteers, or the less-than-dynamic campaigning of Jackson, Humphrey won New Hampshire by a decisive twelve-point margin. His April victories in Wisconsin and Massachusetts not only ended Jackson's campaign but led to an event almost unheard-of in Democratic presidential history.

It was the President himself who engineered it.

"We're in for a hell of a fight," he said to his political team in early May, demonstrating once more his grasp of the political terrain. "In '60, Nixon won 219 electoral votes. With reapportionment, those same states would give him 238. Throw in Texas and South Carolina, and he's president. And don't forget, he damn near took Illinois, Missouri, and New Jersey. If Reagan somehow pulls it off—and I'm not convinced he can't—then Wallace stays out of November and Reagan takes the whole South. And if you don't think Reagan can win in those big Midwestern states, take a look at the working-class and middle-class suburbs when he ran for governor. We're going be drawing to an inside straight in November, and the last thing we need is a brawl in Chicago."

Four days later, one of America's best-known columnists shared an off-the-record coffee with Kennedy in the Oval Office, and two days later Walter Lippmann wrote that "those closest to the President say he is quietly counseling top party leaders to fall in behind the presidential campaign of Hubert Humphrey."

("When it's in a Lippmann column," one senator cracked, "it's about as 'quiet' as a stick of dynamite.")

When Chicago mayor Richard Daley, California assembly speaker Jesse Unruh, and New Jersey governor Richard Hughes all threw their backing behind Humphrey in a single forty-eight-hour period, the Democrats—for the first time anyone could remember—produced a consensus candidate.

"It may be the most unexpected turn of events in modern American political history," wrote R. W. Apple in the *New York Times*. "A party whose presidential campaigns look like a meeting of the Hatfields and the McCoys has suddenly taken on the appearance of the Trapp Family Singers. Those devotees of fractious conventions may want to rethink their travel plans to Chicago this August."

That proved to be an understatement. Even the traditional last-minute choice of a running mate was abandoned in favor of a Sunday-night rally, where Humphrey introduced Tennessee senator Al Gore as his running mate.

"Hubert knows the South is pretty much gone," Gore said to his son, Al Gore Jr., when he got the call. "But he thinks I could make a difference in some of the border states—may give him a shot back home."

"Makes sense," Al Gore Jr. said. "It'd be damn hard for a national candidate to lose his home state."

When the convention swiftly unseated the all-white Southern delegations and rushed the platform through by voice vote, NBC's David Brinkley observed that "while political predictions are notoriously unreliable, you can take this one to the bank: as Lincoln would have put it, the world will little note nor long remember a single moment from the 1968 Chicago Democratic convention."

"Mr. President? Mrs. Kennedy said to tell you she's waiting in the Oval Room."

"Okay, George," Kennedy said to his butler as he was eased out of the tub and slipped into a polo shirt and a pair of chinos. The Yellow Oval Room was one of her proudest accomplishments, a centerpiece of the years-long White House restoration she had supervised. The room opened out onto the Truman Balcony, with its spectacular views of the Mall and the Monuments; it was where many of the Kennedys' close friends ended up after a White House dance or dinner party. Now only his wife awaited him, wearing a pink cashmere sweater and high-waist trousers, her hair long, loose, and straight.

It was ending the way his own campaign had ended: too close to call, too many states in the balance. Not the South—that was going to be all Reagan, once Wallace had decided to take a pass. Reagan had said nice, safe things about Wallace: "He's dwelling mainly on law and order, patriotism, and so forth, and these are very attractive subjects, and I'm sure there are very few people in disagreement." Reagan had told a story about standing up for a Negro football player back in college, and explained how the civil rights laws Wallace opposed weren't about race at all, just about an overbearing federal government. *Well,* Kennedy thought, *that'll be part of my legacy: a Democratic president who delivered the South to the Republican Party for a generation.*

In fact, it *would* be his legacy on the line in so many ways. He'd pulled the country away from its cold war outlook, but how much would they respond to Humphrey's plea to "keep the peace!" after Reagan began quoting lines from Kennedy's own speeches. ("For only when our arms are sufficient beyond doubt," Reagan would intone, "can we be certain beyond doubt that they will never be employed"—and then he'd ask with a chuckle, "Guess what warmonger said that?")

That's why the Humphrey campaign was beaming an unprecedented number of TV commercials into American homes during the daytime, when women were home.

"I was talking to a poli-sci professor last week," said adman Tony Schwartz. "He says if Humphrey wins, it'll be because of what he called a 'gender gap.' I'll put it more simply: if we win, it'll be because five million American women lied to their husbands about how they voted. If their husbands see Reagan and say 'Tough guy,' we need their wives to see Reagan and say 'Dangerous guy.'"

And it wasn't just the war-and-peace question on which his eight years would be judged. He'd brought a whole new generation to public service, but another part of that generation had put fear into the hearts of their elders with their behavior, and it was still unclear whether voters saw him as an inspiration or a baleful influence. He'd opened doors once closed to Negroes—William Hastie now sat on the Supreme Court, its first Negro justice after he'd replaced retiring Chief Earl Warren with Justice Arthur Goldberg—but would those open doors be seen as a step toward equality or special privilege? Would he get credit for trying to resolve an ancient American dilemma, or for feeding agitation? He'd presided over a strong economy, no doubt about that, but his onetime Senate colleague Al Gore cautioned him against excessive optimism.

"I was talking with Al Jr. last week," Gore said. "Bright kid. He was worried that after such a long run of good times, voters might take it for granted. I told him he could test it out when *he* ran for president some day, but he might have a point."

Well, Kennedy thought, *our labor friends are all in.* They were sending mail to every union household in thirty states—millions of pieces of mail, pounding away at Reagan's opposition to social programs; replaying a speech of his where he'd called the new Medicare program for the elderly "right out of Karl Marx's playbook"; warning of his hostility to Social Security and other New Deal programs. *But how strong are those arguments?* he wondered. *The New Deal was more than thirty years ago, and those working-class kids are suburban parents worried about their schools and taxes.*

Whatever the outcome two days from now, there was his own future to consider. He'd be fifty-one when his term ended, and his future had been one of the press's favorite guessing games. Only Teddy Roosevelt had been younger when his presidency ended, and Kennedy had neither the health nor the inclination to set out on a worldwide hunting trip. As for his quest to reclaim the White House, the two-term limit took care of that.

And it wasn't as if Bobby was going to be able to extend the Kennedy legacy in the Oval Office. Bobby had wanted to run, even stepped down as Defense secretary in mid-1967 to take over the Office of Community Development. "I need to be seen putting people to work, and opening businesses," he'd said. "All I've done for seven years is chase bad men and watch men in uniform march around and blow things up."

Still, there was no way to leverage that work into a presidential run in 1968: not without ever having run for office, not with the specter of "dynasty!" hanging over the family, not with Bobby still carrying the image of the "ruthless" family enforcer. He needed distance, and a political life of his own. But where? A second "Senator Kennedy" from Massachusetts might be a bit much. Bobby's home was in Virginia, and as far as a Kennedy winning a Senate seat in Virginia . . . *yes, right after they elect a black man as governor.*

The President had often talked about staying in public life. After John Quincy Adams had lost the White House, he won election to the House of Representatives, where he became a champion of the anti-slavery movement. But the House was simply not a platform significant enough for an ex-president, and as for the Senate, he'd have the same problem as Bobby: the idea of two Kennedys from Massachusetts seemed excessive.

For the near future, then, there was a memoir to write—maybe two or three volumes, if he could find the time and patience. He'd be in a footrace with Schlesinger and Sorensen, but on the other hand, the eight years' worth of tapes he had would give him a hell of a leg up. Churchill had once said, "History will treat me very kindly, for I intend to write it." Well, he'd also had the wit to *record* it. *Let's see Ted and Arthur compete with the tapes.*

———

"How was the trip?" she asked as he set aside the crutches and eased himself onto the sofa next to her.

"Endless," he said.

"J.B. said you wanted to see me," Kennedy said. "If this is about Wexford—"

"No," she said. "I love the house; you don't. No, we need to talk about what comes next."

He sighed and started to go over the familiar ground. Maybe he'd buy a newspaper or start a magazine, a *Time* or *Life* with a liberal bent. In another election or two, if his health allowed, he might wind up as Bobby's or Teddy's secretary of state, although . . .

"Jack?" She was holding up a cautionary hand. "I'm not talking about what comes next for you. I'm talking about what comes next for *me*."

And then she began talking for several minutes, uninterrupted, as he sat and listened.

"We had some of Caroline's friends over for a movie the other night: *The Wizard of Oz*. There's a line in that movie, after Dorothy finds out the Wizard's just a hot-air-balloon man. She says to him, 'You're a bad man.' And he says, 'No, I'm a good man; I'm just a very bad wizard.' It's the other way with you, isn't it, Jack? You've been a very good president—the country's been lucky to have you. But as a man? A husband?"

She talked of what she'd always known, about the women at dinner parties and excursions whom she knew had shared his bed, about her long absences from the White House, about the way she'd carefully alerted the staff about her travel plans, about the people she'd sought out for advice and counseling. "After Dallas—after you almost died in my arms—I really thought things would change . . . and I think for a time they did . . . for months, maybe a year or more. And then they didn't." She told him of a doctor in Washington she'd met years earlier, an obstetrician with whom she'd felt a strong connection—"No, not that kind—not your kind—but I've talked with him over the years about everything. He helped me come to a decision."

"If you're talking about divorce—"

"No," she said. "I grew up in a broken family. I wouldn't do that to the children. I'm talking about something else: when we leave the White House, I'm going to New York. I've been looking at apartments, and there are publishers who would love to have me work with them as an editor. And I don't think we'll have much trouble getting Caroline and John into good schools. As far as the world knows, we'll be together . . . it isn't as if we haven't spent months of every year apart."

"I can't believe you'd do this to me," he said.

"I'm not doing it *to you*," she said, "I'm doing it *for me*. I'm not Nora at the end of *A Doll's House*, slamming a door. I'm just closing one, very quietly, very politely, and maybe opening another one. I've always said my purpose was to live my life through a significant man, and God knows I have. That's what I thought a woman does. Maybe when it's Caroline's time, she'll be able to live her life through herself."

For a long time after she left, he sat out on the Truman Balcony, his flight jacket around his shoulders, smoking a Havana. His wife's decision was a wound, but he had been wounded before. By the smallest accidents of fate, he had lived through those wounds; and those same accidents had put him, with all his strengths and weaknesses, at the helm of his country with the fate of tens of millions in his hands. Whatever judgment history would render on what he had done with the life he had been granted, he could live with that too.

THE SOURCES OF
SPECULATION

This is a book of what might have happened. It is, necessarily, a book of speculation. It is perfectly reasonable to argue that history would *not* have turned out this way: that John Kennedy would not have survived Dallas even if the bubble top had covered his car, or that Lyndon Johnson would not have been driven from office, or that Kennedy would have made very different judgments about Vietnam or civil rights, or that his private life would not have been the target of his political enemies.

If alternate history is a work of imagination, the "alternate historian" has one obligation to readers: plausibility. That's why many of the words spoken here have been taken from real life, although not at the same time and place as they appear here. The thoughts and opinions have been drawn, wherever possible, from the historical record. In telling this story, I've tried as much as possible to draw conclusions based on what the principals said and thought in "real life." I've also sought the guidance of others to help me paint as plausible a portrait as possible.

What follows is in no sense a "bibliography." It's simply a way of letting you know some of the sources for this speculation—apart, of course, from my fevered imagination.

DALLAS, TEXAS, NOVEMBER 22, 1963: The events of that day, the political atmosphere in Texas, the feud within the Democratic Party, as well as the conversations, are drawn from three books: Richard Reeves's *President Kennedy: Profile of Power* (1993); Robert Dallek's *An Unfinished Life* (2003); and Robert Caro's *The Passage of Power: The Years of Lyndon Johnson, Vol. IV* (2012).

Kennedy's instructions to Michael Forrestal to organize a top-to-bottom review of Vietnam after the first of the year, and his assessment of the 1964 political climate, can be found verbatim in Reeves's book.

JOSEPH KENNEDY JR.: The political ambitions of the eldest Kennedy son are recounted in *The Lost Prince* (1969) by Hank Searls and in *The Patriarch* (2012) by David Nasaw. Nasaw also details Joe Sr.'s influence on John Kennedy's career.

LUCKY TO BE ALIVE: Dallek, who had unprecedented access to Kennedy's health records, has detailed accounts of the President's lifelong health woes in his book, and in an *Atlantic* magazine piece (2002). The best account of John Kennedy's ordeal in the South Pacific can be found in Caro's LBJ book, which argues that Kennedy in fact performed heroically.

TWO TELEPHONE CALLS: The most detailed account of the phone calls that helped free Martin Luther King Jr. from a Georgia jail—and thus may have helped determine the 1960 election—is found in *The Bystander: John F. Kennedy and the Struggle for Black Equality* (2006) by Nick Bryant, a largely critical account of Kennedy's record. The specific election results I cite, and many more, are also taken from Bryant's book.

SHE CAME TO THE DOOR: The near death of JFK in Palm Beach at the hands of a suicide bomber has been largely forgotten by history. The most detailed account I have found is in a newspaper article by Robin Erb in the *Toledo Blade* of November 21, 2003. In his memoir, *Secret Service Chief*, U. E. Baughman provides a brief account.

I dealt at length with this incident in my previous alternate history book, *Then Everything Changed*, which imagines what might have happened had Mrs. Kennedy not come to the door, and had Pavlick in fact killed Kennedy.

THE DALLAS VENUE: The dispute over where JFK was to appear at a luncheon is described by Kennedy's advance man, Jerry Bruno, in his book *The Advance Man* (1971), which I cowrote.

JIM LEHRER AND THE BUBBLE TOP: Jim Lehrer recounted his experience in Dallas, when his inquiry to the Secret Service led to the call downtown, and the decision to remove the bubble top, in an interview marking the fortieth anniversary of the assassination. It can be found here: http://www.pbs.org/newshour/bb/white_house/kennedy/lehrer.html. I've altered the interview to make it conform to the alternate history.

THE SHOOTING, THE AFTERMATH, AND THE MEDICAL CARE: The details of the motorcade come from a variety of sources, including extensive viewing of the on-air coverage, both network and local. The reporters and anchors described here all appear more or less as they did on November 22. Moments after the shooting, KRLD's Eddie Barker was reporting live from the Dallas Trade Mart, where he noted that weather forecasters had been predicting rain all day, and that the skies had cleared shortly before the President arrived in Dallas. The actions of the Secret Service detail are taken from Warren Commission testimony, as are the accounts of the medical personnel. Admiral Burkley, Kennedy's personal physician, in fact told the doctors treating the President to "get him some steroids . . . because he's an Addisonian."

RFK: The accounts of Robert Kennedy's actions on November 22 come from Evan Thomas's *Robert Kennedy: His Life* (2000), including his immediate suspicion that the CIA, or organized crime, or the Teamsters, may have been involved with the shooting. Both Thomas's book and David Talbot's *Brothers* (2007) describe Robert Kennedy's suspicions that others besides Oswald were involved in the President's death. There is no concrete account of any specific evidence Robert Kennedy had for this suspicion, but it is clear that he was fully aware of any number of people who would have been happy to see either Kennedy dead.

Thomas's book tells of a Teamster enforcer who set out to assassinate RFK until Teamster chief Jimmy Hoffa called him off, fearing government reprisals against the Teamsters.

While this is speculation, it is possible that Robert Kennedy's doubts stemmed from the same feeling millions had: How could one insignificant, dysfunctional, trouble-plagued individual have committed so historically significant an act?

OSWALD'S CAPTURE: The details of Lee Harvey Oswald's capture come from Gerald Posner's book *Case Closed* (1993, 2003), which argues that Oswald was in fact the lone assassin. He drew his account in large measure from the Warren Commission testimony of police officers and other witnesses to the shooting of Officer Tippit and the capture of Oswald in the Texas Theatre. Obviously, the shooting of Oswald in the theater did not happen.

KENNEDY'S RECOVERY: The imagined recovery of Kennedy is patterned after President Reagan's 1981 recovery after being shot by John Hinckley. A photograph of the Reagans, cropped to hide the nurse standing beside the President, appeared in newspapers all over the world. I've "reframed" the most memorable image of the post-assassination period, that of three-year-old John Kennedy Jr. saluting his father's coffin.

More broadly, given the impact of that four-day period, captured with special vividness in Caro's *The Passage of Power*, it is not hard to imagine the sense of relief that would have greeted Kennedy's survival. Indeed, we don't have to imagine it: Look back to the surge in good feeling toward President Reagan after he lived through an assassination attempt. The Acheson letter is a reworking of a letter he wrote to a British friend after JFK's death, portions of which are quoted in *Dean Acheson: The Cold War Years, 1953–71* (1994) by Douglas Brinkley.

LYNDON JOHNSON'S FALL: The Senate and *Life* magazine investigations into Lyndon Johnson are reported in great detail in Caro's *The Passage of Power*. After JFK's assassination, Caro reports, the Senate investigation faded away, and *Life* magazine's editors decided, in effect, that the new president needed a chance. NBC did launch a topical political comedy program, *That Was the Week That Was*, in January 1964. Johnny Carson's joke about an "im*peach*ment"-flavored ice cream was told by the comedian about Nixon after the Watergate scandal emerged.

"PARKLANDERS": The tradition of a president punctuating a State of the Union speech by citing people in attendance began in 1982, when President Reagan acknowledged Leonard Skutnik, who helped rescue victims of a Washington plane crash. In the years that followed, such individuals were labeled "Skutniks" by the press.

CIA-FBI MALFEASANCE: For the CIA's performance in the weeks and months preceding JFK's assassination, see Jefferson Morley's "JFK at 49: What We Know for Sure," *Huffington Post*, November 22, 2012. The FBI's performance, and Hoover's directive to destroy a note from Oswald to the Dallas FBI bureau, is covered in *J. Edgar Hoover: The Man and the Secrets* (1994) by Curt Gentry.

THE FIGHT FOR A SECOND TERM; JFK'S REELECTION PROSPECTS: Richard Reeves's book has a detailed account of the first (and only) reelection strategy meeting, which took place ten days before the President's death. The quotes from the participants are all real. Many books (including the Caro and Dallek books) offer assessments of Kennedy's political strengths and weaknesses. For an exhaustive look at the Democratic Party's prospects before and after Kennedy's death, see *JFK, LBJ and the Democratic Party* by Sean Savage (2004).

NRA: The organization did endorse a ban on mail-order gun sales in the words quoted, before pressure from its members forced it to retreat.

RACE AND POLITICS: See Savage's book for descriptions of the emergence of "backlash," and for Governor George Wallace's campaigns in the 1964 Democratic presidential primaries. See also Rick Perlstein's book *Before the Storm: Barry Goldwater and the Unmaking of the American Consensus* (2001) for a vivid account of the emergence

of "backlash" as a political issue. Representative Griffiths' letter to
the President is quoted by Reeves. The assessments by *Time* and
Look are real.

Richard Russell told colleagues that JFK could not have passed a
civil rights bill, but that Lyndon Johnson could (the actual comment is in Caro's book). I have reversed it, of course.

Teddy White's prescient words about backlash come from his
classic *The Making of the President 1960*.

THE MOYNIHAN REPORT: In 1965, a leaked, incomplete account of
Daniel Moynihan's report *The Negro Family* created a political firestorm, forcing President Johnson to retreat from its findings and
triggering a blaming-the-victim controversy. For a contemporary,
measured account, see Thomas Meehan's article in the *New York
Times Magazine*, July 3, 1966. For a current "revisionist" assessment, see "Revisiting the Moynihan Report" by Ta-Nehisi Coates
in the *Atlantic*, June 18, 2013.

THE PEACE ISSUE: Kennedy's "discovery" of the peace issue's potency
is described by advance man Jerry Bruno in our book. The World's
Fair speech borrows a few lines delivered by President Johnson when
he opened the Fair, and adds lines that JFK delivered on several occasions, including his American University speech of June 10, 1963.

JFK'S MOSCOW VISIT: Artist and Kennedy friend Bill Walton did
meet with Soviet officials shortly after JFK's death. Details of Kennedy's "visit" are borrowed from Richard Nixon's 1972 journey to
the Soviet Union.

THE GOLDWATER CAMPAIGN: The movement that led his nomination
is the subject of Rick Perlstein's *Before the Storm: Barry Goldwater*

and the Unmaking of the American Consensus (2009). Hillary Rod-ham (Clinton), a "Goldwater Girl" in 1964, used language strik-ingly similar to the line quoted from his acceptance speech in her Wellesley College commencement address in 1969.

THE HAWKS' DISAFFECTION: The critical comments about Kennedy are found in David Talbot's *Brothers*.

SYMINGTON AS VICE PRESIDENT: By all accounts (see, for example, White's *Making of the President 1960*) Stuart Symington was Ken-nedy's likely pick as running mate.

DEBATES: Barry Goldwater often spoke of conversations he'd had with Kennedy, about the possibility of "Lincoln-Douglas" debates held across America. Historian Michael Beschloss, in a phone in-terview on April 9, 2013, discounted the likelihood of debates. "He wouldn't have debated Goldwater in a million years. Can you imagine Kennedy giving a platform to someone that far be-hind him?"

By contrast, former Kennedy aide Richard Goodwin, in an in-terview in Concord, Massachusetts, on May 17, 2013, thought Ken-nedy would have debated, "but no more than one or two."

RESOLVING THE VIETNAM DILEMMA: WHAT WOULD JFK HAVE DONE? It is at the center of speculation about what would have happened if Kennedy had lived: What would he have done about Vietnam? It is often entangled in motives; "keepers of the flame" are certain he would not have escalated the war; Kennedy skeptics suggest he would have been compelled by the same "facts on the ground" as Johnson was, or note that his avowed goal to begin withdrawing

U.S. forces had been overtaken by the coup that deposed Ngo Dinh Diem less than three weeks before Dallas.

There is, of course, no definitive way to answer this question. An excellent starting point, however, is *Vietnam: If Kennedy Had Lived* (2009) by James Blight, Janet Lang, and David A. Welch. The book contains the transcripts of a three-day conference held at the Musgrove Plantation in 2005 among historians, other academics, and policy makers from the Kennedy-Johnson era. It also includes extensive declassified documents from the National Security Council and other sources (many of the quotes in this section of the book come from those documents).

At the end of the conference, a majority of participants concluded that Kennedy would *not* have escalated the war in Vietnam and would have been willing to accept the political cost of disengagement. Kennedy raised the idea of a Geneva-conference-Laos-like solution to Vietnam in a conversation with the State Department's Roger Hilsman, according to Hilsman's oral history at the JFK library.

All of the pre–November 1963 comments by Kennedy, his advisors, and media voices are real.

THE CAMP DAVID MEETING: Paul Kattenburg was the head of the State Department Working Group. He recounted his "emperor has no clothes" moment during a National Security Council ExComm meeting on August 31, 1963, in a 1981 interview with WGBH:

"I blurted out, perhaps it was imprudent for me to do it, but I blurted out that we consider the possibility of withdrawing with honor, that this was, in other words, a time to review our stake . . ." A few weeks later, Kattenburg was removed as head of the Vietnam Working Group.

KHRUSHCHEV AND VIETNAM: The fictional "understanding" here parallels the diplomatic maneuvering that led to the neutralization in Laos in 1961.

RICHARD RUSSELL: The phone call between Kennedy and Russell is a near-verbatim rendering of a call between Russell and President Johnson on May 27, 1964. The audio and the transcript are available from many sources, including the University of Virginia's Miller Center Presidential Recordings Program. The frustration of both men is apparent, as is the chilling sense of foreboding. Both seem to know disaster is coming; neither can figure out how to avoid it. My premise is that a president inclined to disengage would have seen the Russell conversation as a potential opening.

A DIFFERENT COUNTRY—BUT HOW DIFFERENT? THE VOTING RIGHTS ACT: The idea of a deposed Vice President Johnson calling JFK to offer advice is a fantasy. What is true is that the Kennedy White House did not possess anything like the legislative shrewdness of Johnson; he had offered advice to Ted Sorensen in 1963 about the timing of civil rights legislation and the advice was ignored.

The biographies of the African-American participants at the imagined "Vets for the Vote" rally are all historically accurate.

LIBERAL OPTIMISM AND THE SIXTIES: Would the protest movements of the 1960s been different had President Kennedy lived? An affirmative answer comes from both sides of the political spectrum. In interviews conducted in the spring of 2013, SDS founders Tom Hayden and Todd Gitlin argue that—with one crucial caveat—the counterculture would have had a very different tone.

"I think you have a very different history if JFK lives," Todd Gitlin says. "The whole left would have had a soft landing; you'd have had cultural estrangement but not bitterness." But Gitlin's premise rests on the idea that Kennedy would not have escalated Vietnam.

"The Vietnam War is what drives the movement crazy," he says. "Without Vietnam, there's no way to get from anger to 'Blow it up!'"

Tom Hayden, who described the early sixties SDS as "reform-ist . . . the model was peaceful transition," says that the assassination drained a sense of optimism out of the movement.

"There was a sense that 'if *this* could happen, *anything* can happen.'"

Author David Talbot argues that "if there's no JFK death, and no Vietnam, there's no Weather Underground, no bomb throwers, no 'cops as pigs' . . . [T]he assassination robbed us of the possibility of change."

At least one view from the right shares some of this view. In his book *Camelot and the Cultural Revolution: How the Assassination of John F. Kennedy Shattered American Liberalism* (2007), James Piereson argues that the essentially optimistic, patriotic liberal outlook was fatally damaged by the failure to acknowledge that JFK had been killed by a deluded Marxist. Assigning blame on a "culture of hate" meant a much harsher, less benign view of the United States, which enabled conservatives to "capture the flag" as the champions of patriotic values. Two points here: First, if you believe that Kennedy was in fact killed by a right-wing conspiracy, this argument is fatally flawed. Second, it may not put enough emphasis on the way the Vietnam War darkened the assumptions of the protest movement. The speculative question I do *not* deal with is: If JFK had lived and escalated the war, would the darker, more violent aspects of the protest movement still have emerged?

TEDDY WHITE AND CHINA: Richard Reeves's book says JFK had a conversation with Theodore H. White in 1961 about the possible benefit of a meeting in Asia with Mao Tse-tung. Dean Rusk is cited in several works as saying Kennedy intended to normalize relations with China in his second term.

THE THREAT: JFK'S PRIVATE LIFE: The accounts of President Kennedy's sexual behavior range from the cautious to the salacious; at one level or another, they are recounted in Reeves's and Dallek's books; in Sy Hersh's *The Dark Side of Camelot* (1997); in *John F. Kennedy's Women: The Story of a Sexual Obsession* (2011) by Michael O'Brien; and in others too numerous to list. O'Brien's book contains a detailed look at the efforts by the Katers to expose Kennedy's affair with Pam Turnure. The most recent book, *Once Upon a Secret* by Mimi Alford (2012), tells the story of her affair with the President while working in the White House Press Office.

BOBBY KENNEDY AS PROTECTOR: Evan Thomas's *Robert Kennedy: His Life* (2000) provides specific details of Bobby Kennedy's efforts at damage control, including his concessions to FBI director Hoover as the price of keeping John Kennedy's behavior private.

TEDDY WHITE'S CHINA REPORTING AND THE FALLOUT: The author-journalist did go to China, but not until February 1972, when he was part of the press entourage that followed President Nixon on his historic visit to the country. Some of Kennedy's press conference remarks on diplomatic recognition are taken from a speech he delivered in Salt Lake City, Utah, on September 26, 1963.

JFK, MARY PINCHOT MEYER, DRUGS, AND TAPES: Here are the facts that underlie this leap into the speculative: Mary Pinchot Meyer was both a social intimate of the Kennedys and one of the President's lovers. She had a close relationship with LSD proselytizer Timothy

Leary, and was convinced that the use of hallucinogenic drugs by powerful decision makers was the key to a peaceful, spiritual revolution. Her murder on October 12, 1964, officially labeled "unsolved," is treated by some conspiracy theorists as evidence that she was killed to silence her. A book by Nina Burleigh, *A Very Private Woman: The Life and Unsolved Murder of Presidential Mistress Mary Meyer* (1998), the fullest account of her story, suggests that the man acquitted of her murder was very probably the killer; most likely the murder was the result of a robbery or assault gone wrong. Burleigh's book, and other writings, report that during one White House visit, Meyer and the President shared a small amount of marijuana.

Other, more sensational allegations come largely from James Jesus Angleton. He was for more than twenty years chief of the CIA's counterintelligence staff, more formally the associate deputy director of operations for counterintelligence. His wife, Cecily, was one of Meyer's closest friends. The truth-is-stranger-than-fiction dimensions of Angleton's CIA work, his conviction that enemies had penetrated every level of the agency, and his often contradictory allegations about moles and conspiracies are examined most thoroughly in David Martin's book *A Wilderness of Mirrors: Intrigue, Deception, and the Secrets that Destroyed Two of the Cold War's Most Important Agents* (2003). It is in this context that Angleton's assertions that Meyer and Kennedy may have experimented with LSD, or that Angleton tapped Mary Meyer's phones and bugged her town house—allegations that can be found in David Talbot's *Brothers*—have to be weighed. His widow told Sally Bedell Smith that he would have had no means of wiring her home. (You can read this in Smith's 2004 book, *Grace and Power: The Private World of the Kennedy White House.*) It is, of course, reasonable to ask how the wife of a covert operations official would know the limits of her husband's professional abilities.

BY ANY MEANS NECESSARY: The use and abuse of official power during the fight over rising steel prices is reported in Thomas's Robert Kennedy book and in Reeves's book—which also asserts that the phones of congressmen, lobbyists, and journalists were tapped. The President's jocular references to official overreach are taken verbatim from Reeves's book.

END OF TERM: KENNEDY'S HEALTH: While the regimen of exercise and hot baths had eased Kennedy's discomfort in the months before his death, the lifelong litany of ills, and the likely effects of the corticosteroids he was taking, made the prospect of eventual decline a reality. Secret Service agents (Reeves reports) expressed fears that if Kennedy served eight years, he'd be in a wheelchair by the end of his presidency.

RACIAL POLITICS: For the real-life racial tensions that arose between 1965 and 1968, see Rick Perlstein's *Nixonland: The Rise of a President and the Fracturing of America* (2009). The impact of these tensions on the Democratic Party is examined at length in Savage's *JFK, LBJ and the Democratic Party*. White's *The Making of the President 1968* has much on the subject, as do several hundred other books on the politics of the period.

CULTURAL BACKLASH: Would the counterculture have produced a socially conservative backlash even without the flag burning and the rhetorical (and at times actual) violence of the antiwar movement? Perlstein's *Nixonland* suggests that the rising crime and cultural upheaval at Berkeley and other California campuses was a huge asset to Ronald Reagan's campaign for governor in 1966; and the first major disruptions at Berkeley, in late 1964, occurred *before* the Vietnam escalation, and had nothing to do with the war at all. It's reasonable to assume that long hair, drug use, open sexuality, and other signs of the cultural apocalypse would have led to a strong reaction from those embracing more traditional social values.

John Kennedy's Berkeley speech is a reworked version of a 1967 speech that Robert Kennedy delivered to Americans for Democratic Action, where he described the movement of many of the young "from SDS to LSD."

THE GOP BATTLE FOR THE NOMINATION: In 1968, Reagan did not officially announce his presidential candidacy until he arrived at the Miami convention. By then three conservative stalwarts—Barry Goldwater, Strom Thurmond, and John Tower—had lined up most of the Southern delegates behind Richard Nixon. An unpublished monograph by Glenn Moore (date unavailable) argues that if Reagan had made an earlier declaration of candidacy, he might well have won all the delegates from Florida and Mississippi—in both states, *all* the delegates voted for the majority's choice—and denied Nixon a first-ballot nomination. In fact, Nixon won the nomination with a margin of only twenty-five votes to spare. The kind words Reagan speaks about Wallace were in fact spoken by Reagan during his Southern swing in May 1968. The convention speech Reagan gives is taken verbatim from a speech he actually gave at the 1976 Republican convention in Kansas City, when, just after his acceptance speech, President Ford, who had narrowly defeated him for the nomination, invited Reagan to address the delegates.

THE DEMOCRATIC BATTLE FOR THE NOMINATION: To those who lived through the 1968 campaign, or who have absorbed its history, the idea of Hubert Humphrey as a peace candidate may seem absurd. Before he was Johnson's vice president, however, he was an early proponent of disarmament; a key Senate supporter of the Nuclear

Test Ban Treaty; and an originator of the Food for Peace program. As vice president he sent a prescient memo to President Johnson in early 1965, warning of the political consequences of escalation. (This can be found in full in an appendix to Blight et al., *Vietnam: If Kennedy Had Lived.*) For his troubles, Humphrey was exiled from White House deliberations for months, until he was permitted to return as a full-fledged supporter of escalation. It is easy to imagine Humphrey as a strong supporter of President Kennedy's efforts to ease cold war tensions . . . because he was.

My conclusion that Robert Kennedy would not have been able to seek the presidential nomination in 1968 is based on . . . a surmise. As Lowenstein argues in this book, it would have defied historical precedent; moreover, the Robert Kennedy who would have served his brother for eight years would have been a very different Robert Kennedy than the one we know: the one who had spent five years in exile, who had felt firsthand what fate can do to assumptions and certainties, and who was a symbol for those voters hungry for a sense of restoration.

Howard Hughes' fear of nuclear testing led him to offer a large cash contribution to Robert Kennedy's 1968 campaign.

THE END: This is fictional speculation, pure and simple. Jacqueline Kennedy *did* have a private confidant, a Washington obstetrician named Frank Finnerty, with whom she felt a strong sense of empathy. At her request, he became a telephone "counselor" of sorts. According to Sally Bedell Smith's *Grace and Power*, which contains the first public account of Finnerty's role, he discussed with her the most intimate details of her private life. Whether that included her post–White House life is unknown.

Before dismissing the idea of separate lives, it should be remembered that the Kennedys spent long periods apart: months at a time.

A new book by Thurston Clarke, *JFK's Last Hundred Days: The Transformation of a Man and the Emergence of a Great President* (2013), says that the two grew closer after the death of their infant son Patrick, in September 1963, and that John Kennedy may have put aside his sexual pursuits. His near death might well have drawn the two even closer. The question then would be: Given John Kennedy's lifelong compulsions, could he have resisted those compulsions for five years?

ACKNOWLEDGMENTS

A month or so into 2013, I sent Sterling Lord, my literary agent, a vague notion about an alternate history look at John Kennedy. "I think this is a book," he said, and within ten days he had brought the idea to Putnam. If you want to know why he has been my agent for more than forty years, that's one damn good answer.

At Putnam, I've had the great good fortune to have publisher and editor in chief Neil Nyren as my editor on my last three books. It was he who signed on to this book idea and who nurtured this project through the birthing process. His mix of firm direction and gentle demeanor—or is it gentle direction and firm demeanor?—is everything a writer could want in an editor.

As with my past excursions into alternate history, I was blessed with a platoon of creative, politically savvy friends and colleagues who were generous with their time and inventive with their suggestions. Many thanks to journalists Walter Shapiro and Meryl Gordon; to Norm Ornstein of the American Enterprise Institute; to Dick and Doris Goodwin, whose wisdom came in the course of a lengthy, celebratory evening in Concord, Massachusetts; and to novelist and friend Richard North Patterson. I also had the benefit this time around of the assistance of historian Michael Beschloss, who went above and beyond the call of duty in providing counsel and encouragement.

Insight into the political and cultural currents of the 1960s was supplied by SDS founders Tom Hayden and Todd Gitlin; by author David Talbot; and by social historian Fred Kaplan. Fred's 2009 book *1959: The Year Everything Changed* is one of the best guides to the events that roiled the decade that followed.

A special thank-you to Dr. Howard R. Bromley, associate professor of anesthesiology, critical care, and pain management at the University of Tennessee Health Science Center, for helping me describe the medical treatment that the doctors at Parkland Hospital would have provided to a wounded President Kennedy.

As with all my work, I owe a huge debt of gratitude to researcher Beth Goodman. She has worked with me for fifteen years, at two TV networks and through three books. There is simply no one better.

My thanks as well to Richard Hutton, executive director of the Carsey-Wolf Center at the University of California, Santa Barbara, and Cristina Venegas, chair of UCSB's Film Studies Department, for providing me office space for the last stages of my writing.

I cannot ignore the signal contribution of "The Palmeni Group": a group of miscreants with whom I have been having lunch with on a regular basis for decades. Without the unending ridicule of Andrew Bergman, Jerry Della Femina, Dr. Gerald Imber, and Michael Kramer, I would never have found the motive to finish this book. And I know our late companion, Joel Siegel, would have been urging on me an "alternate alternate" history in which Kennedy finds his Jewish roots.

Finally: to my children, Casey and Dave; to my stepdaughter and son-in-law, Justine and Alan Yerushalmi; to my grandchildren, Rory Greenfield and Ella, Ava, and Rebecca Yerushalmi; and to my wife, Dena Sklar . . .

. . . my alternate history would be far less rich without your presence.

Jeff Greenfield is a five-time Emmy Award–winning analyst and has been a correspondent and commentator for CBS, ABC, CNN, and PBS; a columnist for *Time* magazine; and a writer for *Harper's* and *The New York Times Magazine*. He has also worked in politics as a Senate aide, a speechwriter for such men as Senator Robert F. Kennedy and New York mayor John Lindsay, and a political strategist. He is the author or coauthor of thirteen books, including the national bestseller *Then Everything Changed*; an insider's account of the contested 2000 presidential election, *"Oh, Waiter! One Order of Crow!"*; and a national bestselling novel, *The People's Choice*. Greenfield lives in New York and Santa Barbara.

CONNECT ONLINE

jeffgreenfield.net
facebook.com/jeffgreenfieldwriter
twitter.com/greenfield64